EDEXCEL
A LEVEL
HISTORY

ActiveBook included

Paper 3:
Civil rights and race relations in the USA, 1850–2009

Derrick Murphy
Series editor: Rosemary Rees

ALWAYS LEARNING

PEARSON

Published by Pearson Education Limited, 80 Strand, London, WC2R 0RL

www.pearsonschoolsandfecolleges.co.uk

Copies of official specifications for all Edexcel qualifications may be found on the website: www.edexcel.com

Text © Pearson Education Limited 2016

Designed by Elizabeth Arnoux for Pearson

Typeset and illustrated by Phoenix Photosetting, Chatham, Kent

Produced by Out of House Publishing

Original illustrations © Pearson Education Limited 2016

Cover design by Malena Wilson-Max for Pearson

Cover photo/illustration © Getty Images/Joe Raedle

The rights of Derrick Murphy to be identified as author of this work have been asserted by him in accordance with the Copyright, Designs and Patents Act 1988

First published 2016

19 18 17 16

10 9 8 7 6 5 4 3 2 1

British Library Cataloguing in Publication Data

A catalogue record for this book is available from the British Library

ISBN 978 1 447 985358

Printed in the UK by CPI

Websites

Pearson Education Limited is not responsible for the content of any external internet sites. It is essential for tutors to preview each website before using it in class so as to ensure that the URL is still accurate, relevant and appropriate. We suggest that tutors bookmark useful websites and consider enabling students to access them through the school/college intranet.

A note from the publisher

In order to ensure that this resource offers high-quality support for the associated Pearson qualification, it has been through a review process by the awarding body. This process confirms that this resource fully covers the teaching and learning content of the specification or part of a specification at which it is aimed. It also confirms that it demonstrates an appropriate balance between the development of subject skills, knowledge and understanding, in addition to preparation for assessment.

Endorsement does not cover any guidance on assessment activities or processes (e.g. practice questions or advice on how to answer assessment questions) included in the resource, nor does it prescribe any particular approach to the teaching or delivery of a related course.

While the publishers have made every attempt to ensure that advice on the qualification and its assessment is accurate, the official specification and associated assessment guidance materials are the only authoritative source of information and should always be referred to for definitive guidance.

Pearson examiners have not contributed to any sections in this resource relevant to examination papers for which they have responsibility.

Examiners will not use endorsed resources as a source of material for any assessment set by Pearson.

Endorsement of a resource does not mean that the resource is required to achieve this Pearson qualification, nor does it mean that it is the only suitable material available to support the qualification, and any resource lists produced by the awarding body shall include this and other appropriate resources.

Contents

Aspects in breadth: Changing perceptions of race relations, 1850–2009

Aspects in depth: Emancipation and moves towards greater equality

How to use this book

STRUCTURE

This book covers Paper 3, Option 39.1: Civil rights and race relations in the USA, 1850–2009 of the Edexcel A Level qualification.

You will also need to study a Paper 1 and a Paper 2 option and produce coursework in order to complete your qualification. All Paper 1/2 options are covered by other textbooks in this series.

EXAM SUPPORT

The examined assessment for Paper 3 requires you to answer questions from three sections. Throughout this book there are exam-style questions in all three section styles for you to practise your examination skills.

Section A contains a compulsory question that will assess your source analysis and evaluation skills.

> **A Level Exam-Style Question Section A**
>
> *Study Source 1 before you answer this question.*
>
> Assess the value of the source for revealing the aims of Reconstruction during Abraham Lincoln's presidency.
>
> Explain your answer, using the source, information given about its origins and your own knowledge about the historical context. (20 marks)
>
> **Tip**
>
> *It is important to consider the intended audience for the source, and the extent to which the information contained within the source provides sufficient information on the aims of Reconstruction in 1865.*

Section B contains a choice of essay questions that will look at your understanding of the studied period in depth.

> **A Level Exam-Style Question Section B**
>
> 'The failure to pass federal anti-lynching legislation was due to the inaction of Democrat President Franklin D. Roosevelt.'
>
> How far do you agree with this statement? (20 marks)
>
> **Tip**
>
> *This type of question requires a balanced, analytical response. You will be expected to provide evidence that southern white Democrats brought failure. However, this should be balanced with evidence to state that President Roosevelt could have acted after 1936 but failed to do so.*

Section C will again give you a choice of essay questions but these will assess your understanding of the period in breadth.

> **A Level Exam-Style Question Section C**
>
> How far did the period 1915–41 see a major change in the geographical pattern of black Americans? (20 marks)
>
> **Tip**
>
> *You will need to identify the degree of change in the pattern of black American distribution within the United States brought about by the Great Migration. You will need to identify how far it changed from the years before 1915.*

The Preparing for your exams sections at the end of this book contains sample answers of different standards, with comments on how they could be improved.

FEATURES

Extend your knowledge

These features contain additional information that will help you gain a deeper understanding of the topic. This could be a short biography of an important person, extra background information about an event, an alternative interpretation, or even a research idea that you could follow up. Information in these boxes is not essential to your exam success, but still provides insights of value.

> **EXTEND YOUR KNOWLEDGE**
>
> **Frederick Douglass (1818–95)**
> Frederick Douglass was a prominent American abolitionist, author and public speaker. He was born a slave, but escaped at the age of 20 and went on to become a world-renowned anti-slavery activist. He wrote three autobiographies which are considered important works of the slave tradition. Douglass' work as a reformer ranged from his abolitionist activities in the early 1840s to his attacks on Jim Crow and lynching in the 1890s. For 16 years, he edited an influential black newspaper and achieved international fame as an inspiring and persuasive orator and writer. In thousands of speeches and editorials, he levied a powerful indictment against slavery and racism.

Knowledge check activities

These activities are designed to check that you have understood the material that you have just studied. They might also ask you questions about the sources and extracts in the section to check that you have studied and analysed them thoroughly.

> **ACTIVITY**
> **KNOWLEDGE CHECK**
>
> **The failure to address black grievances**
>
> 1 Draw a spider diagram identifying what you regard as the three most important grievances that black Americans had during the New Deal years.
>
> 2 Compare your answers with a partner and decide your combined top three answers.
>
> 3 What reasons can you give for the failure of anti-lynching laws in the USA during the New Deal years?

Summary activities

At the end of each chapter, you will find summary activities. These are tasks designed to help you think about the key topic you have just studied as a whole. They may involve selecting and organising key information or analysing how things changed over time. You might want to keep your answers to these questions safe – they are handy for revision.

> **ACTIVITY**
> **SUMMARY**
>
> **The changing geography of civil rights issues**
>
> 1 Create a spider diagram which shows the main changes in the changing geographical distribution of black Americans in the USA. Include different:
> - push factors
> - pull factors.
>
> 2 How did the pattern of settlement of black Americans change in the years 1850–2009?
>
> 3 What was the difference between legal (*de jure*) and *de facto* segregation?

Thinking Historically activities

These activities are found throughout the book, and are designed to develop your understanding of history, especially around the key concepts of evidence, interpretations, causation and change. Each activity is designed to challenge a conceptual barrier that might be holding you back. This is linked to a map of conceptual barriers developed by experts. You can look up the map and find out which barrier each activity challenges by downloading the progression map from this website: www.pearsonschools.co.uk/ historyprogressionsapproach.

progression map reference

> **THINKING HISTORICALLY** Evidence (6b)
>
> **The strength of argument**
>
> Read Extracts 1, 2 and 3 from historians and then answer the questions below.
>
> 1 Read Extract 1.
>
>   a) What is weak about this claim?
>
>   b) What could be added to it to make it stronger?
>
> 2 Read Extract 2.
>
>   a) Is this an argument? If yes, what makes it one?
>
>   b) How might this argument be strengthened?
>
> 3 Read Extract 3.
>
>   a) How have they expanded their explanation to make the claim stronger?
>
>   b) Can you explain why this is the strongest claim of the three sources?
>
> 4 What elements make a historian's claims strong?

Getting the most from your online ActiveBook

This book comes with three years' access to ActiveBook* – an online, digital version of your textbook. Follow the instructions printed on the inside front cover to start using your ActiveBook.

Your ActiveBook is the perfect way to personalise your learning as you progress through your A Level History course. You can:

- access your content online, anytime, anywhere
- use the inbuilt highlighting and annotation tools to personalise the content and make it really relevant to you.

Highlight tool – use this to pick out key terms or topics so you are ready and prepared for revision.

Annotations tool – use this to add your own notes, for example links to your wider reading, such as websites or other files. Or, make a note to remind yourself about work that you need to do.

*For new purchases only. If the access code has already been revealed, it may no longer be valid. If you have bought this textbook secondhand, the code may already have been used by the first owner of the book.

Introduction
A Level History

WHY HISTORY MATTERS

History is about people and people are complex, fascinating, frustrating and a whole lot of other things besides. This is why history is probably the most comprehensive and certainly one of the most intriguing subjects there is. History can also be inspiring and alarming, heartening and disturbing, a story of progress and civilisation and of catastrophe and inhumanity.

History's importance goes beyond the subject's intrinsic interest and appeal. Our beliefs and actions, our cultures, institutions and ways of living, our languages and means of making sense of ourselves are all shaped by the past. If we want to fully understand ourselves now, and to understand our possible futures, we have no alternative but to think about history.

History is a discipline as well as a subject matter. Making sense of the past develops qualities of mind that are valuable to anyone who wants to seek the truth and think clearly and intelligently about the most interesting and challenging intellectual problem of all: other people. Learning history is learning a powerful way of knowing.

WHAT IS HISTORY?

History is a way of constructing knowledge about the world through research, interpretation, argument and debate.

Building historical knowledge involves identifying the traces of the past that exist in the present – in people's memories, in old documents, photographs and other remains, and in objects and artefacts ranging from bullets and lipsticks to field systems and cities. Historians interrogate these traces and *ask questions* that transform traces into *sources of evidence* for knowledge claims about the past.

Historians aim to understand what happened in the past by *explaining why* things happened as they did. Explaining why involves trying to understand past people and their beliefs, intentions and actions. It also involves explaining the causes and evaluating the effects of large-scale changes in the past and exploring relationships between what people aimed to do, the contexts that shaped what was possible and the outcomes and consequences of actions.

Historians also aim to *understand change* in the past. People, states of affairs, ideas, movements and civilisations come into being in time, grow, develop, and ultimately decline and disappear. Historians aim to identify and compare change and continuity in the past, to measure the rate at which things change and to identify the types of change that take place. Change can be slow or sudden. It can also be understood as progressive or regressive – leading to the improvement or worsening of a situation or state of affairs. How things change and whether changes are changes for the better are two key issues that historians frequently debate.

Figure 1 Fragment of a black granite statue possibly portraying the Roman politician Mark Antony.

Debate is the essence of history. Historians write arguments to support their knowledge claims and historians argue with each other to test and evaluate interpretations of the past. Historical knowledge itself changes and develops. On the one hand, new sources of knowledge and new methods of research cause *historical interpretations* to change. On the other hand, the questions that historians ask change with time and new questions produce new answers. Although the past is dead and gone, the interpretation of the past has a past, present and future.

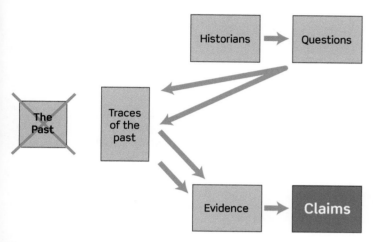

Figure 2 Constructing knowledge about the past.

THE CHALLENGES OF LEARNING HISTORY

Like all other Advanced Level subjects, A Level history is difficult – that is why it is called 'advanced'. Your advanced level studies will build on knowledge and understanding of history that you developed at GCSE and at Key Stage 3 – ideas like 'historical sources', 'historical evidence' and 'cause', for example. You will need to do a lot of reading and writing to progress in history. Most importantly, you will need to do a lot of thinking, and thinking about your thinking. This book aims to support you in developing both your knowledge and your understanding.

History is challenging in many ways. On the one hand, it is challenging to build up the range and depth of knowledge that you need to understand the past at an advanced level. Learning

about the past involves mastering new and unfamiliar concepts arising from the past itself (such as the Inquisition, Laudianism, *Volksgemeinschaft*) and building up levels of knowledge that are both detailed and well organised. This book covers the key content of the topics that you are studying for your examination and provides a number of features to help you build and organise what you know – for example, diagrams, timelines and definitions of key terms. You will need to help yourself too, of course, adding to your knowledge through further reading, building on the foundations provided by this book.

Another challenge is to develop understandings of the discipline of history. You will have to learn to think historically about evidence, cause, change and interpretations and also to write historically, in a way that develops clear and supported argument.

Historians think with evidence in ways that differ from how we often think in everyday life. In history, as Figure 2 shows, we cannot go and 'see for ourselves' because the past no longer exists. Neither can we normally rely on 'credible witnesses' to tell us 'the truth' about 'what happened'. People in the past did not write down 'the truth' for our benefit. They often had clear agendas when creating the traces that remain and, as often as not, did not themselves know 'the truth' about complex historical events.

A root of the word 'history' is the Latin word *historia*, one of whose meanings is 'enquiry' or 'finding out'. Learning history means learning to ask questions and interrogate traces, and then to reason about what the new knowledge you have gained means. This book draws on historical scholarship for its narrative and contents. It also draws on research on the nature of historical thinking and on the challenges that learning history can present for students. Throughout the book you will find 'Thinking Historically' activities designed to support the development of your thinking.

You will also find – as you would expect given the nature of history – that the book is full of questions. This book aims to help you build your understandings of the content, contexts and concepts that you will need to advance both your historical knowledge and your historical understanding, and to lay strong foundations for the future development of both.

Dr Arthur Chapman
Institute of Education
University College London

QUOTES ABOUT HISTORY

'Historians are dangerous people. They are capable of upsetting everything. They must be directed.'

Nikita Khrushchev

'To be ignorant of what occurred before you were born is to remain forever a child. For what is the worth of human life, unless it is woven into the life of our ancestors by the records of history.'

Marcus Tullius Cicero

Civil rights and race relations in the USA, 1850–2009

In the Declaration of Independence of 4 July 1776, leaders of the American colonies declared: 'We hold these truths to be self-evident that all men are created equal, that they are endowed by their Creator with certain unalienable rights.' This statement was the main reason why 13 American colonies declared independence from Britain and became the United States. However, from the very foundation of the USA the nation faced a major dilemma. A significant proportion of the new country's population were black slaves. In many northern states, black Americans were free men with the same civil rights as white Americans. Slavery proved to be the most divisive issue in American politics in the first half of the 19th century, becoming a major issue in the Civil War of 1861–65. Even though slavery was abolished at the end of that war, the issue of black American civil rights has been a dominant theme in US politics until the present day.

How far did the geographical distribution of black Americans change in the years 1850–2009?

In 1850, there were 3.2 million black slaves in the USA, approximately ten percent of the population. The vast majority of black Americans were slaves and lived in the south-east states of the USA. By 2009, the geographical distribution of black Americans had changed dramatically, with black Americans living across the USA, mostly in the urban areas, working in towns and cities rather than engaged in agriculture. In what came to be called the Great Migration, hundreds of thousands of black Americans had migrated north, out of the south-eastern former Confederate states. They escaped rural poverty and racial discrimination to seek work in manufacturing in northern and western cities. However, even though they escaped rural poverty in the Old South, black Americans continued to face racial discrimination in housing, and northern cities possessed black American ghettoes with racially segregated housing, particularly in the suburbs.

How did the portrayal of black Americans in literature, the arts and the media change in the years 1850–2009?

In 1850, black Americans were usually portrayed as childlike song-and-dance performers in theatres, which were the most popular form of entertainment. However, in literature, a more tragic and sinister portrayal of the black plight appeared in novels such as *Uncle Tom's Cabin*, published in 1852, which became a best-seller in the north and graphically outlined life as a slave. However, in literature, black Americans were invariably portrayed in subservient positions.

One of the great American contributions to world arts and entertainment in the 20th century was cinema. Here, black Americans, in the years before American engagement in the Second World War (1941–45), appeared in comic and servile roles. It was only in the 1960s that black Americans received lead roles in US films, most notably Sidney Poitier, who won the Best Actor Oscar in 1963.

The medium which did most to change and reflect changing perceptions of race relations was American television. By 2009, the portrayal and perception of black Americans in film and television had changed dramatically, especially since the Second World War. Black Americans now appeared in a variety of lead roles.

1866 – Rise of Ku Klux Klan and other white supremacist groups in former Confederate states — 1866

1877 – End of Reconstruction — 1877

1880s-1890s – Jim Crow Laws introduce racial segregation and exclude many black Americans from voting — 1880s-189

1915 – Refounding of Ku Klux Klan and rise of white supremacist groups across the USA — 1915

1954 – US Supreme Court ends school segregation in the *Brown* case — 1954

1964 – Civil Rights Act — 1964

1966 – Rise of black radicalism with Black Panthers — 1966

2004 – Election of Barack Obama as US senator for Illinois — 2004

2009 – Barack Obama is sworn in as USA's first black president — 2009

1865	**1865 – End of Civil War** Thirteenth Amendment to US Constitution abolishes slavery
1867–77	**1867–77 – Period of Radical Reconstruction of the former Confederate states**
1883	**1883 – US Supreme Court overturns much of civil rights legislation of Reconstruction in civil rights cases**
1896	**1896 – *Plessy* v *Ferguson* Supreme Court case supports 'separate but equal'**
1933–45	**1933–45 – New Deal offers limited support for black Americans**
1955	**1955 – Montgomery bus boycott and rise to prominence of Martin Luther King**
1965	**1965 – Voting Rights Act**
1968	**1968 – Assassination of Martin Luther King**
2008	**2008 – Barack Obama wins presidential election**

SOURCE 1

From a late 19th-century magazine, *Topsy*, advertising the theatrical production of *Uncle Tom's Cabin*. It shows how black Americans were depicted at the time. What image is it trying to portray?

Emancipation and moves towards greater equality

In 1865, slavery was abolished, and in the period of Reconstruction from 1865 to 1877 black Americans received the same civil rights as white Americans. However, black Americans still faced racial discrimination in jobs and housing across the USA. In the South, white supremacist organisations, such as the Ku Klux Klan, used violence and intimidation to ensure that black Americans were treated as second-class citizens.

After the end of Reconstruction, white-dominated state governments were formed in the former Confederate states. From the 1880s, they began passing laws which introduced legal racial discrimination against their black American citizens. Known collectively as Jim Crow Laws, these changes enforced racial segregation between the white and black races. They also disenfranchised large numbers of potential black voters. These changes were upheld by the US Supreme Court, which, in 1896, in the landmark court case *Plessy* v *Ferguson* supported legal segregation.

An important change, involving black Americans, took place in the 1930s, during the social and economic reforms of the Democrat administration of President Franklin Roosevelt, known as the New Deal. Welfare and relief programmes to aid the poor and unemployed provided help for black Americans affected by the economic depression that gripped the USA from 1929. However, compared to white Americans, black people received less help. A major issue which black organisations wished to see brought in was federal anti-lynching legislation, which was introduced into the US Congress but never passed.

The major change in the move towards greater equality occurred in the years 1954–68, a period associated with Martin Luther King and the civil rights movement. Martin Luther King acted as the unofficial leader of the civil rights movement until his assassination in April 1968. In that period, black Americans campaigned successfully for the end of legal segregation in the South. They were assisted in their quest by decisions of the US Supreme Court, which outlawed legal segregation. In addition, presidential and congressional action reinforced the changes made by the Supreme Court. By 1968, legal segregation had ended and black Americans had acquired full civil rights.

However, although black Americans had achieved full civil rights, many still faced major social and economic deprivation in the mid-1960s. Black Americans rioted against poor living conditions and lack of job opportunities in many cities, such as Los Angeles and Newark, New Jersey. The period also witnessed the fragmentation of the black civil rights movement due to the impact of the views of Malcolm X and the rise of the Black Panther Party.

In the 1980s, for the first time a senior black American politician, Jesse Jackson, stood for the nomination as Democrat Party presidential candidate. Although unsuccessful, his actions paved the way for other black American politicians. In 2008, a historic event took place with the election of the first black American president, Barack Obama.

Civil rights and race relations have been central issues throughout the history of the USA. Eventually, the country was able to live up the central pledge of the Declaration of Independence of 1776.

3.1

The changing geography of civil rights issues

KEY QUESTIONS

- How far did the geographical distribution of black Americans change in the years 1850–2009?
- To what extent did the changing pattern of settlement and segregation impact on civil rights issues in the years 1850–2009?

INTRODUCTION

The period 1850–2009 saw a transformation in the geographical distribution and nature of **civil rights** issues associated with **black Americans**. The first black Americans arrived for **slavery** in 1607, at England's first permanent colony at Jamestown, Virginia. They were transported across the Atlantic from the coast of West Africa. By the 18th century, tens of thousands of black Africans had been transported to America. They were sold to white Americans and were used as domestic servants and as agricultural labourers on large farms, known as plantations. These plantations grew crops such as tobacco, cotton and sugar cane. By the mid-19th century, the geographical distribution of black Americans spread across the southern United States, from Virginia in the east to Texas in the west.

As slaves, black Americans possessed no civil rights; they were the property of their white owners, to be bought and sold like any other form of property. Slaves were housed by their owners and were subject to the owners' own version of justice. Occasionally, slaves fled their plantations. Others rebelled. In 1831, the Nat Turner slave rebellion occurred in Virginia but was suppressed quickly through the use of military force.

In 1850, the centre of black America and civil rights issues was located in the south-east of the USA, the **Old South**, where the vast majority of black Americans lived as slaves. However, black Americans also lived in the northern states, but in small numbers. These were freemen. Even though they had civil rights in theory, like white Americans, they also faced racial discrimination. Occasionally, free black Americans were captured and sold into slavery. In 2014, the film that won the Best Picture US Academy Award (Oscar) was *12 Years a Slave*. It was based on the real-life story of a black freeman, Solomon Northup, who was sold into slavery in the southern state of Louisiana in 1841.

KEY TERMS

Civil rights
The rights of individuals to political and social freedom and equality.

Black Americans
Over time, the term to describe the black population of the United States has changed. In the period 1850 to the beginning of the 20th century, the term usually used was 'coloured'. One of the major civil rights organisations of the 20th century, founded in 1909, was the National Association for the Advancement of Colored People (NAACP). For the period from the early 20th century to the 1960s, the term 'negro' was used. Since 1970, the term 'black American' has come into use. Most recently, the term 'African American' has become widespread.

Slavery
A condition of involuntary service. Black Africans were brought to America as slaves from 1607. Until the abolition of slavery in 1865, black American slaves were treated as the property of their white owners, without rights. Even those black Americans who were free, in northern states, suffered racial discrimination because of their ethnic background and, in many cases, were treated as second-class citizens.

1850 - United States is divided between free and slave states; majority of black Americans are slaves

1863 - Emancipation Proclamation on freeing slaves under Confederate control

1877 - End of Reconstruction and beginning of legal segregation in the Old South

1910 onwards - Beginning of the Great Migration to the north

| 1845 | 1850 | 1855 | 1860 | 1865 | 1870 | 1875 | 1880 | 1900 | 1905 | 1910 | 1915 |

1861 - Outbreak of the Civil War

1865 - Slavery is abolished End of the Civil War

1865 onwards - Slow migration of black Americans north and west from Old South

1905 - Beginning of mass migration of black Americans to Harlem in New York City

KEY TERM

Old South
The area of the USA which comprised the Confederate States of America, which had seceded from the USA in 1861 to defend slavery, thus causing the Civil War. These states included Mississippi, Louisiana, Alabama, Georgia, North Carolina, South Carolina, Virginia, Florida, Tennessee and Arkansas. East Texas was also an area with extensive slavery. The area known as 'the Deep South' is usually associated with Mississippi, Alabama, Georgia, Louisiana and North and South Carolina. Other states which allowed slavery up to the time of the Civil War were Missouri, Kentucky, Maryland and Delaware. These stayed loyal to the USA and were termed 'border states'.

Up to 1865, a major issue in American politics was black slavery and the denial of civil rights to black Americans. By 1861, just over half the US states were free states, which meant they had abolished slavery. The other states, in the South, retained slavery as it was seen as vital to the economic prosperity of the region. The tension between free and slave states eventually led to the Civil War in 1861, when a president was inaugurated who wished to prevent the spread of slavery westward. Most slave-owning states decided to secede from (leave) the USA to form their own country, the **Confederate States of America**. The northern states, which also contained four slave states, went to war with the Confederacy in order to preserve the unity of the United States. During that war, the US president Abraham Lincoln, in order to win the conflict, made the abolition of slavery a northern war aim. Shortly before the end of the war, in January 1865, slavery was abolished.

KEY TERM

Confederate States of America
A country created as a result of the American Civil War. It comprised 11 states, which were formerly part of the USA: Alabama, Mississippi, Louisiana, Arkansas, Texas, Tennessee, Virginia, North Carolina, South Carolina, Florida and Georgia. Four slave states did not officially join the Confederacy. These were Missouri, Kentucky, Maryland and Delaware. Volunteers from these states joined the Confederate army and Missouri was split throughout the war between federal- and Confederate-controlled areas. The western part of Virginia seceded from Virginia, as it was an anti-slavery area. In 1863, it became the new state of West Virginia.

The abolition of slavery allowed black Americans from the Old South to migrate north and west to seek new economic opportunities and to try to escape racial discrimination. This slow migration became a flood during and after the First World War. From 1915 to 1945, hundreds of thousands of black Americans migrated to the north in what became known as the Great Migration. By 2009, most black Americans lived in urban areas and had become a significant population in many northern and western cities, as well as urban areas in the South.

The change in geographical distribution of black Americans did not lead to an end of racial discrimination against them. Race riots occurred in many northern and western cities after the First World War and racially based housing areas became a feature of most towns, with white populations migrating to suburbs, leaving the central districts of cities to become primarily black American areas. In the Old South, racial **segregation** was enshrined in law up to the 1960s. In the north and west, racial segregation occurred informally. As a result of the change in geographical distribution of black Americans between 1850 and 2009, civil rights issues, once associated with the Old South, became a nationwide phenomenon.

KEY TERM

Segregation
The separation of black and white in the USA in terms of education, housing, recreational facilities, transportation and the armed forces. In some states, primarily in the Old South, segregation was enforced by law and was known as legal or *de jure* segregation. In other parts of the USA, racial discrimination of an informal nature, usually in housing, was known as *de facto* segregation.

The migration to the north and west, away from the South, had been fuelled by the introduction of legal racial discrimination by white-dominated southern state governments, from the 1890s. However, by the 1970s legal segregation had come to an end. In addition, the Old South began to go through a period of rapid economic growth. These factors led to a migration of some black Americans back to the Old South by 2009.

1919 – Red Summer and Chicago race riot

1941–45 – Second World War increases black migration north and west

1950s – Civil rights movement launches campaign against legal segregation

1965 – Watts race riot in Los Angeles

1970s – Desegregation of Old South is completed

1992 – Rodney King riots in Los Angeles

| 1920 | 1935 | 1940 | 1945 | 1950 | 1955 | 1960 | 1965 | 1970 | 1990 | 2005 | 2010 |

1921 – Tulsa race riot

1920s – Harlem Renaissance

1945 onwards – Growth of suburbia leads to creation of black and white housing areas across the USA

1967 – Newark race riot and Kerner Report

1960s onwards – Migration back to Old South begins

2008 – Barack Obama is elected first black American president

SOURCE
1 The number of black Americans in the USA and the proportion of the total population they comprised from 1790 to 2009.

Year	Population (millions)	Percent of population
1790	0.8	19.3
1800	1.0	18.9
1850	3.6	15.7
1900	8.8	11.6
1910	9.8	10.7
1920	10.5	9.9
1930	11.9	9.7
1940	12.9	9.8
1950	15.0	10.0
1960	18.9	10.5
1970	22.6	11.1
1980	26.5	11.7
1990	30.0	12.1
2000	34.6	12.3
2009	38	11.0

HOW FAR DID THE GEOGRAPHICAL DISTRIBUTION OF BLACK AMERICANS CHANGE IN THE YEARS 1850–2009?

The position in 1850

The Atlantic slave trade brought black West Africans to work as slaves in the Americas. By the time the USA held its first census in 1790, there were roughly 700,000 black Americans, approximately 19 percent of the US population. In the 19th century, white Americans referred to slavery as 'the peculiar institution' because it was unique to a number of states in the south-east. These states comprised Delaware, Maryland, Virginia, North and South Carolina, Georgia, Florida, Alabama, Mississippi, Kentucky, Tennessee, Arkansas, Missouri and Texas. The capital territory of the District of Columbia also allowed slavery. The other states were called free states; over the period 1777–1850, slavery had been abolished in these states. By 1850, there were 3.2 million black slaves, and approximately 400,000 free black Americans in the USA.

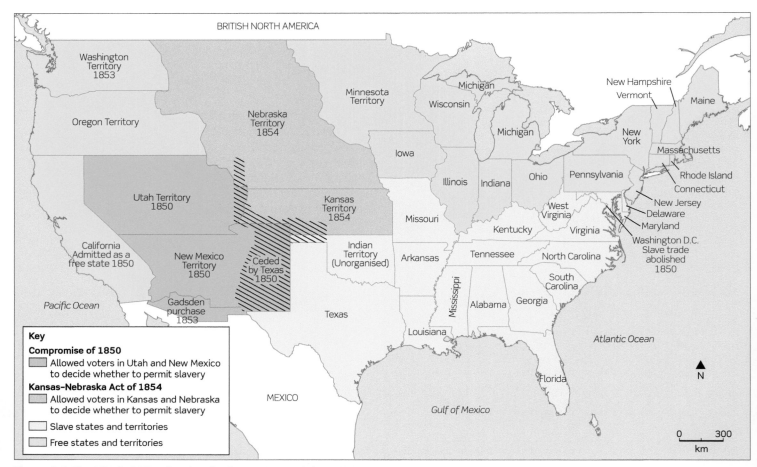

Figure 1.1 The USA in 1854, showing the free states and slave states.

TIMELINE: THE FINAL ABOLITION OF SLAVERY IN THE FREE STATES, 1777–1850

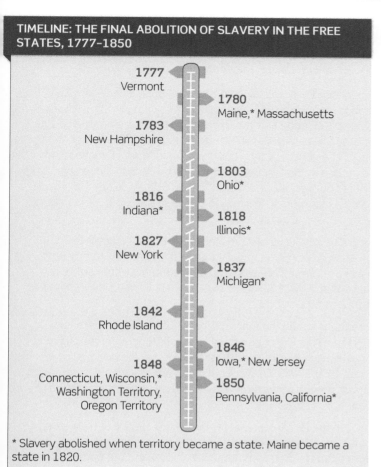

1777 Vermont

1780 Maine,* Massachusetts

1783 New Hampshire

1803 Ohio*

1816 Indiana*

1818 Illinois*

1827 New York

1837 Michigan*

1842 Rhode Island

1846 Iowa,* New Jersey

1848 Connecticut, Wisconsin,* Washington Territory, Oregon Territory

1850 Pennsylvania, California*

* Slavery abolished when territory became a state. Maine became a state in 1820.

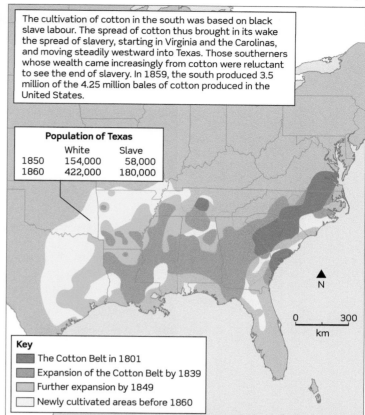

The cultivation of cotton in the south was based on black slave labour. The spread of cotton thus brought in its wake the spread of slavery, starting in Virginia and the Carolinas, and moving steadily westward into Texas. Those southerners whose wealth came increasingly from cotton were reluctant to see the end of slavery. In 1859, the south produced 3.5 million of the 4.25 million bales of cotton produced in the United States.

Population of Texas

	White	Slave
1850	154,000	58,000
1860	422,000	180,000

N

0 — 300 km

Key

■ The Cotton Belt in 1801
■ Expansion of the Cotton Belt by 1839
■ Further expansion by 1849
□ Newly cultivated areas before 1860

Figure 1.2 The cultivation of cotton in the South, 1801–60. © Sir Martin Gilbert (2009).

When the **US Constitution** was written and approved at a Constitutional Convention in Philadelphia, Pennsylvania in 1787, the issue of slavery appeared only once in that document. Black American slaves were mentioned only in the section of the Constitution that dealt with the allocation of seats in the **US Congress** House of Representatives. There were 435 seats allocated to states based on population, with the most populous states gaining the largest allocation of seats. For this purpose, black American slaves were included in the calculation. Even though black American slaves had no civil rights and could not vote, a slave was worth three-fifths of a free, white person in allocating seats.

KEY TERMS

US Constitution
A document that embodies the fundamental laws and principles by which the USA is governed.

US Congress
The national legislative body of the USA, consisting of the Senate, or upper house, and the House of Representatives, or lower house, as a continuous institution.

Slaves were primarily used as agricultural workers in the slave states. The main crops associated with slave labour were cotton, tobacco and rice production. The most valuable agricultural commodity in the USA before the Civil War was cotton. Cotton was grown mainly to provide the raw material for Britain's cotton manufacturing industry. The wealth of the Old South was inextricably associated with slave labour.

Northern states, free of slavery, were the recipients of hundreds of thousands of white immigrants from Europe, which swelled cities such as New York, Boston and Philadelphia. The newly arrived white immigrants saw slave labour as a rival to them in the labour market. In addition, many voters in free states saw the concept of slavery as contrary to the civil rights given to all other Americans. A rivalry developed between free states and slave states. In 1819, the Missouri Compromise admitted Missouri as a slave state to the USA. It was balanced by the admission of a free state, Maine, in 1820. The rivalry between the northern and mid-western free states and the slave-owning southern states was termed 'sectional conflict'.

Freedom in 1865

The potential geographical expansion of slavery became an issue of conflict between those who supported it and those who opposed it during the 1850s and laid the foundations for the Civil War. Attempts had been made in the Missouri Compromise of 1820 and the Compromise of 1850 to maintain a parity between free and slave states, as each US state was allotted two **senators** in the US Senate. The Kansas–Nebraska Act of 1854 opened up the possibility of extending slavery westward (see Figure 1.1). The Act declared that when new states were created out of the Kansas–Nebraska territory, the decision to become either a free state or a slave state would be decided by the adult, male population. The process was known as 'popular sovereignty'. This resulted in large numbers of pro-slavery and anti-slavery white

KEY TERM

Senator
Each state has the right to elect two senators to the US Congress. Each senator is elected for a six-year term. The 100 senators have considerable power. They have the power to approve or reject presidential nominations to the president's cabinet and justices to the Supreme Court. They also have the power to ratify treaties with foreign governments. As one of the two houses of Congress, the US Senate has to pass any proposal for legislation before it is sent to the president for signature to become law.

migrants entering the territory, in particular the Kansas area. An armed conflict occurred in Kansas in the late 1850s even before the outbreak of civil war. The Act also encouraged anti-slavery political groups to come together to oppose the westward movement of slavery. In the same year, 1854, the Republican Party was created. It opposed the creation of any new slave states in the west.

In 1860, Abraham Lincoln of the Republican Party was elected sixteenth president of the USA. Within a month of Lincoln's inauguration, in March 1861, the country was plunged into civil war. Southern slave-owning states saw Lincoln's election as a major threat to the future of slavery. The wealth of these states was based on slave labour. Also, southern states saw the USA as a voluntary union of states created initially in 1776. They believed they had the right to leave or secede from the USA if they so wished. South Carolina was the first southern state to secede in December 1860, just after the presidential election. Other southern states followed in 1861. They decided to form their own country, the Confederate States of America, in order to preserve slavery. In all, 11 states seceded.

The northern states viewed the issue differently. They believed the USA was an indissoluble union which, once a state joined, it could not leave. The north initially fought the Civil War to preserve the union of states. They called the war the 'Great Rebellion' and Confederates were known as 'rebels'. Only later in the war, from the autumn of 1862, did the issue of abolishing slavery within Confederate-held areas become a northern war aim.

During the Civil War, many black Americans joined the federal (Union) army. By the war's end, over 300,000 black Americans had served in the US armed forces. Also, as federal forces began to penetrate areas occupied by the Confederate states, tens of thousands of black slaves fled to join the federal forces, acting as civilian workers. In 1862, the Confederate Congress issued a declaration that any former slaves caught in the federal army would be summarily executed, along with any white officers leading black American troops.

Black Americans were not allowed to join the Confederate army until April 1865, just before the end of the war. A small token force of a few hundred was based in Richmond, Virginia. Confederate troops openly tried to kill all black American Union troops, as at Fort Pillow and the Battle of the Crater, both in 1864.

The Civil War transformed the position of black Americans. In January 1863, President Lincoln issued the Emancipation Proclamation which declared all slaves under Confederate control free. In 1865, the Thirteenth Amendment of the US Constitution declared slavery to be abolished. In 1868, the Fourteenth Amendment granted all US citizens equal protection of the law and, in 1870, the Fifteenth Amendment granted all adult male US citizens the right to vote. These Civil War Amendments meant that all black Americans in the USA were now free and equal, in theory, with white citizens. Over 3.5 million black Americans had been removed from slavery. In the period 1863–77, the federal government made attempts to assist black Americans in the transition from slavery to freemen. A Freedmen's Bureau was established and former slaves were promised land to cultivate. However, as a South Carolina slave said in 1865, just because his master said he was free, it did not mean he was white and did not mean he was equal.

Hopes of landownership for former slaves failed to materialise for most black Americans in the former Confederate states, in spite of efforts by the US government. The Southern Homestead Act was passed by the US Congress in 1866, setting aside 44 million acres (approximately 20 million hectares) for freed slaves. However, very few freed slaves could avail themselves of this opportunity, due to lack of money to buy land and farm implements and opposition from southern whites.

These developments led to sharecropping for freed black and poor white Americans. Old plantations which employed hundreds of slaves before abolition were divided into small farms of 30 to 50 acres, where rent for use was paid by giving the white landowner a share of the crop. To raise money to buy crops and farm tools a local credit system was introduced, which led to many sharecroppers facing debts caused by high rates of interest for borrowing money. By 1880, sharecropping was commonplace from east Texas to South Carolina. The hopes that the abolition of slavery would lead to a better life for freed black slaves proved illusory.

ACTIVITY
KNOWLEDGE CHECK

Freedom in 1865

1 Identify four reasons why black Americans did not have the same civil rights as other Americans in the years to 1865.

2 Identify the ways in which the Civil War of 1861-65 helped to improve the position of black Americans within US society.

The slow drift north and west

On the eve of the abolition of slavery, the northern and western states comprised approximately 500,000 free black citizens. Faced with harsh economic conditions and continued racial discrimination in the former Confederate states, black Americans in that region began to migrate north and west. In the years 1865–1917, there was a slow migration out of the Old South. Even though migration took place, by 1910, 50 years after the Civil War, 89 percent of black Americans still lived in the former Confederate states, with 80 percent of these still living in rural areas. The cost of relocating proved prohibitive for many.

Before the Civil War, some black Americans had escaped from slavery, aided by northern white Americans in the **abolitionist movement**, which campaigned to end slavery. Of those who escaped from slavery, many moved north through what was known as the **underground railroad**, organised by northern sympathisers.

KEY TERMS

Abolitionist movement
From the 1830s until 1870, this movement attempted to achieve immediate emancipation of all slaves and the ending of racial segregation and discrimination. In early 1831, William Lloyd Garrison, in Boston, began publishing a newspaper, the *Liberator*, supported largely by free black Americans, who always played a major role in the movement. By 1835, the movement had received substantial moral and financial support from black American communities in the north. It had also established hundreds of branches throughout the free states, flooding the north with anti-slavery literature, agents and petitions demanding that Congress end all federal support for slavery.

Underground railroad
The network of safe houses and helpers who assisted black slaves in their journey to the northern free states and Canada.

After 1865, the slow migration north continued. Northern cities such as Cincinnati, on the Ohio River and just north of the slave state of Kentucky, had 3,700 black Americans by 1877, of whom 70 percent had come from the South. More popular destinations were the northern cities like New York, Philadelphia, Detroit and Cleveland. Black Americans tended to take the shortest route north. Those who lived in Mississippi, Alabama and Tennessee tended to move to Chicago, while those on the east coast gravitated towards New York, Philadelphia and Boston. By 1917, all these cities had sizeable black American communities, with areas such as the South Side of Chicago and Harlem in New York City becoming distinctive black areas.

Clearly push factors help to explain this migration. Lack of job opportunities, racial intimidation by groups such as the Ku Klux Klan, an d the in troduction of racial segregation by southern state governments dominated by whites all explain the desire to move north and west. Also, in 1914, a small insect, called the boll weevil, had a very destructive effect on the cotton crop, causing a major economic depression.

However, there were also pull factors. The north, to many southern black Americans, was the 'promised land'. It was the northern president, Abraham Lincoln, who made the Emancipation Proclamation which came into force on 1 January 1863, and it was Lincoln who helped push through the Thirteenth Amendment of the US Constitution that abolished slavery. The image of the north as a land of liberation was central in the minds of many southern black Americans. Northern black newspapers, such as the *Chicago Defender*, reinforced this view with advertisements by northern recruiters for industrial jobs. The move north was also aided by family members who had moved north and had written home highlighting the advantages of living and working in the north. Northern recruiters also saw advantages in hiring southern black Americans. They were willing to work for lower wages than white people and could also be used as non-union labour in breaking strikes by white workers, such as the 1911 strike on the Illinois Central Railroad, as they were forbidden in the vast majority of trade unions.

Migration also saw black Americans move westward. In 1879, approximately 6,000 black Americans from the Old South migrated to Kansas, Missouri and Iowa. This was the prelude to more extensive black American migration which occurred in the mid-western states in the early 20th century.

In 1914, the First World War broke out in Europe. This brought an abrupt halt to the flow of white European migration across the Atlantic. The labour shortage which resulted offered greater opportunities for black Americans and helped speed up the rate of migration north to work in war-related industries.

Overall, the slow migration north and west was the result of a combination of both 'push' and 'pull' factors. As life in the former southern slave states became more difficult, both economically and politically, migration to the north and west became more attractive.

SOURCE 2 Black migrants entering Kansas in 1879 to escape an outbreak of yellow fever in the Old South.

EN ROUTE FOR KANSAS—FLEEING FROM THE YELLOW FEVER.—DRAWN BY SOL EYTINGE, JUN., FROM A SKETCH BY H. J. LEWIS.

SOURCE 3

Attacks and intimidation by white supremacist groups such as the Ku Klux Klan were major push factors and forced black Americans to leave the Old South. This is an illustration from a magazine, the *Richmond Whig*, a southern magazine from Virginia, published in 1872 highlighting the issue.

"ONE VOTE LESS."—*Richmond Whig.*

EXTEND YOUR KNOWLEDGE

Ku Klux Klan

The Ku Klux Klan (KKK) was a white supremacist organisation which committed widespread acts of violence and intimidation against black Americans, including lynching. It was formed in 1866 to defend southern whites during the period of Reconstruction in the Old South. Members of the KKK hid their identity by wearing hoods and white robes. The KKK publicised its presence by burning a large cross ('the fiery cross') which acted as its symbol. It was suppressed by the federal government and went into decline following the end of Reconstruction in 1877 and the introduction of legal segregation by states in the Old South.

The organisation was revived in 1915 by W. Simmons at Stone Mountain, Georgia. This can be explained in part by the impact of D.W. Griffith's film *Birth of a Nation*, which was released in 1915 (see Chapter 2). The film dealt with the issues of the Civil War and Reconstruction and portrayed black Americans as exploitative and under the influence of northern white Americans. The KKK grew rapidly in the years from 1915 to become a nationwide institution with hundreds of thousands of members. It suffered a major loss in influence following scandals involving the KKK leader in 1926, but remained an important institution in intimidating black Americans and engaging in acts of violence, including lynching and murder, up to the 1970s.

SOURCE 4

From an article written by Booker T. Washington in 1908 for the monthly magazine, *Outlook*. This was one of the most popular magazines in the USA and was published in New York City. Among its contributors were Theodore Roosevelt (president 1901–09) and Booker T. Washington. Washington was a major black American civil rights activist. Here he highlights pull factors behind the black American migration to the north and west.

BOLEY, A NEGRO TOWN IN THE WEST

Boley, Indian Territory, is the youngest, the most enterprising, and in many ways the most interesting of the negro towns in the United States. A rude, bustling, Western town it is a characteristic product of the negro immigration from the South and Middle West into the new lands of what is now the State of Oklahoma.

The large proportions of the northward and westward movement of the negro population recall the Kansas Exodus of thirty years ago, when within a few months more than forty thousand helpless and destitute negroes from the country districts of Arkansas and Mississippi poured into eastern Kansas in search of 'better homes, larger opportunities, and kindlier treatment.'

It is a striking evidence of the progress made in thirty years that the present northward and westward movement of the negro people has brought into these new lands, not a helpless and ignorant horde of black people, but land-seekers and home-builders, men who have come prepared to build up the country.

ACTIVITY
KNOWLEDGE CHECK

Slow migration north and west

1 Identify reasons which help to explain why black Americans wished to migrate north and west in the second half of the 19th century.

2 What do you regard as more important in explaining black migration: push factors or pull factors?

A Level Exam-Style Question Section C

How far can the end of the US Civil War in 1865 be regarded as a turning point in the changing geography of civil rights issues in the USA in the period 1850–2009? (20 marks)

Tip

It is important to consider the importance of the end of Civil War in the changing geography. It led to slow migration to the north and west initially, leading to greater migration after the First World War. It also led to change in where black Americans lived. Before 1865, they lived predominantly in the rural south on plantations. After 1865, they migrated to urban areas, as well as out of the Old South.

The Great Migration, 1915–45

The slow migration of black Americans out of the Old South in the second half of the 19th century became a flood in the years after the First World War. In what became known as the 'First Great Migration', 1.6 million black Americans left the south-east of the USA, predominantly from rural areas to live in cities in the north. In 1910, seven million of the country's eight million black Americans resided in the area known as the Cotton Belt. In the next 15 years, more than ten percent of the country's black American population voluntarily moved north. By 1930, black Americans lived in large numbers across the USA, north and south.

As with the migration in the second half of the 19th century, both pull and push factors help to explain such a mass movement of population. Between 1910 and 1930, the black American population increased by 40 percent in northern states, with some of the biggest increases in cities such as Detroit, Cleveland, Chicago and New York City.

Pull factor: the impact of the First World War

It is estimated that 400,000 black Americans left the Old South from 1916 to 1918 to take advantage of job opportunities created by the war. The outbreak of war in Europe, in 1914, had led to a drop in European migration. Combined with the demand for US-produced armaments by the Allied powers fighting the First World War, job opportunities arose. By 1916, war production was in full swing. The shortage of labour was met from two sources: white women and black Americans. To fill that gap, many black Americans moved from a life of poverty in the rural south to northern industrial cities. Recruiting agents representing northern industrial companies went south to entice black Americans north with promises of a better lifestyle, higher wages and an end to poverty. The most widely read black newspaper in the Old South was the *Chicago Defender*, produced in the north. The newspaper urged southern black Americans already working in the north to publish their own letters in the newspaper, which stated that life was much better in the north. One example came from the sister of black American Julia Hunt of Texas. Her sister, R.V., moved north to find a job in Boston, Massachusetts. In letters to her sister, R.V. wrote about meeting black people from Africa, attending concerts with her white friends and earning a degree in music from a white school. Southern black Americans also heard about life in the north from friends and relatives who came back to the South for visits. They came home dressed in their finest clothes. Some drove brand new cars, which were often rented or soon to be repossessed. Others told tall stories. A 'great job' at US Steel, for example, actually meant pushing a broom.

SOURCE 5

Black American sharecroppers leaving their home in the Old South to migrate north during the 1930s.

The editorial of the newspaper praised the north as a land of opportunity and freedom and, at the same time, condemned the South as a land of poverty and repression. Many of the claims made in the *Chicago Defender* were borne out in reality. A black American man could earn $2.50 a day in a meat-packing factory in Chicago, and as much as $5.00 a day on the assembly line of a car and truck manufacturer in Detroit. This was far more than what black Americans could earn in the rural south, where sharecropping and domestic service offered very poor rates of pay. In Alabama, for example, black American domestic servants received just a few dollars a week.

In addition to moving north to work in war-related industries, thousands of black Americans decided to join the US armed forces, which at this time remained segregated between black and white. Several black regiments fought with distinction on the Western Front in the First World War in 1918.

Pull factor: the economic boom of the 1920s

The migration which began with the First World War was sustained with the economic changes affecting the USA in the 1920s. From 1922, the US economy experienced a major economic boom. The development of the car industry characterised the changes. The growth of mass production through the use of assembly-line techniques lowered the prices of manufactured goods and increased demand. Detroit became the car manufacturing capital of the world. Companies like General Motors and Ford recruited tens of thousands of black Americans in their plants (see Source 6). The demand for workers meant that black Americans were afforded greater job opportunities in the north and west.

SOURCE 6

Increase in population of Detroit, Michigan, the centre of US car manufacturing, 1910–30. Over the period, the population of Detroit grew by 300 percent, while the black American population of Detroit grew by 2,400 percent.

Year	Total population	Black American population
1910	465,766	5,741
1920	993,675	40,838
1930	1,568,662	120,066

At the same time, agriculture went through a difficult period. The boom in agricultural prices and increased demand during the First World War came to an end in the 1920s as Europe recovered from war and sourced supplies from elsewhere. As the Old South was heavily dependent on agriculture, the economic changes of the 1920s acted as both pull and push factors on black migration.

SOURCE 7

From *The Negro at Work During the First World War and Reconstruction* produced by the Department of Labor, Bureau of Negro Statistics, published in 1921. It provides official government information on the migration of black Americans to the north during the First World War.

MIGRATION.

Shortage of labor in northern industries was the direct cause of the increased Negro migration during the war period. This direct cause was, of course, augmented by other causes, among which were the increased dissatisfaction with conditions in the South – the ravages of the boll weevil, floods, change of crop system, low wages and poor houses and schools.

A previous bulletin of the department summed up the causes as follows:

Other causes assigned as the southern end are numerous: General dissatisfaction with conditions, ravages of boll weevil, change of crop system, low wages, poor houses on plantations, poor school facilities, unsatisfactory crop settlements, rough treatment, lynching, desire for travel, labor agents, the Negro press, letters from friends in the North, and finally advice of white friends in the South where crops had failed.

The Department of Labor estimates the Negro migration in figures of from 400,000 to 500,000. Other estimates, ranging from 300,000 to 800,000, have been made by individual experts and by private bureaus. Such a variation of figures goes to show the wide scope of the migration. Prior to the war period the Negro worker had been sparsely located in the North, but the laws of self-preservation of the industrial and agricultural assets of our country and the law of demand and supply turned almost overnight both into war and private industries hundreds of thousands of Negro workers, among whom there were laborers, molders, carpenters, blacksmiths, painters, janitors, chauffeurs, machinist laborers, and a mass of other workers, comprising, probably, nearly every type of skilled, semiskilled and unskilled labor.

The most marked effects of the migration were easily determinable. First, the agricultural regions of the Southern States, particularly Mississippi and Louisiana, began to suffer for want of the Negro worker who had so long tilled the soil of those regions. On the other hand, the Negro workers who had been turned into the plants of the North faced the necessity of performing efficient work in the minimum amount of time, of adjusting themselves to northern conditions and of becoming fixtures in their particular line of employment, or becoming 'floaters.'

It is interesting to review for a moment some of the wage scales in Southern States. In 1917 about $12 a month was being paid for farm labor in many sections. In other sections 75 cents and $1 a day were considered equitable wages. During the harvesting of rice in the 'grinding season' the amount was usually increased to $1.25 and $1.75 per day, with a possible average of $1.50. Cotton was always considered a cheap labor crop, about which one man has said:

'The world has gone on thinking that the farm labor in the South should work for 75 cents or $1 a day when all other labor is getting $1.50 and $2 per day.'

EXTRACT

The view of Peter Gottlieb, a historian writing in 1978, about the migration of black Americans into the western Pennsylvania city of Pittsburgh, which was an important centre for steel production. It outlines the reasons for migration from the Old South and the impact black Americans had on Pittsburgh.

Beginning in 1916 and continuing until the depression of the 1930s, Pittsburgh received thousands of southern black migrants who were participants in the Great Migration which carried a million and a half black men and women from the South to the North. Most of those new arrivals in Pittsburgh left the states of Virginia, North Carolina, South Carolina, Georgia and Alabama. They moved north basically for the same reason the southern and eastern Europeans had come to America – to seek jobs in the iron and steel mills. Between 1910 and 1930, the black population of Pittsburgh grew 115 percent – from 25,623 to 54,983. The number of black iron- and steelworkers in Pittsburgh in this period increased from 786 to 2,853, or 626 percent.

The experience of southern black migrants to Pittsburgh represents a chapter in the epic story of rural people lured from their homelands by the possibilities of higher wages in the industrial city. The pattern of life among rural blacks in the South after Reconstruction, the particular aspirations they brought with them to the North, and their opinions of Pittsburgh as a new home and as a place of work produced a unique variation on the country-to-city theme.

Pull factor: the Great Depression and New Deal

The period 1929 to 1941 saw the USA plunged into economic depression and then, from 1933, a period of economic recovery known as the New Deal. The federal government established a number of federal agencies through which black Americans obtained jobs. The Works Progress Administration (WPA), the National Youth Administration (NYA) and the Civilian Conservation Corps (CCC) allocated ten percent of their budgets for black Americans, who comprised ten percent of the population but 20 percent of the poor. However, the intervention of southern white Democrats meant that social security was denied to most black Americans and many trade unions excluded black Americans from membership. Attempting to prevent black Americans from being discriminated against was extremely difficult in the states of the Old South that had introduced legal segregation.

Push factor: the slump in the cotton industry

The pull factors which encouraged black Americans to move north were strengthened by severe problems associated with the Old South's agricultural economy, in particular in the cotton-growing areas.

In 1914, the southern cotton industry suffered a major catastrophe. A tiny insect called the boll weevil appeared in the cotton fields of east Texas and spread across the cotton-growing areas of the South, destroying the crop. Thousands of black Americans faced acute poverty which forced them to look for work elsewhere.

After the end of the First World War, the cotton-producing areas faced a major slump in prices. This was due to a massive drop in demand for cotton as a result of the end of the war. The wholesale price of cotton stood at 42 cents a pound in 1920. It then dropped to 10 cents a pound in 1921. By 1932, it had fallen even further to 5 cents a pound. This had a major impact on those black Americans who were sharecroppers. Facing poverty and destitution, many moved north.

Push factor: the rise of discrimination and violence against black Americans in the old south

An important push factor in the Great Migration was the growth of discrimination and violence against black Americans in the Old South. Between 1890 and the outbreak of the First World War, white-dominated southern state governments introduced laws which denied black Americans many of their civil rights. Although the Fifteenth Amendment of the US Constitution of 1870 guaranteed all American adult males the right to vote, this was effectively removed from black Americans in the Old South. Southern governments introduced literacy tests for registration and a poll tax to be paid if people wished to vote. These laws affected poor white people too, but as most black Americans living in the Old South lived in poverty, it disproportionately discriminated against them. In some states, a Grandfather Clause was inserted into the registration process. If a person's grandfather could not vote, then nor could that person. As the vast majority of black Americans had been slaves before 1865, their grandfathers could not have voted.

Increased legal discrimination was also associated with the rise of violence against black Americans, and **lynching** of black Americans increased. In 1915, the white supremacist group, the Ku Klux Klan, was revived and grew rapidly to become a major force in American life in the years 1915 to 1926. Indiscriminate violent attacks on black Americans occurred in their thousands across the Old South. The move north was seen by many in biblical terms. Just as Moses had led the Israelites out of bondage in Egypt, the north became the new 'Promised Land'.

THINKING HISTORICALLY   Change (8a, b & c) (I)

Imposing realities

Black American musicians in Harlem, New York, in 1938.

Answer the following question.

1 Explain why the conversation in the photograph above would not have happened.

The shape of history is imposed by people looking back. People who lived through the 'history' did not always perceive the patterns that later historians identify. For example, some people living through the Industrial Revolution may have understood that great change was taking place, but they would not have been able to understand the massive economic, social and political consequences of industrialisation.

Answer the following questions.

2 Consider the beginning of the Great Migration of black Americans north and west.

   a) Who would have made the decision as to when the Great Migration began?

   b) Could anybody have challenged this decision?

   c) Explain why someone living in the early 20th century would have been unable to make a judgement about the beginning of a new era.

3 Who living at the present time might regard the beginning of the Great Migration as an important event?

4 What does this photograph tell us about the structure of history as we understand it?

Black American population in selected cities, 1920.

City	Number of black Americans	Percent of total
New York City	152,467	2.7
Philadelphia	134,229	7.4
Washington DC	109,966	25.1
Chicago	109,457	4.1
Baltimore	108,322	14.8
New Orleans	100,930	26.1
Birmingham	70,320	39.3
St Louis	69,854	9.0
Atlanta	62,796	31.3
Memphis	61,181	37.1
Richmond	54,041	31.5
Norfolk, VA	43,392	37.5
Jacksonville	41,520	45.3
Detroit	40,838	4.1
Louisville	40,087	17.1
Savannah	39,179	47.1
Pittsburgh	37,725	6.4
Nashville	35,633	30.1
Indianapolis	34,678	11.8
Cleveland	34,451	4.3
Houston	30,960	24.6
Kansas City, MO	30,719	9.5
Cincinnati	30,079	7.5

The Great Migration

1 Suggest five reasons why you think the Great Migration took place.

2 What impact did the Great Migration have on the geographical distribution of black Americans?

A Level Exam-Style Question Section C

How far did the period 1850–2009 see a major change in the geographical distribution of black Americans? (20 marks)

Tip

You will need to identify the degree of change in the pattern of black American distribution within the United States brought about by the slow drift north and west and the Great Migration. You will need to identify how far it changed over the years stipulated.

The impact of the Second World War: migration north and west, 1941–45

The Second World War transformed the US economy. In the five wartime years of 1941–45, national income, wealth and industrial production more than doubled. In 1940, the gross national product was $99.7 billion; by 1945, it had risen to $211 billion. When Franklin Roosevelt (FDR) came to power as president in 1933, there were 12.8 million out of work, 25 percent of the workforce. By 1940, after six years of the New Deal, unemployment had fallen to 8.1 million, 14.6 percent of the workforce; and by 1945, unemployment had fallen to one million, 1.9 percent of the workforce. By conscripting nearly 12 million men into the armed forces, and placing the economy on a war footing, FDR had brought unrivalled prosperity. The war created 17 million new jobs, with average wages rising by 30 percent. These dramatic changes in the US economy led to greater job opportunities for black Americans.

When millions of Americans joined the military, they moved to bases away from home. So did millions of military civilian employees. However, more important permanent shifts in population occurred because of the war. Fifteen million black and white Americans moved permanently. Black Americans continued the Great Migration of the 1920s and 1930s, moving north from the Old South. Seven hundred thousand left the Old South, many taking the traditional route to Chicago, Philadelphia and New York. However, a new trend in population movement was occurring, with many people moving to the Pacific Coast to war industries such as aircraft production and shipbuilding. For instance, 120,000 black Americans moved west into the Los Angeles area.

 One of the impacts of black migration during the Second World War was the creation of tensions in the housing market between black and white people. Historian Albert Broussard highlights the issue in his study, *Black San Francisco*, published in 1993.

The assimilation of 27,000 black migrants into San Francisco within a span of four years, 1941-1945, was not easy. An even larger influx of white migrants during the same period exacerbated the problems of housing, race relations, and the black migrants' adjustment. Perhaps under the best of circumstances, race relations would be strained in the wake of a sizable black migration. Yet even though San Francisco suffered from racial tensions in a number of areas, conditions never resembled the volatile situations in Los Angeles or Detroit, where race riots erupted. Black and white San Franciscans coexisted in a state of relative peace and mutual toleration. Indeed, the two races came into contact more frequently than ever before in housing, employment, recreation and public accommodations. But some whites were visibly disturbed over the growing black presence and showed disdain for blacks. After all, longtime residents, both white and black, had to adjust to the presence of tens of thousands of blacks in a city where less than 5,000 had lived in 1940. The process was often fraught with racial antipathy and bitterness, but the black migration was also welcomed in some circles as the dawning of a new era in San Francisco's race relations. This duality – tolerance and ambivalence – made the adjustment of wartime black migrants unpredictable and uncertain in a city that had been renowned for its racial toleration.

KEY TERM

Rust Belt
The area of the USA associated with declining industry in the 1970s and 1980s, usually associated with large-scale industry such as steelmaking and car manufacture. States regarded as being in the Rust Belt were Michigan, Pennsylvania and New York state.

KEY TERM

Reconstruction, 1863–77
The period of US history associated with the readmission of Confederate states back into the United States. Officially, it began in 1863 in those areas of the Confederacy already recaptured by the northern Union army. The main period of Reconstruction occurred after the end of the Civil War, from April 1865. Northern troops occupied and administered the former Confederate states until such time that the US Congress deemed they could be readmitted back into the USA with their own elective state governments.

Migration after the Second World War: the move back to the Old South

The migration of black Americans since the end of the Civil War had a profound impact on their economic, political and social lives. By the end of the Second World War, in 1945, more black Americans lived in urban areas than in rural areas. By 1970, black Americans were more urbanised than the average American population. Eighty percent of black Americans lived in cities compared to 70 percent of the general American population. Also, by 1970, only 53 percent of black Americans lived in the Old South. Forty percent of black Americans lived in the north-east and mid-western states and seven percent lived in the west.

However, a profound change occurred to the pattern of black migration. After the Second World War, and in particular from the 1960s, black Americans began to move back to the Old South from the north. Approximately two-thirds of black American migrants who moved to the Old South in the years 1965–70 returned to the area of their birth or their parents' birth. From 1975 to 1980, at least 41 percent of black American migrants moving south were return migrants.

The migration of black Americans back to the Old South occurred for a variety of reasons. Many were fleeing life in the inner cities of the north, noted for their high crime rates and limited job opportunities. Others sought new job opportunities in what became known as the 'Sun Belt', which included areas such as Florida, Georgia and Texas. From the 1970s, the Old South offered far better job opportunities as the region experienced rapid economic growth. In contrast, the north-east and mid-western states became known as the **Rust Belt** as heavy industry went into decline, particularly after the oil crisis of 1973. Once booming cities in Michigan, like Flint, became areas of social deprivation and high unemployment. For instance, in Detroit – the heart of the nation's auto-manufacturing industry – jobs were cut by more than half in the 30 years following the end of the Second World War. In 1947, the city had 3,272 manufacturing firms, which employed approximately 338,400 people; in 1977, the number of firms had withered to 1,954, employing 153,300 people. In 1963, the east north central region (primarily Michigan and Illinois) produced 30 percent of the nation's manufacturing output, while the South produced 21 percent, and the west 14 percent. By 1989, however, the eastern north central's manufacturing output had been cut almost in half, while the output in the South and west grew to 29 percent and 18 percent, respectively.

Nevertheless, coming home to family remained one of the most important factors pulling black Americans to the South, especially in the early years. In a 1973 survey of return migrants to Birmingham, Alabama, for example, the majority of respondents (52 percent) cited various kinship and family reasons, the single most important of which (cited by 12 percent of returnees) was to care for an ill or aging parent or relative. In a distant second, respondents mentioned various economic reasons (almost 20 percent) as the impetus for their return. Non-family social reasons (16 percent) and health/climate reasons (12 percent) also influenced decisions to return south.

ACTIVITY
KNOWLEDGE CHECK

The move back to the Old South

1 In what ways did the pattern of migration of black Americans remain the same in the years after 1933?

2 In what ways was the pattern of black migration different in the years from 1933?

3 Did the reasons for black migration change in the years after 1933? Explain your answer.

TO WHAT EXTENT DID THE CHANGING PATTERN OF SETTLEMENT AND SEGREGATION IMPACT ON CIVIL RIGHTS ISSUES IN THE YEARS 1850–2009?

The changing pattern of settlement of black Americans, in particular since the abolition of slavery by the Thirteenth Amendment of the US Constitution in 1865, had a major impact on the relations between white and black Americans. In the states of the Old South following the end of **Reconstruction** in 1877, white-dominated state governments began introducing legal segregation of their white and black populations. From the 1880s to the 1960s, black Americans faced legal segregation in housing, schooling, transportation and recreational facilities. The US Supreme Court case of *Plessy* v *Ferguson* of 1896 reinforced this development by declaring that segregation created 'separate but equal' treatment of white and black Americans, and was, therefore, not against the Fourteenth Amendment of the US Constitution which afforded all US citizens 'equal protection of the law'.

Discrimination against black Americans was not confined to the legal restrictions enforced in the Old South. Black Americans across the USA faced discrimination in housing and jobs. Even the US armed forces were racially segregated until 1948. The years 1850–2009 witnessed the continued struggle of black Americans to gain full and equal civil rights with other Americans.

The mass migration into Harlem from 1905

Perhaps the most famous black American community created in the north of the USA was Harlem, on Manhattan Island in the middle of the city of New York. The development of Harlem witnessed many of the problems faced by black Americans as they migrated north out of the old slave states into an area many regarded as the promised land of freedom. Harlem also saw the blossoming of a distinct black American urban culture which began with the Harlem Renaissance in the 1920s.

A major boost to black migration to Harlem came in 1905, when black American Philip Payton and his company the Afro-American Realty Company almost singlehandedly encouraged the growth of Harlem as a black American neighbourhood. Incorporated in 1904, Payton's company saw the potential of the Harlem area as the subway was extended to the area in that year. His company bought, leased and sold empty white-owned properties to black Americans. The availability of housing in the middle of the city helped fuel the Great Migration from the Old South. Although Payton died of liver cancer in 1917, his foresight and efforts were central to creating the Harlem black community. Between 1920 and 1930, approximately 87,000 black Americans arrived from the Old South and the West Indies. At the same time, over 118,000 white Americans moved out, helping to create a black community. Harlem became what the black American poet, Claude McKay, called a black metropolis and the black capital of the world.

A key feature of the development of Harlem was the Harlem Renaissance – the development of a distinct black American urban culture which encompassed music, song, poetry and literature. In 1925, the *New York Herald Tribune* newspaper was declaring the emergence of the Harlem Renaissance. This creative movement was grounded in the belief that race relations could be improved – and society reshaped – through art. Using black experiences and disappointments to mirror a 'democratic society' that did not treat its citizens equally, writers such as Countee Cullen, Langston Hughes and Zora Neale Hurston made up the literary arm of the movement. Visual artists such as Aaron Douglas, William H. Johnson and Malvin Gray Johnson contributed unforgettable images that emphasised the emotional and daily realities of black life. However, the energy and exuberance of these and many other Harlem Renaissance artists buckled in the 1930s under the weight of the Great Depression. The social changes that the movement had hoped for would not be realised until the Second World War pulled America, both black and white, out of its economic morass.

Although the Harlem Renaissance reflected the positive side of the development of a distinct black community within the centre of New York City, the existence of such a community created racial tension. The city had been no stranger to black–white conflict. In the anti-conscription riots of 1863, free black Americans were targeted by white mobs, who lynched them and burnt down black-owned property. In 1935 and 1943, Harlem faced its own race riots.

However, following the end of the Second World War, the economic fortunes of Harlem declined. The black American community was crammed into a relatively small area of Upper Manhattan Island, mainly due to discrimination against black Americans in relation to housing. In 2000, the population density of the whole of Manhattan Island was 2,000 people per square mile. In the 1920s, Harlem suffered a population density of 215,000 per square mile. Crammed into such a small area, Harlem also suffered from high levels of poor accommodation and unemployment, which were double that of New York City as a whole. Also, a 1990 study suggested life expectancy for a 15-year-old female resident of Harlem would be roughly on a par with that of a 15-year-old girl living in India. She would have about a 65 percent chance of surviving to 65, while a black man would have about a 37 percent chance of making it to the same age, on a par with an Angolan male in West Africa. As with other areas of deprivation and desperation, crime and drug abuse took a hold. In the 1960s, Harlem became an important base for radical black American groups such as the Nation of Islam, Malcolm X and his followers, and the Black Panther Party. Yet, at the same time, Harlem was the focus of a vibrant black culture and a strong religious life. However, from the 1960s Harlem experienced an influx of middle-class black Americans, Asians and Hispanics, attracted by the low housing prices. The influx, linked with a marked drop in crime, led to a revitalisation of the area.

SOURCE

9 From *Freedomways* by Langston Hughes, published in 1963. Hughes was a major figure in the Harlem Renaissance of the 1920s and recounts his early life in Harlem.

On a bright September morning in 1921, I came up out of the subway at 135th and Lenox into the beginnings of the Negro Renaissance. I headed for the Harlem Y.M.C.A. down the block, where so many new, young, dark, male arrivals in Harlem have spent early days. The next place I headed to that afternoon was the Harlem Branch Library just up the street. There, a warm and wonderful librarian, Miss Ernestine Rose, white, made newcomers feel welcome, as did her assistant in charge of the Schomburg Collection, Catherine Latimer, a luscious café au lait. That night I went to the Lincoln Theatre across Lenox Avenue where maybe one of the Smiths – Bessie, Clara, Trixie or Mamie – was singing the blues. As soon as I could, I made a beeline for *Shuffle Along*, the all-colored hit musical playing on 63rd Street in which Florence Mills came to fame.

I had come to New York to enter Columbia College as a freshman, but *really* why I had come to New York was to see Harlem. I found it hard a week or so later to tear myself away from Harlem when it came time to move up the hill to the dormitory at Columbia. That winter I spent as little time as possible on the campus. Instead, I spent as much time as I could in Harlem, and this I have done ever since. I was in love with Harlem long before I got there, and I still am in love with it. Everybody seemed to make me welcome. The sheer dark size of Harlem intrigued me. And the fact that at that time poets and writers like James Weldon Johnson and Jessie Fauset lived there, and Bert Williams, Duke Ellington, Ethel Waters, and Walter White, too, fascinated me. Had I been a rich young man, I would have bought a house in Harlem and built musical steps up to the front door, and installed chimes that at the press of a button played Ellington tunes.

The riots in Chicago, 1919

Black Americans saw the removal of their civil rights by the white-dominated state governments of the Old South from the 1880s. Denial of civil rights was also associated with an escalating incidence of random violence against black Americans in the form of lynching. Mob justice became a permanent feature of life for black Americans living in the Old South. Matters were made worse from 1915 with the revival of the white supremacist group, the Ku Klux Klan. Violence and intimidation against black Americans reinforced legal segregation, making black Americans second-class citizens.

However, violence against black Americans was not confined to the areas of legal segregation. Wherever black Americans migrated, they faced similar levels of discrimination occasionally linked to extreme violence. Such a period was the Red Summer of 1919. In that year, 26 race riots took place across the USA, both north and south. In July 1917, the Red Summer was preceded by a major race riot in East St Louis, Illinois, where black workers were being used to break a strike by white workers in an aluminium plant. In the ensuing riot, instigated by white workers, 48 black Americans were killed and hundreds injured. In addition, more than 300 buildings were destroyed.

Of all the 26 race riots affecting the USA in the hot summer of 1919, Chicago was the worst. The riot erupted on 27 July when the summer temperature soared to above 30 degrees Celsius. The spark that ignited the riot occurred when a black youth, 17-year-old Eugene Williams, entered a public beach on Lake Michigan usually reserved for white people. The 29th Street beach had traditionally been reserved for white people and the 25th Street beach for black people. Several white bathers attacked Eugene Williams, resulting in his death by drowning. When a black American was arrested, a group of black Americans attacked the police. The ensuing rioting was mainly confined to the South Side of Chicago where 90 percent of the black American population lived. The race riot lasted for five days and resulted in the deaths of 38 people, 23 of whom were black, and 537 were wounded. The homes of black Americans were attacked and 1,000 black families were made homeless. The riot was finally brought to an end by the intervention of the Illinois **National Guard**, and a large thunderstorm that dispersed the rioters.

KEY TERM

National Guard
The reserve forces of the USA. Each state possesses a volunteer organisation called the National Guard who are part-time members of the US armed forces, but equipped with similar equipment. They are under the command of the governor of each state, who can use them to maintain law and order if the police require assistance. As commander-in-chief of all US armed forces, the US president can 'federalise' the National Guard and place them under his direct command. As part-time members of the armed forces, the National Guard do not have the same degree of training or professionalism as the regular armed forces.

SOURCE 10   Two white men stoning a black American to death during the Chicago riots of 1919.

The underlying cause of the race riot was typical of race riots across the USA that summer. Drawn north by the promise of employment, the black American population of Chicago had doubled in the years 1916–18. Black Americans were discouraged from joining white-dominated trade unions. Most important of all, the competition for housing and the creation of black-dominated areas, like the South Side, helped divide the city of Chicago on clear racial lines. As black Americans moved in, white people moved out. The resulting tension sparked the riot.

Tulsa race riot, 1921

Two years after the Red Summer, an even greater attack occurred on black Americans in the Oklahoma city of Tulsa. It was a boom town due to the discovery and exploitation of its oil, and the city attracted a large number of migrants, both white and black. On 30 May 1921, a young black American, Dick Rowland, was accused of sexually assaulting a white girl in a lift and was subsequently arrested by the police. On the following day, the local newspaper, the *Tulsa Tribune*, published a fictitious story claiming that Rowland had scratched the hands and face of the white girl in an alleged assault. By 10.30pm that evening, nearly 2,000 white Americans had surrounded the gaol where Rowland was imprisoned and attempted to lynch him. Some black sympathisers went to the gaol to protect Rowland. They had come from Greenwood, a predominantly black American area of Tulsa. By the end of that night, Greenwood had been attacked by white mobs. In an orgy of violence and burning, the Tulsa race riot claimed the lives of 200 to 300 black Americans and approximately 1,000 black homes and businesses were burned. The intensity of the attacks led to half of Tulsa's black population, numbering 2,500, leaving Tulsa.

SOURCE 11

'A Crowd of Howling Negroes.' A report from the *Chicago Daily Tribune* on the Chicago race riot, 28 July 1919. The newspaper had a reputation for being antagonistic towards black American migrants.

Report Two Killed, Fifty Hurt, in Race Riots

Bathing Beach Fight Spreads to Black Belt

All Police Reserves Called to Guard South Side.

Two colored men are reported to have been killed and approximately fifty whites and negroes injured, a number probably fatally, in race riots that broke out at south side beaches yesterday. The rioting spread through the black belt and by midnight had thrown the entire south side into a state of turmoil.

Among the known wounded are four policemen of the Cottage Grove avenue station, two from west side stations, one fireman of engine company No. 9, and three women.

One Negro was knocked off a raft at the Twenty-ninth street beach after he had been stoned by whites. He drowned because whites are said to have frustrated attempts of colored bathers to rescue him. The body was recovered, but could not be identified.

A colored rioter is said to have died from wounds inflicted by Policeman John O'Brien, who fired into a mob at Twenty-ninth street and Cottage Grove avenue. The body, it is said, was spirited away by a colored man.

Drag Negroes from Cars.

So serious was the trouble throughout the district that Acting Chief of Police Alcock was unable to place an estimate on the injured. Scores received cuts and bruises from flying stones and rocks, but went to their homes for medical attention.

Minor rioting continued through the night all over the south side. Negroes who were found in street cars were dragged to the street and beaten.

Scores of conflicts between the whites and blacks were reported at south side stations and reserves were ordered to stand guard on all important street corners. Some of the fighting took place four miles from the scene of the afternoon riots.

When the Cottage Grove avenue station received a report that several had drowned in the lake during the beach outbreak, Capt. Joseph Mullen assigned policemen to drag the lake with grappling hooks. The body of a colored man was recovered, but was not identified.

Boats Scour Lake.

Rumors that a white boy was a lake victim could not be verified. The patrol boats scoured the lake in the vicinity of Twenty-ninth street for several hours in a vain search.

John O'Brien, a policeman attached to the Cottage Grove avenue station, was attacked by a mob at Twenty-ninth and State streets after he had tried to rescue a fellow cop from a crowd of bawling Negroes. Several shots were fired in his direction and he was wounded in the left arm. He pulled his revolver and fired four times into the gathering. Three colored men dropped.

Man Cop Shot Dies.

When the police attempted to haul the wounded into the wagon the Negroes made valiant attempts to prevent them. Two were taken to the Michael Reese hospital but the third was spirited away by the mob. It was later learned that he died in a drug store a short distance from the shooting.

Cop Refuses to Interfere.

Indignant at the conduct of the policeman, the Negroes set upon Stauber and commenced to pummel him. The whites came to his rescue and then the battle royal was on. Fists flew and rocks were hurled. Bathers from the colored Twenty-fifth street beach were attracted to the scene of the battling and aided their comrades in driving the whites into the water.

SOURCE

12 A leading American activist, Walter White, secretly entered Tulsa and wrote an article for *The Nation* magazine entitled 'The Eruption of Tulsa', published on 29 June 1921.

A hysterical white girl related that a nineteen-year-old colored boy attempted to assault her in the public elevator of a public office building of a thriving town of 100,000 in open daylight. Without pausing to find whether or not the story was true, without bothering with the slight detail of investigating the character of the woman who made the outcry (as a matter of fact, she was of exceedingly doubtful reputation), a mob of 100-per-cent Americans set forth on a wild rampage that cost the lives of fifty white men; of between 150 and 200 colored men, women and children; the destruction by fire of $1,500,000 worth of property; the looting of many homes; and everlasting damage to the reputation of the city of Tulsa and the State of Oklahoma. This, in brief, is the story of the eruption of Tulsa on the night of May 31 and the morning of June 1.

What are the causes of the race riot that occurred in such a place? First, the Negro in Oklahoma has shared in the sudden prosperity that has come to many of his white brothers, and there are some colored men there who are wealthy. This fact has caused a bitter resentment on the part of the lower order of whites, who feel that these colored men, members of an 'inferior race,' are exceedingly presumptuous in achieving greater economic prosperity than they who are members of a divinely ordered superior race. There are at least three colored persons in Oklahoma who are worth a million dollars each; J. W. Thompson of Clearview is worth $500,000; there are a number of men and women worth $100,000; and many whose possessions are valued at $25,000 and $50,000 each. The white man was killed while attacking the plant. Oklahoma is largely populated by pioneers from other States. Some of the white pioneers are former residents of Mississippi, Georgia, Tennessee, Texas, and other States more typically southern than Oklahoma. These have brought with them their anti-Negro prejudices. Lethargic and unprogressive by nature, it sorely irks them to see Negroes making greater progress than they themselves are achieving.

Another cause was the rotten political conditions in Tulsa. A vice ring was in control of the city, allowing open operation of houses of ill fame, of gambling joints, the illegal sale of whiskey, the robbing of banks and stores, with hardly a slight possibility of the arrest of the criminals, and even less of their conviction. For fourteen years Tulsa has been in the absolute control of this element. Most of the better element, and there is a large percentage of Tulsans who can properly be classed as such, are interested solely in making money and getting away. They have taken little or no interest in the election of city or county officials, leaving it to those whose interest it was to secure officials who would protect them in their vice operations.

The race riots of the 1917–21 period took place against a background of increasing discrimination against black Americans. The creation of legal segregation in the Old South, supported by violence and intimidation by white supremacist groups like the Ku Klux Klan, witnessed a major deterioration in black American civil rights. The gains in rights at the end of the Civil War of 1861–65 had all but disappeared. Ironically, discrimination against black Americans increased after the First World War, partly in response to the fear of thousands of returning black American servicemen who had served their country fighting.

ACTIVITY
KNOWLEDGE CHECK

Changing patterns of settlement and segregation

1 What were the main problems facing black Americans as they migrated out of the Old South in the 19th century and the first half of the 20th century?

2 What do you regard as the most important problem black Americans faced? Explain your answer.

The Watts riot in Los Angeles, August 1965

The circumstances surrounding the riots of the 1960s were very different from those at the time of the Chicago and Tulsa riots. By 1965, the civil rights movement had made substantial gains in achieving civil equality for black Americans. In 1954, the US Supreme Court had declared the idea of 'separate but equal' treatment for black Americans constitutional in terms of public education. This had been followed by a wide variety of initiatives by both president and Congress to ensure greater equality. Beginning with President J.F. Kennedy, affirmative action was introduced in federal employment and through federal contracts guaranteeing black Americans a proportion of jobs. More significantly, under President Lyndon Johnson, Congress passed the Civil Rights Act of 1964 and the Voting Rights Act of 1965 which, together, gave black Americans civil equality with white Americans.

Although black Americans may have achieved civil equality, they continued to face major social and economic problems, which formed the background for much racial unrest in the period 1964–68.

The inner-city areas of the north and west were largely untouched by the gains achieved by the civil rights movement. These areas were characterised by high unemployment, crime and poor housing. The Watts riot, in south central Los Angeles, took place between 11 and 15 August 1965. Over 3,500 black rioters participated. They were protesting against the poor housing and poor unemployment prospects in the Watts district, as well as police harassment. The Watts riot was one of 239 outbreaks of racial violence in over 200 American cities in the period 1964–68. Other cities facing serious racial violence were: Cleveland, Ohio, in 1966 and 1968; Oakland, California in 1965 and 1966; Detroit, Michigan in 1967; and Chicago, Illinois in 1967 and 1968. In 1967, another major riot occurred in Newark, New Jersey. All these outbreaks were borne out of the frustration of living in poor housing, in inner cities, with poor job opportunities and harassment by the local police.

The Watts riot started following an incident on 11 August 1965, when Marquette Frye, a young black American motorist, was arrested by Lee W. Minikus, a white California highway patrolman, on suspicion of driving while drunk. As a crowd of onlookers gathered at the scene of Frye's arrest, tension between police officers and the crowd erupted into a violent exchange. The outbreak of violence that followed Frye's arrest immediately sparked off a large-scale riot centred in the commercial section of Watts, a deeply impoverished black American neighbourhood in south central Los Angeles. For several days, rioters overturned and burned cars and looted grocery stores, liquor stores, department stores and pawnshops. Over the course of the six-day riot, over 14,000 California National Guard troops were mobilised in south Los Angeles, and a curfew zone encompassing over 45 miles was established in an attempt to restore public order.

The final statistics of the Watts riot are staggering. There were 34 people killed and 1,032 reported injuries, including 90 Los Angeles police officers, 136 firemen, 10 national guardsmen, 23 people from other governmental agencies and 773 civilians. Of the injuries, 118 resulted from gunshot wounds. Of the 34 killed, one was a fireman, one was a deputy sheriff and one a Long Beach policeman. Property damage exceeded $40 million, mainly to white-owned businesses.

SOURCE

13 From the governor of California's commission into the Watts riot, 12 August 1965. The riot began on 11 August and lasted until 15 August. The governor called out the California National Guard (the reserve army) to restore law and order in the Watts district.

By 12:20 a.m. approximately 50 to 75 youths were on either side of Avalon Blvd. at Imperial Highway, throwing missiles at passing cars and the police used vehicles with red lights and sirens within the riot area perimeter in an effort to disperse the crowd. As they did so, the rock throwing crowd dispersed, only to return as the police left the scene. Some of the older citizens in the area were inquiring, 'What are those crazy kids doing?' A number of adult Negroes expressed the opinion that the police should open fire on the rock throwers to stop their activity. The police did not discharge firearms at rioters. It was estimated that by 12:30 a.m. 70% of the rioters were children and the remainder were young adults and adults. Their major activity was throwing missiles at passing vehicles driven by Whites. One rioter stationed himself a block from the intersection of Avalon Blvd. and Imperial Highway, where the major group of rioters was centered, and signaled to this group whenever a vehicle driven by a Caucasian approached the intersection, so that it could be stoned.

Supervisor Kenneth Hahn and his assistant, Mr. Pennington, drove to the riot scene at about 12:35 a.m. and did not observe road blocks or policemen in the area. Rioters continued to attack vehicles in the vicinity of Imperial Highway and Avalon Blvd. Some spectators described the crowd as having the appearance of a carnival, with persons acting with abandon and some spectators apparently enjoying the activity as if it were a sporting event.

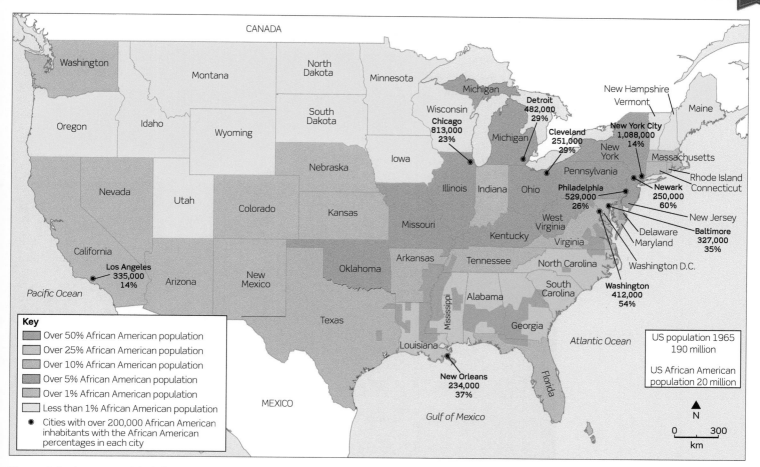

Figure 1.3 The geographical distribution of black Americans in 1965. © Sir Martin Gilbert (2009).

SOURCE 14

The changes in the pattern of black American migration in the period 1965–80.

	1965–70	1975–80
North-east		
Massachusetts	7,701	−5,766
Connecticut	8,356	−3,012
New York	7,053	−128,143
New Jersey	24,936	−6,462
Pennsylvania	2,182	−25,849
Mid-west		
Ohio	17,857	−16,503
Indiana	9,177	−2,040
Illinois	12,670	−37,220
Michigan	56,72	93,592
Wisconsin	7,910	6,964
Missouri	253	−10,428
Kansas	1,248	4,215
South		
Maryland	40,750	54,793
District of Columbia	−18,876	−58,454

	1965–70	1975–80
Virginia	−8,448	22,295
North Carolina	−25,887	14,456
South Carolina	−23,462	9,238
Georgia	−19,643	29,616
Florida	−5,466	15,900
Kentucky	−5,255	5,500
Tennessee	−15,577	4,436
Alabama	−53,854	−7,843
Mississippi	−56,367	−20,106
Arkansas	−23,465	−9,236
Louisiana	−34,346	−5,315
Oklahoma	−946	7,192
Texas	5,009	47,685
West		
Colorado	4,764	8,861
Washington	3,550	10,861
California	83,318	75,746

The Newark riot, 1967

In 1967, two years after the Watts riot, riots occurred in Detroit and Newark. At the time, the outbreak of rioting was partly blamed on the exceptionally hot weather. However, Newark was an area where housing segregation between black and white Americans had caused racial tension. In 1967, Newark had the highest percentage of substandard housing in the USA and the second highest percentage of crime and infant mortality.

SOURCE 15 Rioting in Newark in July 1967. The top photograph shows the result of looting and destruction by the rioters and the photograph below shows the deployment of the New Jersey National Guard in a bid to restore law and order.

SOURCE

 16 Report from the National Advisory Commission into Civil Disorders, known as the Kerner Commission, into the causes of rioting in the USA in 1967.

The summer of 1967 again brought racial disorders to American cities, and with them shock, fear and bewilderment to the nation. The worst came during a two-week period in July, first in Newark and then in Detroit. Each set off a chain reaction in neighboring communities. On July 28, 1967, the President of the United States established this Commission and directed us to answer three basic questions:

What happened?

Why did it happen?

What can be done to prevent it from happening again?

To respond to these questions, we have undertaken a broad range of studies and investigations. We have visited the riot cities; we have heard many witnesses; we have sought the counsel of experts across the country.

This is our basic conclusion: Our nation is moving toward two societies, one black, one white – separate and unequal.

Reaction to last summer's disorders has quickened the movement and deepened the division. Discrimination and segregation have long permeated much of American life; they now threaten the future of every American.

This deepening racial division is not inevitable. The movement apart can be reversed. Choice is still possible. Our principal task is to define that choice and to press for a national resolution.

To pursue our present course will involve the continuing polarization of the American community and, ultimately, the destruction of basic democratic values.

The alternative is not blind repression or capitulation to lawlessness. It is the realization of common opportunities for all within a single society.

This alternative will require a commitment to national action – compassionate, massive and sustained, backed by the resources of the most powerful and the richest nation on this earth. From every American it will require new attitudes, new understanding, and, above all, new will.

The vital needs of the nation must be met; hard choices must be made, and, if necessary, new taxes enacted.

Violence cannot build a better society. Disruption and disorder nourish repression, not justice. They strike at the freedom of every citizen. The community cannot – it will not – tolerate coercion and mob rule.

Violence and destruction must be ended – in the streets of the ghetto and in the lives of people.

Segregation and poverty have created in the racial ghetto a destructive environment totally unknown to most white Americans.

What white Americans have never fully understood – but what the Negro can never forget – is that white society is deeply implicated in the ghetto. White institutions created it, white institutions maintain it, and white society condones it.

It is time now to turn with all the purpose at our command to the major unfinished business of this nation. It is time to adopt strategies for action that will produce quick and visible progress. It is time to make good the promises of American democracy to all citizens – urban and rural, white and black, Spanish-surname, American Indian, and every minority group.

Our recommendations embrace three basic principles:

* To mount programs on a scale equal to the dimension of the problems;

* To aim these programs for high impact in the immediate future in order to close the gap between promise and performance;

* To undertake new initiatives and experiments that can change the system of failure and frustration that now dominates the ghetto and weakens our society.

Two further issues fuelled racial resentment in Newark. One was the mayor's selection of secretary to the Newark School Board, which caused fighting between black and white Americans. The other was the plan to build the New Jersey College of Medicine and Dentistry on a 50 acre site that black Americans thought should be used to relieve the housing problem. By July 1967, the social situation was made worse by outbreaks of what the black community saw as police brutality towards them. In July, the arrest of a black American taxi driver charged with assaulting a policeman plunged Newark into four days of rioting. The governor of New Jersey decided to restore law and order through the deployment of the National Guard. On day three of the riot, the National Guard opened fire on the rioters. By the end of the riot, 26 black Americans had been killed, including ten-year-old Edward Moses, and 1,000 black Americans had been injured. Damage to the value of $10 million had been done to property.

In response to the Newark riot and similar riots across the USA, President Johnson set up the Kerner Commission to report on the causes of the riots.

The development of *de facto* segregation against black Americans in Levitt estates

White exodus to the suburbs post-1945 in the north

After the end of the Second World War, racial tension was increased in the north and west through the development of segregated housing policies associated with developers in suburbia. This resulted in *de facto* segregation against black Americans.

The 1950s was a period of affluence in the USA. The US gross national product rose from $227 billion in 1940 to $355 billion in 1950. By 1960, it had leapt to $448 billion. Wages rose and consumer credit, an indicator of personal buying, increased from $8.4 billion in 1950 to $45 billion in 1960. This period of unprecedented growth in wealth was reflected in changes in the nature of cities across the USA. However, there were important differences between white and non-white Americans. In 1953, the median income of a white family was $4,392 per year, compared to only $2,461 for black American families. By 1960, the gap had grown to $5,835 for white families and $3,233 for black American families. This difference was reflected in the changing nature of cities. By 1955, America was growing rapidly, both in size of population and where people lived. The population rose from 130 million in 1940 to 165 million by the mid-1950s, the biggest increase in the history of the USA. A considerable number of people were moving from rural areas and small towns into cities. The number of those living in urban areas rose from 96.5 million in 1950 to 124.7 million in 1960. At the same time, the numbers living on rural farms fell from 23 million in 1950 to 13.4 million in 1960. Many took the opportunity to have a new life where consumer goods were plentiful and the standard of living higher. Many black Americans escaped rural poverty and racial discrimination in the Old South as they had done in the Great Migration of the 1920s and 1930s. In the 1950s, the USA's 12 largest cities gained 1.8 million black American residents.

By the 1960s, many cities were becoming racially segregated. Central cities were becoming the preserve of non-white people. Areas such as the Watts district of Los Angeles, west and north Philadelphia, the South Bronx and Harlem in New York City were becoming black American areas. On the edge of cities, new suburbs were dominated by white Americans. Where interracial tension in the past had been centred in the Old South, now interracial tensions were developing in northern and western cities and the nature of these cities changed.

Matters were made worse by federal housing policy. The Federal Housing Administration (FHA) supported anti-Jewish and anti-black **restrictive covenants** on new suburban housing developments. The FHA's aim was to ensure that neighbourhoods had racial cohesion. In reality, it meant that non-white residents of cities were barred from much suburban development. Instead, they were forced to live in privately owned rental accommodation in inner-city areas, which became rundown racial ghettoes. In addition, many cities failed to provide the public housing required for these areas. In the period 1949–59, only 320,000 houses were funded under President Truman's Public Housing Act. Even where public housing areas were provided, known in many cities as 'the projects', much of the accommodation was cramped. To save on costs, the projects were built in massive high-rise blocks. As a result, densely populated areas with poor public amenities became a feature of many inner cities. Northern and western cities were developing into two societies: a predominantly non-white inner city and a predominantly white suburbia.

While US cities grew in size, the centre of many cities declined. In the 1950s, many white residents left city centres for life in the suburbs, leaving old city centre residential areas to non-white residents. The rapid expansion of cities in the 1950s was essentially the growth of suburbia. This growth was the result of the rising affluence of many Americans as the economy grew throughout the 1950s. However, it was also aided by developments such as **Levittowns**, purpose-built new communities of affordable private housing, initially for white residents only. Levittowns of over 17,000 houses each developed in New York state and Pennsylvania. Growth was also helped by cheap home loans from organisations such as the Veterans Administration and the FHA. The latter financed 30 percent of all new homes in the USA in the 1950s.

By 1960, home ownership had become the norm for the first time in American history, with three in every five families owning a home. Between 1950 and 1960, 18 million people moved to the suburbs. The term used to describe the suburban growth from Boston, Massachusetts to Washington DC, which encompassed New York City, Philadelphia and Baltimore was megalopolis.

KEY TERMS

Restrictive covenant
A condition attached to the sale of a house, in this case that the house could not be sold to black American families or individuals.

Levittown
New suburbs built near New York City and in eastern Pennsylvania in the late 1940s and early 1950s that were regarded as typical of the development across the USA in the 1950s. They discriminated against black Americans and other minorities.

Not only did people migrate from inner cities to suburbs, they also migrated across the USA. Many deserted the north-east for life in the Sun Belt. Cities in Florida, Texas and California all grew rapidly in the 1950s. These included Dallas, San Diego, Los Angeles, Houston and Miami. By 1970, 80 million Americans lived in suburbs, 15 million more than lived in central cities.

Increasing desegregation of the Old South post-1970

The decades of the 1950s and 1960s saw great moves towards offering black Americans greater equality with white Americans. In 1954, in the landmark case *Brown* v *Board of Education, Topeka, Kansas*, the US Supreme Court declared that racially separated public schools were unconstitutional. In 1956 and in cases in the early 1960s, racially segregated public transportation was also declared illegal. In 1964, the Civil Rights Act and, in 1965, the Voting Rights Act gave black Americans full civil equality with white Americans.

However, the implementation of these changes was slow in the Old South. Massive white resistance, both in state government and by way of acts of violence and intimidation, slowed the process of integration of black and white Americans. Part of the problem was the existence of local community schools in areas with distinct black and white populations.

In 1969 and 1971, the US Supreme Court demanded greater integration. In the October 1969 case *Alexander* v *Holmes County School Board*, the Court demanded racial integration at once. In April 1971, in the *Charlotte Mecklenburg* case, the Court demanded that children should be bussed from black-only and white-only areas to ensure full racial integration in public schools. By the 1970s, the pattern of racial public schooling had gone through a social revolution. The events of Central High School, Little Rock, Arkansas in 1957, when the armed forces were used to allow seven black students to attend an all-white school, seemed a distant memory. In 1969, when Richard Nixon became president, 68 percent of black American children attended segregated schools. By the time of Nixon's resignation as president, in 1974, that figure had fallen to 8 percent.

In addition, the Voting Rights Act ensured that black Americans could play a full and active role in politics in the Old South. Black Americans were elected to Congress for southern districts and were elected mayors for cities such as Atlanta, Georgia and New Orleans, Louisiana. For instance, in 1973, Maynard Jackson became the first black American since 1877 to win such a post in a southern city. In 1996, Atlanta became the host of the summer Olympic Games. It won that honour under black American mayor, Andrew Young, a close aide of Martin Luther King.

In addition to the end of legal impediments to the civil rights of black Americans in the Old South, opportunities developed in other areas. Housing areas which were once exclusively white now allowed black Americans to purchase and rent homes. Sports teams which had been exclusively white, such as baseball, now contained black American players.

However, not all black Americans benefited from these changes. Black American society was divided in two following the end of legal segregation and the federal legislation of 1964–65. Many black Americans benefited, received college educations and developed into a black American middle class. Others stayed in the same poorly paid, poorly housed existence they had before the end of legal segregation. This bifurcation of southern black American society became a feature of southern society from 1970 to 2009.

> **A Level Exam-Style Question Section C**
>
> How far were the 1950s a turning point in the changing pattern of segregation in the USA against black Americans in the period 1850–2009?
> (20 marks)
>
> **Tip**
>
> *It is important that you organise your answer in a balanced way. Assess the ways discrimination diminished with the end of legal segregation and support and sustain your argument with factual evidence. Then assess the continued existence of de facto segregation and social problems in the* same *way. Your conclusion must contain a judgement of how far the 1950s were a turning point.*

ACTIVITY
KNOWLEDGE CHECK

Race riots in the USA

1 In what ways were the causes of race riots in the 1960s similar?

2 In what ways were they different?

3 What do you regard as the most important reason for race riots in the 1960s?

4 What reasons can you give for the existence of continued segregation of black and white Americans in the USA after 1950?

THINKING HISTORICALLY Change (7a)

Convergence and divergence

The changing geographical distribution of black Americans, 1850–2009				
1865 Abolition of slavery	**1870s–80s** Slow movement north and west	**1915–41** The Great Migration	**1941–45** Impact of the Second World War	**1970–2009** Migration back to the Old South
The changing pattern of settlement and segregation, 1850–2009				
1877–1900 Introduction of Jim Crow Laws in the South	**1905 onwards** Mass migration into Harlem, New York City	**1919–21** Chicago and Tulsa riots	**1945–70s** *De facto* segregation in housing	**1970–80s** Increasing desegregation in the Old South

1 Draw a timeline across the middle of a landscape piece of A3 paper. Cut out ten small rectangular cards and write the above changes on them. Then place them on the timeline, with changing geographical distribution events above the line and changing pattern of settlement and segregation events below the line. Make sure there is a lot of space between the changes and the line.

2 Draw a line and write a link between each change within each strand, so that you have four links that join up the changes in the changing geographical distribution of black Americans part of the timeline and four that join the changing pattern of settlement and segregation changes. You will then have two strands of change: *Changing geographical distribution* and *Changing pattern of settlement and segregation*.

3 Now make as many links as possible across the timeline between *Changing geographical distribution* and *Changing pattern of settlement and segregation*. Think about how they are affected by one another and think about how things can link across long periods of time.

You should end up with something like this:

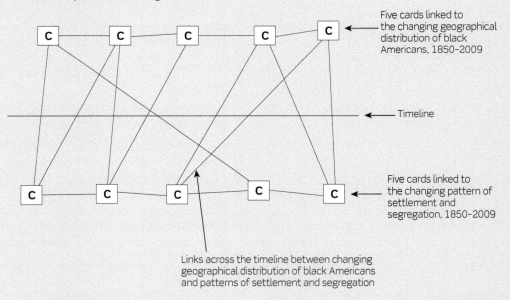

Five cards linked to the changing geographical distribution of black Americans, 1850–2009

Timeline

Five cards linked to the changing pattern of settlement and segregation, 1850–2009

Links across the timeline between changing geographical distribution of black Americans and patterns of settlement and segregation

Answer the following questions.

4 How far do different strands of history interact with one another? Illustrate your answer with two well-explained examples.

5 At what point do the two strands of development converge (i.e. when do the changes have the biggest impact on one another)?

6 How useful are the strands in understanding the changing geography of civil rights issues in the years 1850 to 2009?

ACTIVITY
SUMMARY

The changing geography of civil rights issues

1 Create a spider diagram which shows the main changes in the changing geographical distribution of black Americans in the USA. Include different:

- push factors

- pull factors.

2 How did the pattern of settlement of black Americans change in the years 1850–2009?

3 What was the difference between legal (*de jure*) and *de facto* segregation?

WIDER READING

Mauk, D. and Oakland, J. *American Civilisation: An Introduction*, Routledge (2013)

Paterson, D., Willoughby, S. and Willoughby, D. *Civil Rights in the USA 1863 to 1980*, Heinemann (2001)

Tuck, S.G.N. (ed.) *We Ain't What We Ought To Be: The Black Freedom Struggle from Emancipation to Obama*, Harvard University Press (2011)

3.2

Changing portrayal of civil rights issues in fiction and film

KEY QUESTIONS

- To what extent did literature shape and reflect changing perceptions of race relations, 1850–2009?
- How far did film and television influence and reflect changing perceptions of race, 1850–2009?

INTRODUCTION

The struggle for civil rights and equality between white Americans and black Americans has been a long and ongoing process. In that process, literature, film and television have played an important role. The way black Americans have been portrayed in fiction, and later film and television, from 1850 to 2009 has had an important impact on relations between the races within the USA. In the period 1850 to 2009, fiction, film and television portrayals of black Americans have both helped and hindered the achievement of civil rights for all Americans. In 1850, the USA was one of the most literate societies in the world. Most adult white Americans could read and write. As a result, the portrayal of black Americans in literature would have a potentially wide audience. This made literature very important in both reflecting and changing perceptions of how black Americans were treated within US society.

In the 20th century, the USA was at the forefront of the development of film and television. Hollywood films dominated world cinema and US television became a very important social medium within the USA after the Second World War. Both of these media, like literature, had the power and influence to shape perceptions of black Americans and how they lived. Slavery and segregation were both referred to as the South's 'peculiar institution', peculiar in the sense that it was unique to that region. This meant that the lives of black Americans in the South were far different from the lives of those black Americans living in the north and west. In addition, as racially distinct districts developed in urban areas across the USA, those white Americans living in white suburbs had very little idea of life in black-dominated inner-city districts. Film and television both played a major role in creating and changing perceptions of how white Americans viewed black Americans.

Eventually, literature, film and television all helped to reflect and change white perceptions of the plight and position in society of black Americans. On occasion, literature, film and television had a positive impact on the struggle to gain civil rights for black Americans.

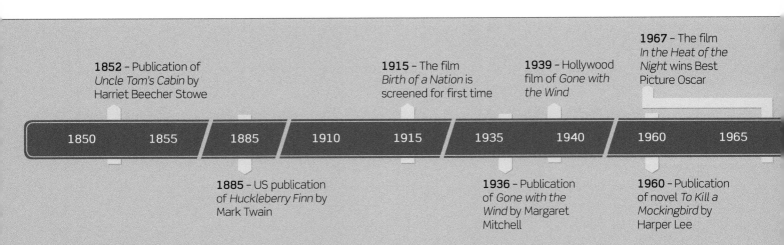

1852 – Publication of *Uncle Tom's Cabin* by Harriet Beecher Stowe

1885 - US publication of *Huckleberry Finn* by Mark Twain

1915 – The film *Birth of a Nation* is screened for first time

1936 – Publication of *Gone with the Wind* by Margaret Mitchell

1939 – Hollywood film of *Gone with the Wind*

1967 – The film *In the Heat of the Night* wins Best Picture Oscar

1960 – Publication of novel *To Kill a Mockingbird* by Harper Lee

| 1850 | 1855 | 1885 | 1910 | 1915 | 1935 | 1940 | 1960 | 1965 |

TO WHAT EXTENT DID LITERATURE SHAPE AND REFLECT CHANGING PERCEPTIONS OF RACE RELATIONS, 1850–2009?

To what extent did *Uncle Tom's Cabin* (1852) by Harriet Beecher Stowe impact on race relations?

The background

In the 1850s, the most divisive issue in American politics was slavery and its possible extension west from the slave-owning areas of the South. In 1850, a Compromise was reached at national level, which was an attempt to maintain a balance between free states and slave states. Among the provisions of the Compromise of 1850 was the creation of a new, stricter, Fugitive Slave Law. Helping runaways had been illegal since 1793, but the 1850 law required that everyone, law enforcers and ordinary citizens, help to catch fugitives. Those who refused to assist slave-catchers, or aided fugitives, could be fined up to $1,000 and jailed for six months. It also eliminated what little legal protection fugitives once had. Before 1850, some northern states had required slave-catchers to appear before an elected judge to determine the validity of a claim. After the 1850 Fugitive Slave Law, anyone could be taken from the street, accused of being a fugitive from slavery, and taken before a federally appointed commissioner who received $5 for every fugitive released and $10 for each one sent south. Free black Americans and anti-slavery groups argued that the system bribed commissioners to send kidnapped people into slavery, and obliged citizens to participate in the slavery system.

Harriet Beecher Stowe was furious about these developments and there is no doubt that they helped to clarify her personal stance on slavery. She believed the country expected her complicity in the slavery system and she disobeyed the law by hiding runaways. As a housewife living in Cincinnati, Ohio, just across the Ohio River from Kentucky, a slave state, she had gained experience of slavery from first-hand accounts from runaway slaves.

When she shared her frustrations and feelings of powerlessness with her family, her sister-in-law Isabella Porter Beecher suggested she do more, saying that if she could use a pen as well as Harriet could, she would write something that would make the whole nation realise what an accursed thing slavery is. Moved by the letter, Stowe swore she would, and in this divisive atmosphere she wrote her novel, *Uncle Tom's Cabin*, published in 1852.

Uncle Tom's Cabin was originally released in serial form in the *National Era*, a weekly newspaper, between 5 June 1851 and 1 April 1852. The serialised version attracted a lot of interest and helped to generate future sales of the whole novel when it appeared. When published as a novel, *Uncle Tom's Cabin* became an immediate best-seller. It sold 10,000 copies in the USA in its first week and 300,000 in its first year. Eventually, it sold over two million copies within ten years in America. In Britain, it sold 1.5 million copies in one year. It was eventually translated into 60 languages.

1977 – Beginning of the miniseries *Roots*

1988 – Film *Mississippi Burning* by British director Alan Parker gets first screening

1992 – First screening of black American Spike Lee's film *Malcolm X*

2002–08 – *The Wire* series appears on the Home Box Office channel of US television

| 1970 | 1975 | 1980 | 1985 | 1990 | 1995 | 2000 | 2005 | 2010 |

1987 – Publication of *Beloved* by Toni Morrison

1993 – Toni Morrison becomes first black American to win the Nobel Prize in Literature

2009 – Publication of *The Help* by Kathryn Stockett

The synopsis of the novel

Uncle Tom's Cabin begins on the Shelby Plantation in Kentucky and deals with two slave families and their predicaments. The main plot focuses on Tom, a strong, religious man living with his wife and three young children. The other plot deals with Eliza, her son Harry and her husband George.

When the novel begins, Eliza's husband George Harris has already escaped to become a runaway slave. He plans to acquire money as a way of purchasing his family's freedom. To protect her son, Eliza also runs away, making a dramatic escape across the frozen Ohio River from the slave state of Kentucky to freedom in the north. Eventually, the Harris family are reunited in British North America, now known as Canada, where slavery did not exist.

Tom protects his family by choosing not to run away, hoping to keep his family together. However, he is sold by the owner of the Shelby Plantation to an owner in another state, Louisiana. There he meets Topsy, a young black girl whose outgoing behaviour hides the pain of slavery. He also meets Eva, a young white girl who is charming but dies tragically young. There is also Simon Legree, a white slave owner who is cruel and violent towards his slaves. It is Tom's strong religious beliefs that enable him to survive his position as a slave.

The novel ends when Tom escapes but is whipped to death by the violent Simon Legree for not revealing the hiding place of two runaway female slaves. Tom's act of self-sacrifice saves the lives of his family.

EXTEND YOUR KNOWLEDGE

Harriet Beecher Stowe (1811–96)

Harriet Elisabeth Beecher was born on 14 June 1811 in Litchfield, Connecticut, to the Reverend Lyman Beecher (1775–1863) and Roxana Foote Beecher (1775–1816), the sixth of 11 children. Roxana Beecher died when Stowe was only five years old. Her later pursuit of painting and drawing honoured her mother's talents in those areas. Her oldest sister, Catharine, became an important maternal influence. Stowe wrote at an early age: at seven, she won a school essay contest, earning praise from her father. Lyman's second wife, Harriet Porter Beecher (1800–35), was a beautiful woman, slightly overwhelmed by the eight boisterous children she inherited. Her own children, Isabella, Thomas and James, added to the noisy household. In 1851, *The National Era*'s publisher Gamaliel Bailey contracted with Stowe for a story that would 'paint a word picture of slavery' and that would run in instalments. Stowe expected *Uncle Tom's Cabin* or *Life Among the Lowly* to be three or four instalments. She wrote more than 40.

Harriet Beecher Stowe published more than 30 books, but it was her best-selling anti-slavery novel *Uncle Tom's Cabin* which catapulted her to international celebrity and secured her place in history. But *Uncle Tom's Cabin* was not Stowe's only work. Her broad range of interests resulted in such varied publications as children's textbooks, advice books on homemaking and childrearing, biographies and religious studies. The informal, conversational style of her many novels permitted her to reach audiences that more scholarly or argumentative works would not, and encouraged everyday people to address such controversial topics as slavery, religious reform and gender roles. Harriet Beecher Stowe believed her actions could make a positive difference.

Reaction to the publication of *Uncle Tom's Cabin*

By relating the institution of slavery through the eyes of the slave and by focusing on the heroic struggle of one woman, Eliza, to gain freedom for herself and her child, Harriet Beecher Stowe's message did much more than hundreds of abolitionist presentations to persuade Americans to oppose slavery. The book, read by hundreds of thousands of Americans, and the plays it inspired, viewed by millions more, proved a powerful weapon in the campaign to end slavery in the USA. Harriet Beecher Stowe's novel was able to personalise the whole issue of slavery in a way political speeches and sermons in churches failed to do. Her style engaged readers, and her portrayal of the inherent cruelty and inhumanity of slavery in the South increased the sectional division between the free north and the slave-owning south. Tom's strong Christian beliefs enabled him to survive his lot as a slave with dignity. In fact, Stowe claimed that God guided her writing.

However, almost immediately after its publication the novel was criticised. The more radical members of the abolitionist movement felt the portrayal of slavery and the treatment of black slaves was not strong enough to encourage Americans to support the immediate end of slavery. In addition, many abolitionists disliked Harriet Beecher Stowe's tacit support for the colonisation movement, which supported the idea of returning black slaves to Africa. The West African state of Liberia was created to offer a homeland for freed black slaves. Pro-slavery groups disliked the attack on the institution as they believed it was sanctioned by the Old Testament of the Bible. They claimed the story was one-sided and showed slave owners in a bad light.

In response to early criticism of the novel, Stowe produced *The Key to Uncle Tom's Cabin*, which included references to the sources of information Stowe used to write the novel. *The Key* reinforced Stowe's open opposition to slavery and claimed in writing the novel it had turned her into an abolitionist. Harriet Beecher Stowe went on to write a second novel which attacked slavery, *Dred, A Tale of the Great Dismal Swamp*, published in 1856. This was even more forceful than *Uncle Tom's Cabin* in attacking slavery and demanding its immediate abolition.

To many, *Uncle Tom's Cabin* put a human face on the issue and horrors of slavery. The black slaves, in particular Tom, are shown as pious Christians, which helps them to endure their fate. However, despite Stowe's desire to portray slavery as a powerful blight upon the nation, she also did much to expand anti-black sentiment through her presentation of stereotypical black characters in the novel. Some of these stereotypes include the dark-skinned 'mammy', 'pickaninny' black children, and Uncle Tom, the obedient and long-suffering servant to his white master. In fact, the term 'Uncle Tom' came to denote a black American who was willing to follow the wishes of white Americans and be subservient to them. Stowe also made clear that white and black people had very different characters, with the black characters in her novel displaying loyalty and subservience.

Yet *Uncle Tom's Cabin* had a popularity that lasted into the 20th century. In 1952, one of the leading black American poets of the Harlem Renaissance of the 1920s and 1930s stated that the novel was a good story with exciting incidences, sharp characterisation and woven humour.

SOURCE

1 From *Uncle Tom's Cabin,* written by Harriet Beecher Stowe and published in 1852. These concluding remarks from Chapter 45 give insight into her motivation for writing *Uncle Tom's Cabin*.

For many years of her life, the author avoided all reading upon or allusion to the subject of slavery, considering it as too painful to be inquired into, and one which advancing light and civilization would certainly live down. But, since the legislative act of 1850, when she hear d, with perfect surprise and consternation, Christian and humane people actually recommending the remanding of escaped fugitives into slavery, as a duty binding on good citizens, — when she heard, on all hands, from kind, compassionate and estimable people, in the free states of the North, deliberations and discussions as to what Christian duty could be on this head, — she could only think, These men and Christians cannot know what slavery is; if they did, such a question could never be open for discussion. And from this arose a desire to exhibit it in a living dramatic reality. She has endeavored to show it fairly, in its best and its worst phases. In its best aspect, she has, perhaps, been successful; but, oh! Who shall say what yet remains untold in that valley and shadow of death, that lies the other side?

To you, generous, noble-minded men and women, of the South, — you, whose virtue, and magnanimity and purity of character, are the greater for the severer trial it has encountered, — to you is her appeal. Have you not, in your own secret souls, in your own private conversings, felt that there are woes and evils, in this accursed system, far beyond what are here shadowed, or can be shadowed? Can it be otherwise? Is man ever a creature to be trusted with wholly irresponsible power? And does not the slave system, by denying the slave all legal right of testimony, make every individual owner an irresponsible despot? Can anybody fail to make the inference what the practical result will be? If there is, as we admit, a public sentiment among you, men of honor, justice and humanity, is there not also another kind of public sentiment among the ruffian, the brutal and debased? And cannot the ruffian, the brutal, the debased, by slave law, own just as many slaves as the best and purest? Are the honorable, the just, the highminded and compassionate, the majority anywhere in this world?

The slave-trade is now, by American law, considered as piracy. But a slave-trade, as systematic as ever was carried on on the coast of Africa, is an inevitable attendant and result of American slavery. And its heart-break and its horrors, can they be told?

The writer has given only a faint shadow, a dim picture, of the anguish and despair that are, at this very moment, riving thousands of hearts, shattering thousands of families, and driving a helpless and sensitive race to frenzy and despair. There are those living who know the mothers whom this accursed traffic has driven to the murder of their children; and themselves seeking in death a shelter from woes more dreaded than death. Nothing of tragedy can be written, can be spoken, can be conceived, that equals the frightful reality of scenes daily and hourly acting on our shores, beneath the shadow of American law, and the shadow of the cross of Christ.

The large volume of sales and its graphic depiction of slavery greatly enhanced the campaign for those who opposed slavery within the USA. In the divisive atmosphere of the 1850s on the issue of slavery, *Uncle Tom's Cabin* helped fuel that conflict. President Abraham Lincoln, who issued the Emancipation Proclamation in September 1862 and was mainly responsible for the Thirteenth Amendment of the US Constitution in 1865 which abolished slavery, borrowed *Uncle Tom's Cabin* from the Library of Congress. In late 1862, after issuing the Emancipation Proclamation, President Lincoln met Harriet Beecher Stowe and allegedly said to her that she was the woman who wrote the book that started the Civil War. Lord Palmerston, British prime minister from 1859 to 1865, read the novel three times.

In 2007, on the eve of the election of America's first black American president, Barack Obama, Henry Louis Gates (one of the most important black literary historians), reprinted *Uncle Tom's Cabin* to convince the black population to revisit the story of Uncle Tom, Eliza and Eva with 19th-century spectacles rather than judge it with 21st-century opinions. *Uncle Tom's Cabin* lent itself to nationwide debate on racial politics that continues to this day.

ACTIVITY
KNOWLEDGE CHECK

Uncle Tom's Cabin

1 Describe the main events of the story of *Uncle Tom's Cabin*.

2 Give reasons why *Uncle Tom's Cabin* helped to change people's perceptions of race in 1850s America.

How important was *The Adventures of Huckleberry Finn* (1885) by Mark Twain in shaping and reflecting changing perceptions of race relations?

The background

The novel *Huckleberry Finn* was published in 1885, 20 years after the end of the Civil War (1861–65). In the period 1865 to 1870, black Americans gained a large number of civil rights. Slavery was abolished in 1865 by the Thirteenth Amendment to the US Constitution; in 1868, in the Fourteenth Amendment, all Americans were given 'equal protection of the law'; and in 1870, the Fifteenth Amendment gave all black American adult males the right to vote, the same rights as white people. However, black Americans faced discrimination and intimidation in the former Confederate states. Vigilante groups like the white supremacist Ku Klux Klan attacked black Americans and their property. After the end of the Reconstruction period, in 1877, governments in the former Confederate states began passing laws, collectively known as Jim Crow Laws, which discriminated against black Americans.

The novel *Huckleberry Finn* was written by Samuel Clemens, who used the pen name Mark Twain. It is set in Missouri, which was a slave state before the Civil War but did not officially join the Confederate states. A civil war between federal and Confederate supporters took place within the state during the war. The novel was preceded, in 1876, by *The Adventures of Tom Sawyer*, which deals with the same area covered in *Huckleberry Finn*, which could be seen as a sequel to that novel. Both novels are set in the town of St Petersburg, Missouri, on the banks of the Mississippi. At the end of *The Adventures of Tom Sawyer*, Huckleberry Finn, a poor boy with a drunk for a father, and a middle-class boy with a keen imagination, Tom Sawyer, find a stash of robber's gold. As a result, Huckleberry Finn gains money which is placed in a bank for him. He is then adopted by a woman, Widow Douglas.

Synopsis of the novel

The novel is written in Missouri dialect and begins where *Tom Sawyer* ends. Huck Finn is living with a new family, but characters from his past, such as his drunken father, Pap, appear. Huck is not happy with his new life of cleanliness, church and school. The local judge, Judge Thatcher, and the widow try to get legal custody of Huck, but another well-intentioned new judge in town believes in the rights of Huck's natural father and even takes the old drunk, Pap, into his own home in an attempt to reform him. This effort fails miserably, and Pap soon returns to his old ways. He harasses his son, who in the meantime has learned to read and to tolerate the widow's attempts to improve him. Outraged, Pap kidnaps Huck and holds him in a cabin across the river from St Petersburg, from which Huck escapes by faking his own death.

The heart of the story begins when Huck meets up with the escaped slave Jim on Jackson's Island in the middle of the Mississippi River, and this is Huck's first step to overcoming society's prejudice and belief that black people are nothing more than uneducated, superstitious slaves and possessions. Jim implores Huck not to tell anyone that he has run away. Despite Huck's uncertainty about the legality or morality of helping a runaway slave in the beginning, Huck doesn't turn Jim in to the authorities for two reasons. One is that he has very little respect for the authorities. Another is that it is not convenient for him to turn Jim in. Without Jim, Huck would be alone and he does not want to deal with that again. However, Huck struggles with his conscience, believing that by not turning Jim in, he is breaking all of society's and religion's tenets. Therefore, in the beginning, Huck does not step far beyond the views of race issues that his society held.

Although the island is blissful, Huck and Jim are forced to leave after Huck learns from a woman onshore that her husband has seen smoke coming from the island and believes that Jim is hiding out there. Huck also learns that a reward has been offered for Jim's capture. They decide to leave the island on a log raft they captured during a storm, with the aim of making it to the free states, where slavery is prohibited.

The pair encounter several characters during their flight, including a group of men looking for escaped slaves. Huck has a brief moral crisis about concealing Jim, but he decides to lie to the men and tell them that his father is on the raft suffering from smallpox. The men are terrified of the disease and quickly leave. They also meet a band of robbers, two southern 'genteel' families who are involved in a bloody feud, and scammers who sell Jim back into slavery.

Huck discovers that Jim is being held captive on Silas and Sally Phelps' farm and resolves to free him. The Phelps think Huck is their visiting nephew, Tom Sawyer, and Huck goes along with the mistake. Tom Sawyer soon arrives and, after Huck explains Jim's captivity, Tom takes on the guise of his own younger brother, Sid.

Tom hatches an elaborate plan to free Jim, adding multiple unnecessary obstacles, even though Jim is only lightly secured. Tom's plan is haphazardly based on several of the prison and adventure novels he has read, and the simple act of freeing Jim becomes a complicated farce with rope ladders, snakes and mysterious messages. Although Huck is sure Tom's plan will get them killed, he complies nonetheless.

When the escape finally takes place, a pursuing farmer shoots Tom in the calf. Huck is forced to get a doctor and because Jim will not leave the injured Tom, Jim is again recaptured and taken back to the Phelps' farm. At the farm, Tom reveals that Jim has actually been a free man all along, as Miss Watson, Jim's owner, had died two months earlier and had made a provision in her will to free Jim. Tom had planned the entire escape idea all as a game.

Huck develops a different view of black Americans through the story. It is not an instant change, but a gradual process. Each of Huck and Jim's adventures brings Huck closer to the realisation that there is something wrong with society's view of black people, but Huck finds it difficult to escape from the influence that society has had on him. He is initially torn between following his conscience and feeling that he has behaved badly in society's view, and how good Jim has been to him and how he is the only friend that Jim has. At the beginning, he believes that society is correct, but he chooses to ignore society and do what he feels is right, regardless of what society believes.

It is Jim's love for his family that affects Huck so strongly, causing him to realise that a black man is capable of loving his family as much as a white man can. This is especially significant considering the abusive nature of Huck's father. Jim becomes a father figure to Huck, although Huck does not necessarily recognise it as such, sheltering him from the more disturbing features of their journey, including the death of Huck's father.

From the point when Huck decides that he will help Jim escape from slavery, he does not care how much society might resent him for it. It feels right to him, and he will do it. This action goes contrary to the social norms. A white person was never expected to care about a black person, much less to help one escape. But Huck did just that. Huck has opened his mind to the view that slavery is wrong; he has taken a big step in this direction. In this manner, Huck Finn attacks the social norm of slavery specifically, and racism in general.

The representations of race and the challenges to social norms of racism make up an important part of the novel *The Adventures of Huckleberry Finn*. Huck himself undergoes a change; he stops accepting the social norms and instead follows his own beliefs. In this way, Twain encourages people to be like Huck and not to accept racism just because society accepts it.

SOURCE 2

From *The Adventures of Huckleberry Finn* by Mark Twain, published in 1885. These excerpts deal with the issue of race relations as they appear in the novel.

A. From Chapter 6. Old Pap, Huckleberry Finn's natural father, and a white character are talking about free black Americans.

... as a free nigger there from Ohio — a mulatter, most as white as a white man. He had the whitest shirt on you ever see, too, and the shiniest hat; and there ain't a man in that town that's got as fine clothes as what he had; and he had a gold watch and chain, and a silver-headed cane — the awful-est old gray-headed nabob in the State. And what do you think? They said he was a p'fessor in a college, and could talk all kinds of languages, and knowed everything. And that ain't the wust. They said he could VOTE when he was at home. Well, that let me out. Thinks I, what is the country a-coming to? It was 'lection day, and I was just about to go and vote myself if I warn't too drunk to get there; but when they told me there was a State in this country where they'd let that nigger vote, I drawed out. I says I'll never vote agin.

B. From Chapter 42. This section gives the views of the doctor who treated the black character, Jim.

I liked the nigger for that; I tell you, gentlemen, a nigger like that is worth a thousand dollars — and kind treatment, too. I had everything I needed, and the boy was doing as well there as he would a done at home — better, maybe, because it was so quiet; but there I WAS, with both of 'm on my hands, and there I had to stick till about dawn this morning; then some men in a skiff come by, and as good luck would have it the nigger was setting by the pallet with his head propped on his knees sound asleep; so I motioned them in quiet, and they slipped up on him and grabbed him and tied him before he knowed what he was about, and we never had no trouble.

The issue of race relations in *Huckleberry Finn*

The story of *Huckleberry Finn* is set at the time of slavery, before the Civil War. Black Americans in Missouri are regarded and treated by white people as inferior. However, as a young person Huck Finn seems unaware of the degree of racial prejudice and racial discrimination and has adventures with Jim, the black American. The novel was a best-seller and has become a major work of American literature. It is a standard text in many American secondary schools and it is second only to Shakespeare in the frequency with which it appears in the American classroom.

SOURCE 3

A lithographic illustration from the novel *Huckleberry Finn* by Mark Twain, 1885. The black character, Jim, thinks Huck Finn is a ghost.

JIM AND THE GHOST

Twain, in *The Adventures of Huckleberry Finn*, was not attempting to write an exposé on slavery or even trying to give an accurate depiction of it. He needed to sell novels, making an outright attack on slavery, racist southern attitudes and Jim Crow Laws unwise. Instead, he used irony, satire and subtlety to make his points. For example, Jim is at the mercy of white characters in the novel, most of whom are morally inferior to him. Jim must follow Huck's schemes and 'adventures', such as exploring the wrecked ship that causes them to lose their raft and supplies, and Tom and Huck's ridiculous escape attempt in the novel's closing chapters. Jim must also take orders from the duke and the dolphin, two of the more reprobate characters.

However, the novel provoked criticism at the time of publication and since about the way black Americans are characterised in the book, in particular the negative characterisation of the main black character Jim and the extensive use of the derogatory term 'nigger' for black Americans, which appears throughout the novel. The novel was completed in 1884 at a time when many black Americans were trying to develop a new life in US society after the abolition of slavery. In defence of Mark Twain, the author attempts to use the language and attitudes of a pre-Civil War slave state, and his use of Missouri black dialect reinforces the idea that Jim is uneducated and lacking basic social skills. However, although Jim is seen as a caricature of black Americans at the time, it does not mean that Jim is not given an opportunity to display his humanity and strong character in the novel. Nowhere in the novel is Jim's humanity more apparent than when he offers the ultimate sacrifice – his freedom – to save Tom's life.

Reactions to the issue of race relations in *Huckleberry Finn*

The use of dialect and the storyline have caused controversy since the publication of *The Adventures of Huckleberry Finn* in the US in 1885. In that year Concord Public Library, Massachusetts, banned the novel, claiming it was vile trash, suitable for the slums. On 17 March 1885, the *St Louis Globe-Democrat* newspaper stated that the novel was irrelevant, and used rough dialect and bad grammar.

However, it is the novel's depiction of race relations which has created the greatest criticism. The black civil rights organisation, the **National Association for the Advancement of Colored People (NAACP)**, declared in 1957 that the novel contained 'racial slurs' in the ways it depicted black characters. The regular use of the term 'nigger' to describe black Americans in the book has caused particular offence since publication, in particular to 20th-century readers. Since 1957, the book has been removed from reading lists in schools across the USA, including the Mark Twain Intermediate School, Fairfax, Virginia. John Wallace, a school administrator there, was quoted in the *Washington Post* newspaper as saying that the reading aloud of the text was humiliating and insulting to black students and contributed to feelings of low self-esteem in the black community and to white students' disrespect for black people. He claimed the book was used by insensitive and unwittingly racist teachers who hailed the book as a classic, disregarding the concerns of black families who thought the book was not good for their children.

Black American writer, Margo Allen, in an article called 'Huck Finn: Two Generations of Pain' described her negative experiences with the book at school. In the work, she stated that she hated the book, but would hide the hurt and pain it caused her from her teacher and classmates.

Yet for all the criticism of racial stereotyping, Mark Twain's *The Adventures of Huckleberry Finn* has been accepted as a masterpiece of American literature with changing attitudes towards race relations since the success of the civil rights movement.

KEY TERM

NAACP
The National Association for the Advancement of Colored People was created in 1909, mainly through the efforts of W.E.B. DuBois. Its aim was to campaign for civil rights for black Americans.

ACTIVITY
KNOWLEDGE CHECK

Huckleberry Finn

1 Explain how Jim, the main black American character, is portrayed in *Huckleberry Finn*.

2 What does the lithograph in Source 3 show about the race relations between black and white people in the novel?

How accurate was the portrayal of race relations in *Gone with the Wind* (1936) by Margaret Mitchell?

The background

Margaret Mitchell published her epic story, set in Georgia in the era of the Civil War, in 1936 and it immediately became a best-seller. In the following year, 1937, the novel was awarded a Pulitzer Prize, one of America's most prestigious literary awards. In 1939, the novel was adapted for cinema and became one of the most successful Hollywood films of all time. In the 1940 Academy Awards (Oscars), *Gone with the Wind* won nine Oscars, including Best Film and Best Director. It was also memorable for having the first ever black American to win an Oscar, Hattie McDaniel for Best Supporting Actress in the role of Mammy.

When *Gone with the Wind* was published, the USA was experiencing economic depression and it was the era of the New Deal, a set of social and economic measures that aimed to return the USA to prosperity. *Gone with the Wind* was a historical novel about a period of US history which had passed, hence the title of the novel. By 1934, legal segregation had been firmly established across the Old South. Many black Americans were denied their constitutional right to vote and were reduced to a position of second-class citizenship. Even outside the Old South, black Americans faced racial discrimination. Serious race riots had broken out in northern and western cities, such as Chicago in 1919 and Tulsa, Oklahoma, in 1921. The portrayal of black Americans proved to be controversial, and considerable criticism of the role of black Americans in the novel, and the language used, affected what appeared in the film screenplay for the 1939 film.

The synopsis of the novel

It is the spring of 1861, on the eve of the Civil War. Scarlett O'Hara, a pretty southern belle, lives on Tara, a large plantation in Georgia. She is looked after by a female black American nurse called Mammy. She helped bring up Scarlett instead of her mother, a common practice on rich white plantations. Mammy is a key character in understanding how *Gone with the Wind* portrays race relations in a southern plantation before the Civil War. Unlike other slaves, Mammy's close relationship with Scarlett allows her to criticise Scarlett's behaviour, such as her flirty behaviour towards the young white bachelors of the area. Scarlett concerns herself only with her numerous suitors and her desire to marry Ashley Wilkes, a wealthy neighbour of the O'Hara family. However, Ashley marries Melanie Hamilton after telling Scarlett that they are too different to be together.

When the Civil War begins, Charles Hamilton, Melanie's timid, dull brother, proposes to Scarlett. She spitefully agrees to marry him, hoping to hurt Ashley. Over the course of two months, Scarlett and Charles marry, Charles joins the army and dies of the measles, and Scarlett learns that she is pregnant. After Scarlett gives birth to a son, Wade, she becomes bored and unhappy. She makes the long trip to Atlanta to stay with Melanie.

KEY TERM

Yankee
Northerner – somebody from the regions of the Union side of the American Civil War.

After the bloody Battle of Gettysburg, in 1863, Ashley is captured and sent to prison, and the northern Union army begins bearing down on Atlanta, the largest city in Georgia. Scarlett is also pursued in romance by a dashing businessman and trader, Rhett Butler. On the night the **Yankees** capture Atlanta, in 1864, and set it on fire, Melanie gives birth to her son, Beau. Rhett helps Scarlett and Melanie escape the Yankees, escorting them through the burning streets of the city, but he abandons them outside Atlanta so he can join the Confederate army.

Scarlett returns to Tara to find that her mother is dead, her father has lost his mind and the Yankee army has looted the plantation. She takes charge of rebuilding Tara, murdering a Yankee thief and putting out a fire set by a spiteful Yankee soldier. At last the war ends, word comes that Ashley is free and on his way home, and a stream of returning soldiers begins pouring through Tara. One soldier informs Scarlett that the taxes have been raised on Tara in a bid to drive out the family. Scarlett turns to Rhett Butler for the money. However, he is in a Yankee jail and cannot help her. Rhett blackmails his way out of prison and he lends Scarlett enough money to buy a sawmill. To the displeasure of Atlanta society, Scarlett becomes a shrewd businesswoman.

A free black man and his white male companion attack Scarlett on her way home from the sawmill one day. That night, the Ku Klux Klan avenges the attack on Scarlett, and Frank, Scarlett's second husband, ends up dead. Rhett proposes to Scarlett and she quickly accepts. Scarlett and Rhett's marriage begins happily, but Rhett becomes increasingly bitter and indifferent towards her.

Scarlett's feelings for Ashley have diminished into a warm, sympathetic friendship, but Ashley's jealous sister, India, finds them in a friendly embrace and spreads the rumour that they are having an affair. Bonnie, the young daughter of Scarlett and Rhett, is killed in a horse-riding accident, Rhett nearly loses his mind, and his marriage with Scarlett worsens. Scarlett concludes that she truly loves Rhett and hurries to tell Rhett of her revelation. Rhett, however, says that he has lost his love for Scarlett, and he leaves her. Grief-stricken and alone, Scarlett makes up her mind to go back to Tara to recover her strength in the comforting arms of her childhood nurse and slave, Mammy, and to think of a way to win Rhett back.

SOURCE 4

From *Gone with the Wind*, a novel by Margaret Mitchell published in 1936. By permission of GWTW Partners, LLC.

From Chapter 9. Melly, a white character, talks about how she sees the possibility of a slave revolt during the Civil War.
And as for all this talk about the militia staying here to keep the darkies from rising—why it's the silliest thing I ever heard of. Why should our people rise! It's just a good excuse of cowards.

From Chapter 28. Scarlett O'Hara talks about black slaves.
Negroes were provoking sometimes and stupid and lazy, but there was loyalty in them that money couldn't buy, a feeling of oneness with their white folks which made them risk their lives to keep food on the table.

From Chapter 31. Two northern troops talk about what is going to happen in the South following a northern victory in the Civil War.
Wilkerson and Hilton furthermore told the negroes they were as good as the whites in every way and soon white and negro marriages would be permitted, soon the estates of their former owners would be divided and every negro would be given forty acres and a mule for his own.

From Chapter 42. A view of Scarlett's neighbours who once owned slaves, when attempting to persuade her not to use convicts for labour.
Slaves were neither miserable nor unfortunate. The negroes were far better off under slavery than they were now under freedom, and if she didn't believe it, just look about her!

SOURCE 5

Scarlett O'Hara, played by Vivien Leigh, and Mammy, played by Hattie McDaniel, in the film version of *Gone with the Wind*, 1939.

The portrayal of race relations in *Gone with the Wind*

In her novel, Margaret Mitchell attempted to create the view that the pre-Civil War south of large plantations was an idyllic world. Scarlett O'Hara, the main character, lives in a world of social events where southern white men take on the role of cavaliers. The society which Mitchell described was supported by subservient black workers either in the fields growing cotton or working as domestic servants in the big plantation mansion. The title of the novel suggests a world lost that had 'gone with the wind', destroyed by the Civil War. Slaves appear as well treated and generally cheerful with their position, loyal to their white master. When they work hard, they are rewarded with gifts from their owner. The main field hand character is Big Sam, who only leaves Tara when ordered to do so by his white owners, and later in the novel he saves Scarlett at a serious risk to his own life.

During the Civil War part of the novel, the northern forces which aimed to end slavery and free black Americans are portrayed in a poor light. The northern army which marched through Georgia pillaged and destroyed plantations. Tara, Scarlett O'Hara's home, is pillaged, and Scarlett kills two of the pillagers, one black and one white.

Ashley Wilkes, one of the leading white characters in the novel, is portrayed as a southern gentleman who fights to defend the South as an officer in the Confederate army. After the southern defeat in 1865, Ashley Wilkes joins the Ku Klux Klan and his escapades are seen as defending a white population under military occupation by northern troops. The glorification of the role of the Ku Klux Klan was one of the more controversial aspects of the novel.

The dominant black character in the novel is Mammy, the black servant who has helped raise Scarlett and acts as her personal domestic servant. The characterisation of a black 'Mammy' figure has been a controversial portrayal of black Americans through history. She is content with her position and 'belongs' to the white family and seems to have no black friends. We are not told Mammy's real name. She merely acts as an ever faithful servant but has the authority to scold Scarlett when she does things wrong. The central role of Mammy allowed Hattie McDaniel to become the first black actor to win an Oscar when the novel was transferred to the screen as a film. Other black characters came off worse. Prissy, another house slave, appears as stupid, squeamish and a liar. Both she and Mammy are clearly uneducated.

Reactions to *Gone with the Wind*

The world portrayed by the novel received almost immediate criticism from America's black community. The NAACP tried to arrange a boycott of the film version of the novel by black audiences. The Hollywood producer, David O. Selznik, who brought *Gone with the Wind* to the screen, stated he could not go too far in being faithful to the novel and had no desire to produce an anti-black film. All direct references to the Ku Klux Klan were removed in the film. Also words like 'darkies' and 'niggers', which appeared in the novel, did not appear on screen. Walter White, the secretary of the NAACP, sent information to Selznik pointing out how the novel was a very biased representation of the Reconstruction period of US history, and Walter White was used by Selznik to play down the overtly racist elements that he saw in the novel. Even with the amendments made by Selznik and White, the film version of *Gone with the Wind* gave a biased view of how slave society operated in the pre-Civil War south and how slaves were treated. It also reinforced the portrayal of black Americans as menial, loyal, uneducated supporters of white society. The novel and film reinforced and reflected the attitude towards black people held by many Americans, particularly in the Old South.

A Level Exam-Style Question Section C

How far did the portrayal of race relations change between the publication of *Uncle Tom's Cabin* in 1851 and *Gone with the Wind* in 1936? (20 marks)

Tip

The question requires you to identify change and continuity in the portrayal of race relations in the novels Uncle Tom's Cabin, *and* Gone with the Wind. *To ensure that you engage in balanced analysis, you will be expected to identify similarities in the way black Americans are portrayed and treated by white Americans, and how far the novels offer different portrayals of black American characters.*

ACTIVITY
KNOWLEDGE CHECK

Gone with the Wind

1 Describe how the issue of race relations appeared in the novel and film of *Gone with the Wind*.

2 Describe how the relationship between black and white American characters in *Gone with the Wind* is portrayed.

3 In what ways did the novel and film of *Gone with the Wind* change perceptions of race relations?

In what ways did *To Kill a Mockingbird* (1960) by Harper Lee reflect the changing nature of race relations?

The background

Harper Lee wrote *To Kill a Mockingbird* in 1959 and it was published the following year. It is set in the economic depression of the 1930s in the town of Maycomb, Alabama, in the Old South. Harper Lee wrote the novel at the height of the civil rights movement. In 1954, the US Supreme Court declared school segregation unconstitutional and called for all American schools to be integrated. This resulted in white resistance in the Old South. One important episode in school integration occurred in 1957 in Little Rock, Arkansas, where President Eisenhower had to deploy paratroopers for a year to ensure seven black children could attend Central High School. In 1955–56, Martin Luther King rose to national prominence when he successfully led a boycott of public transportation in Montgomery, Alabama, against segregation on buses. In 1960, the Student Non-violent Co-ordinating Committee began a protest against segregated lunch counters in stores.

The events portrayed in the novel in Maycomb, Alabama in the 1930s helped to make *To Kill a Mockingbird* a best-selling novel almost overnight. The events concerning race relations portrayed in the novel hit a chord with readers at a time when black and many white Americans were campaigning nationwide for full civil rights for black Americans and an end to legal segregation. It received a Pulitzer Prize in 1960. Like *Gone with the Wind*, the novel's storyline was turned into a Hollywood film. It was released in 1962 and became a box-office success, earning Gregory Peck a Best Actor Oscar for portraying the leading white character, lawyer Atticus Finch.

Synopsis of *To Kill a Mockingbird*

To Kill a Mockingbird is primarily a novel about growing up under extraordinary circumstances in the 1930s in the close-knit town of Maycomb, Alabama, where every family has its social position. A widower and lawyer, Atticus Finch raises his children by himself with the help of a black housekeeper named Calpurnia. One of his children, a girl called Scout, is a tomboy who prefers the company of boys and generally solves her differences with her fists. She hates school, gaining her most valuable education on her own street and from her father.

The main story in the novel is a court trial where Atticus Finch is going to represent a black man named Tom Robinson, who is accused of raping and beating a white woman. Suddenly, Scout and Jem, Atticus Finch's children, have to tolerate a barrage of racial slurs and insults because of Atticus' role in the trial. During the novel's last summer, Tom is tried and convicted, even though Atticus proves that Tom could not possibly have committed the crime of which he is accused. In the process of presenting Tom's case, Atticus inadvertently insults and offends Bob Ewell, a nasty, lazy drunkard whose daughter is Tom's accuser. In spite of Tom's conviction, Ewell vows revenge on Atticus and the judge for besmirching his already tarnished name. The two children are bewildered by the jury's decision to convict. Atticus tries to explain why the jury's decision was in many ways a foregone conclusion.

The story appears to be winding down, but then Bob Ewell starts making good on his threats of revenge. Scout is in the Halloween pageant at school, playing the part of a ham. On the way home, the children hear odd noises, but convince themselves that the noises are coming from another friend who scared them on their way to school that evening. Suddenly, a scuffle occurs. During this attack, Jem breaks his arm badly. Scout gets just enough of a glimpse out of her costume to see a stranger carrying Jem back to their house. The stranger happens to be Arthur 'Boo' Radley, who saves the children by killing Bob Ewell. When Atticus Finch comes home, he finds Scout and Jem safe at home and Boo Radley quietly sitting in a corner. The local police decide not to pursue the case against Boo.

SOURCE 6

From *To Kill a Mockingbird*, written by Harper Lee and published in 1960. The excerpts deal with the issues of race and race relations as portrayed in the novel.

Chapter 12. Atticus Finch's two children, Scout and Jem, confront racial segregation in Maycomb for the first time. They are objects of the black racism of Lula, a black character in the novel.
Lula stopped, but she said, 'You 'ain't got no business bringin' white chillun here – they got their church, we got our'n. It is our church, ain't it, Miss Cal?'

… When I looked down the pathway again, Lula was gone. In her place was a solid mass of colored people.

One of them stepped from the crowd. It was Zeebo, the garbage collector. 'Mister Jem,' he said, 'we're mighty glad to have you all here. Don't pay no 'tention to Lula, she's contentious because Reverend Sykes threatened to church her. She's a troublemaker from way back, got fancy ideas an' haughty ways – we're mighty glad to have you all.'

Chapter 20. This deals with a speech by Atticus Finch in defence of black American, Tom Robinson, during his trial. He is addressing the all-white jury.
Which, gentlemen, we know is in itself a lie as black as Tom Robinson's skin, a lie I do not have to point out to you. You know the truth, and the truth is this: some Negroes lie, some Negroes are immoral, some Negro men are not to be trusted around women – black or white. But this is a truth that applies to the human race and to no particular race of men. There is not a person in this courtroom who has never told a lie, who has never done an immoral thing, and there is no man living who has never looked upon a woman without desire.

Chapter 25. The narrator of the novel, Harper Lee, makes a pessimistic verdict on life in Maycomb, Alabama, and the issue of race relations in the 1930s south. After he was convicted, Tom Robinson tried to escape prison and was killed.
To Maycomb, Tom's death was typical. Typical of a nigger to cut and run. Typical of a nigger's mentality to have no plan, no thought for the future, just run blind first chance he saw. Funny thing, Atticus Finch might've got him off scot free, but wait–? Hell no. You know how they are. Easy come, easy go. Just shows you, that Robinson boy was legally married, they say he kept himself clean, went to church and all that, but when it comes down to the line the veneer's mighty thin. Nigger always comes out in 'em.

Portrayal of race relations in *To Kill a Mockingbird*

Maycomb is a small town in Alabama inhabited by both white and black Americans, but each community lives a separate existence within the town. The racial segregation of Maycomb is apparent throughout the novel, as are the racial taboos about integration or mixing of the races. When a white lawyer, Atticus Finch, offers to defend a black man, Tom Robinson, on the highly emotive charge of raping a white woman, the white community of the town is outraged and Atticus Finch's children suffer ostracism as a result.

Unlike the portrayal of black Americans in *Huckleberry Finn* and *Gone with the Wind*, *To Kill a Mockingbird* has a much more sympathetic view of the lives of black Americans. The main black character, Tom Robinson, who is falsely accused of rape, is portrayed as harmless, innocent and hardworking. As Atticus Finch's daughter, Scout, notes, he would have been a fine specimen of a man if it had not been that his left hand was injured in an accident. Tom Robinson was married, with three children and worked on white man Link Dea's farm. Tom's good manners and courtesy come across during the trial scene in the novel. He refuses to repeat the foul language directed at him by his white accuser, Bob Ewell. Tom refuses to openly accuse a black servant, Mayella, for lying about him in the court case. His dignity in face of racial provocation and abuse stands out as one of his main strengths and makes him a sympathetic, pleasant and intelligent character, even faced with the injustice of being falsely convicted of a crime he did not commit in the racially segregated society of Maycomb.

On a broader note, the black American community of Maycomb also comes across as one of tolerance and dignity faced with a racially divided community. Harper Lee reveals the striking difference between the two racial communities through the medium of the court case. The one character who breaches the racial divide is Atticus Finch. His housekeeper is black and he supports the black community in offering to defend Tom Robinson, knowing full well that an all-white jury will convict Tom no matter what evidence is produced in his defence. In his summing up in the court case, he powerfully states that, yes, all black people lie and, yes, they are basically immoral beings, but he insists that the truth is that there is not a person who has never told a lie, who has never done an immoral thing, and there is not a man living who has never looked at a woman with desire.

Apart from Atticus Finch and his children, the black characters in the novel are portrayed as better, more dignified characters than the white Americans. They stand in marked contrast to the Ewells, who appear as 'white trash', ignorant and full of racial prejudice. Even when Scout and Jem visit an all-black church, they are treated with respect. Harper Lee was able to portray a racially divided society where black Americans appear as more morally upright and dignified compared to the white community. At the end of the novel, the only white character who comes to the aid of Scout and Jem when they are attacked by Bob Ewell is the quiet, lonely outcast, Boo Radley.

EXTEND YOUR KNOWLEDGE

Harper Lee (1926–2016)

While *To Kill a Mockingbird* was the first novel Harper Lee had published, it was not the first one she penned. Her first effort, titled *Go Set a Watchman*, which followed the later lives of the characters from *To Kill A Mockingbird*, was submitted to a publisher in 1957. However, the book was not accepted and Lee was asked to revise the story and make her main character Scout, a child. Lee worked on the story for two years and it eventually became *To Kill a Mockingbird*.

In 2015, the original manuscript of *Go Set a Watchman* was published. The title features Scout as a 26-year-old woman on her way back home to Maycomb, Alabama, from New York City. In *Watchman*, Scout's father Atticus Finch, the upstanding moral conscience of *To Kill a Mockingbird*, is portrayed as a racist with bigoted views and links to the Ku Klux Klan. This shocking portrayal of the beloved character Atticus Finch has caused much controversy and debate.

How far did *Beloved* (1987) by Toni Morrison shape and reflect race relations?

The background

Beloved was published in 1987 and won a Pulitzer Prize that year. It was written by a female black American author, Toni Morrison, who was born Chloe Anthony Wofford in Lorain, Ohio. In 1992, she went on to win the Nobel Prize in Literature. The novel is set in two periods in the past. One is about a brutal life as a slave in Kentucky in the 1850s. The other is during the period of Reconstruction after the Civil War. This was a time when black Americans faced racial discrimination and intimidation from white Americans, even though slavery had been abolished. By 1870, former slaves had been guaranteed equal protection of the law and the right to vote by the US Constitution. However, many white Americans resented the fact that former slaves had been given equal civil rights to those of whites.

In the USA of the late 1980s, black Americans, as a result of the civil rights movement, had seen the end of legal segregation and the renewed guarantee of their civil rights through the Civil Rights Act of 1964 and the Voting Rights Act of 1965. However, although black Americans had received civil equality, there were still major social and economic problems facing black Americans. Many, across the USA, lived in inner-city areas with run-down housing and poor job opportunities. These conditions helped spark off race riots in the Watts district of Los Angeles in 1965 and in Newark, New Jersey, in 1967. These problems were exacerbated by actions of police brutality. After the novel was published, in 1992, another major race riot occurred in the Watts area when Rodney King, a black American, was severely beaten by police. The event was recorded electronically by a bystander. It led to six days of intense rioting. This backdrop made *Beloved* a powerful novel because its portrayal of race relations reflected what was happening in contemporary America.

A synopsis of the story of *Beloved*

Beloved begins in 1873 in Cincinnati, Ohio, where Sethe, a former female slave, has been living with her 18-year-old daughter Denver. On the day the novel begins, Paul D, whom Sethe has not seen since they worked together on Mr Garner's Sweet Home plantation in Kentucky approximately 20 years earlier, stops by Sethe's house. His presence resurrects memories that have lain buried in Sethe's mind for almost two decades. From this point on, the story develops at two levels. The present in Cincinnati constitutes one level, while a series of events that took place around 20 years earlier, mostly in Kentucky, constitutes the other. This latter period is accessed through the fragmented flashbacks of the major characters.

From these fragmented memories, the following story begins to emerge. Sethe was born in the South to an African mother she never knew. When she was 13, she was sold to a white family, the Garners, who own Sweet Home and practise a benevolent kind of slavery. However, after the death of Mr Garner, the widowed Mrs Garner asks her sadistic, vehemently racist brother-in-law to help her run the farm. He is known to the slaves as 'Schoolteacher', and his oppressive presence makes life on the plantation even more unbearable than it had been before. The slaves decide to run.

Schoolteacher anticipates the slaves' escape and captures two of them, Paul D and Sixo. Schoolteacher kills Sixo and brings Paul D back to Sweet Home, where Paul D sees Sethe for what he believes will be the last time. She is still intent on running, having already sent her children ahead to her mother-in-law Baby Suggs' house in Cincinnati. Schoolteacher seizes Sethe in the barn and rapes her. When Schoolteacher finds out that Sethe has reported his misdeeds to Mrs Garner, he has her whipped severely, despite the fact that she is pregnant. Sethe runs away, but along the way she collapses. A white girl, Amy Denver, finds her and nurses her back to health. When Amy later helps Sethe deliver her baby in a boat, Sethe names this second daughter Denver, after the girl who helped her. Sethe spends 28 wonderful days in Cincinnati. On the last day, however, Schoolteacher comes for Sethe to take her and her children back to Sweet Home. Rather than surrender her children to a life of dehumanising, she tries to kill them. Only the third child, her older daughter, dies, her throat having been cut with a handsaw by Sethe.

Meanwhile, Paul D has endured torturous experiences in a chain gang in Georgia, where he was sent after being sold by Schoolteacher. His experiences have caused him to lock away his memories. One day, a rainstorm allows Paul D to escape. He travels northward, and years later he ends up on Sethe's porch in Cincinnati. Both Paul D and Sethe encounter a strange woman sleeping in the porch of their house whom they name 'Beloved'. She is the ghost of Sethe's dead daughter. Sethe's remaining daughter, Denver, develops an obsessive attachment to Beloved, and Beloved's attachment to Sethe is equally, if not more, intense. Paul D and Beloved hate each other, and Beloved controls Paul D by moving him around the house like a rag doll and seducing him against his will. Paul D leaves.

EXTRACT

1   From *The Unspoken Spoken: Toni Morrison's* Beloved *in the context of the African American experience of slavery, and slave narrative*, by Marie Burns, 2008.

Beloved, written in 1987, could be considered a slave narrative of the twentieth century, since, from the unfolding of the story, we follow Sethe's journey from enslavement to freedom. Unlike Jacobs's work, however, it is set exclusively in the black world. A cultural heritage, that includes improvisation, allows Toni Morrison, 'writing a part of herself into the narrative', to envisage for Sethe an experience of motherhood, and intertwining subplots for the other characters.

Through these, she unveils the interior life of the slave. This Morrison deems necessary to give a true representation of African American life, in and after bondage. Her novel 'exposes the unsaid of the narratives, the psychic subtexts that lie within and beneath historical facts'. Like Ella, one of her characters, Morrison 'listens for the holes – the things the fugitives did not say: the questions they did not ask'. She finds them, and in true African American tradition, has Paul D admit to his heartache, 'sang it sometimes but never told a soul'.

The medium of the novel lends itself to the process. In this way, the 'unspeakable things, unspoken', namely, the horrors endured by the black people who inhabit the world of *Beloved*, can be unearthed and shared. Characters in a novel do not hold any secrets. Their inner as well as their outer lives can be exposed so that they are understood completely by the reader.

In the light of Sethe's preoccupation with 'beating back the past' so that she may have a 'liveable life', James Baldwin agrees with Morrison that it is by acknowledging and confronting the darkness and complexity of humanity that 'we find at once ourselves and the power that will free us from ourselves'. This power is 'the power of revelation', which is the business of the novelist.

As a vehicle to address 'the necessity of historical memory, the desire to forget the terrors of slavery and the impossibility of forgetting', Morrison uses this novel to show, also, that 'there is a necessity for remembering the horror… in a manner in which… the memory is not destructive'. She extends the power of revelation to her characters who reveal the hidden degradation and humiliation they suffered, by telling what they want to tell, of their own volition, and at a time they are ready to tell it. When they finally come to putting their memories into words, Morrison demonstrates that, 'the collective sharing of that information heals the individual – and the collective'.

Beloved grows increasingly abusive, manipulative and parasitic, and Sethe is obsessed with satisfying Beloved's demands and making her understand why she murdered her. Worried by the way her mother is wasting away, Denver leaves home for the first time in 12 years in order to seek help from Lady Jones, her former teacher. Afterwards, Paul D comes back to Sethe, who has retreated to her son's bed to die. Mourning Beloved, Sethe laments that she was her best thing. To this, Paul D replies that Sethe herself is her best thing. The novel then ends with a warning that the story is not one to be passed on.

Portrayal of race relations in *Beloved*

On one level, *Beloved* deals with the brutal world of slavery. It stands in marked contrast to the slave world portrayed in *Gone with the Wind*. Far from being an idyllic time in the history of the Old South, slavery is shown as brutal, inhuman and violent. Black slaves are treated as merchandise, everything has its price, and the price is tyranny. The novel contains a number of historical references on the issue of slavery. References are made to the Middle Passage, which describes the Atlantic trade route in slaves from West Africa to America. More importantly it refers to the Fugitive Slave Act of 1850, which was important to Harriet Beecher Stowe in inspiring her to write *Uncle Tom's Cabin*. Even when former slaves escaped north out of slavery, they lived in constant fear of being caught and returned to their former masters. There are also references to the underground railroad, the organisation set up by abolitionists to assist slaves in their escape to freedom by offering safe houses, food and guidance.

White characters like Schoolteacher are portrayed as brutal and savage. Life as a slave is so terrible that Sethe was willing to murder her own child rather than return to a life of slavery. Paul D also suffers while living as a slave in Georgia, where he works on a chain gang. The novel is full of brutal images of black Americans, such as hanging from trees, floating downstream drowned or raped by white Americans. There are few white characters who come out with any credit. One is Amy, a runaway white indentured servant who helps Sethe and her children during their flight to freedom from slavery in Kentucky. There are also members of the abolitionist movement who find Baby Suggs a house and a job when she is freed.

At another level, the novel, when dealing with the period from 1873, in Cincinnati, shows how life as a slave has haunted and traumatised the lives of the chief black characters, Sethe, Denver and Paul D.

As a black American writing, Toni Morrison produced a novel from the perspective of a black American woman, brutalised by slavery and the guilt of murdering her own child. In 2006, in a *New York Times* poll of 200 critics, writers and editors, *Beloved* was named the single best work of American fiction published in the last 25 years.

Did *The Help* (2009) by Kathryn Stockett do more to reflect than shape race relations?

The background

The Help was white American Kathryn Stockett's first novel. It was published in the year the first black American, Barack Obama, was sworn in as president. This was a major event in the advancement of black Americans within US society. It brought together black and white Americans.

In many ways, one of the main themes of *The Help* was the eventual coming together of the black and white communities in Jackson, Mississippi in the novel. However, in the period it was set, 1962–64, racial tensions were acute in Mississippi. In 1962, black American James Meredith attempted to enrol in the all-white University of Mississippi, where the main character of *The Help*, Skeeter, went to college. Meredith's attempted enrolment sparked off major white resistance. President Kennedy had to send in large numbers of federal police to help Meredith enrol. They were met by armed resistance and a firefight occurred. Eventually, Meredith was enrolled on a law course. Mississippi was also the centre of attempts to enrol black Americans as voters in this period. Civil rights volunteers were murdered, which became the subject of the Hollywood film *Mississippi Burning*. The summer of 1964 was known as Freedom Summer, when major efforts were made to enrol black voters. The black community of Mississippi even sent its own delegation to the Democratic Party National Convention in August 1964, known as the Mississippi Free Democratic Party, to rival the all-white representation for the state.

This massive political turmoil that was taking place in Mississippi in 1964 is absent from the novel. Yet the novel does deal with a key aspect of race relations in Mississippi, the separate communities of black and white, who lived in different areas of the city and worked in different jobs.

Synopsis of *The Help*

The novel is set in Jackson, Mississippi between the years 1962 and 1964. It tells the story of black American maids (the help) who work in the homes of Jackson's wealthy white community. The main character of the novel is Eugenia Phelan, nicknamed Skeeter. She is a 22-year-old graduate of the University of Mississippi who has returned home to find that her black maid and nanny, Constantine, has left. Skeeter's main ambition is to be a writer. She gets a job at the *Jackson Journal* writing articles on housekeeping of which she knows virtually nothing. She turns to black American maid Aibileen for advice.

To make their relationship closer, Skeeter reads up about Jim Crow Laws which have forced legal racial segregation on Mississippi and decides to write stories for a New York publisher about the lives of black American maids in Mississippi. In the end, Skeeter gets Aibileen to introduce her to 12 maids who tell her their stories of domestic service to rich white families. An important character is black maid Minny, who has lost many jobs as a maid for speaking her mind. Skeeter, Aibileen and Minny become close friends. The stories Skeeter uncovers show that Constantine, her former nanny, had an illegitimate child, whom she gave up for adoption. It also contains revealing information about the lives of the black maids and white families for whom they work. The book is set in a fictional town called Niceville and it becomes a best-seller nationally. The white women of Jackson soon realise it is about them. One, Hilly Holbrook, is so annoyed she seeks vengeance against Skeeter.

In the end, it is a secret about Hilly, revealed by Minny in the book, that silences Hilly, and the book becomes a powerful force in giving black maids in Jackson a voice in a racially separated community. It leads to a re-evaluation of the relationship between the black and white inhabitants of Jackson, where until that time the two communities had lived very separate lives.

SOURCE

7 From *The Help* by Kathryn Stockett (2009). Skeeter meets Aibileen in order to write down her experiences as a black American maid to a white middle-class family in Jackson, Mississippi.

> I told her we'd try it just to get the project going again.
>
> Aibileen takes a breath, a swallow of Coke, and reads on. She backtracks to her first job at thirteen, cleaning the Francis the First silver service at the governor's mansion. She reads how on her first morning, she made a mistake on the chart where you filled in the number of pieces so they'd know you hadn't stolen anything. 'I come home that morning, after I been fired, and stood outside my house with my new work shoes on. The shoes my mama paid a month's worth a light bill for. I guess that's when I understood what shame was and the color of it too. Shame ain't black, like dirt, like I always thought it was. Shame be the color of a new white uniform your mother ironed all night to pay for, white without a smudge or a speck a work-dirt on it.' Aibileen looks up to see what I think. I stop typing. I'd expected the stories to be sweet, glossy. I realize I might be getting more than I'd bargained for. She reads on. '... so I go on and get the chiffarobe straightened out and before I know it, that little white boy done cut his fingers clean off in that window fan I asked her to take out ten times. I never seen that much red come out a person and I grab the boy, I grab them four fingers. Tote him to the colored hospital cause I didn't know where the white one was. But when I got there, a colored man stop me and say, Is this boy white?' The typewriter keys are clacking like hail on a roof. Aibileen is reading faster and I am ignoring my mistakes, stopping her only to put in another page. Every eight seconds, I fling the carriage aside. 'And I say, Yessuh, and he say, Is them his white fingers? And I say, Yessuh, and he say, Well you better tell em you his high yellow cause that colored doctor won't operate on a white boy in a Negro hospital. And then a white policeman grab me and he say, Now you look a here—' She stops. Looks up. The clacking ceases. 'What? The policeman said look a here what?' 'Well, that's all I put down. Had to catch the bus for work this morning.' I hit the return and the typewriter dings. Aibileen and I look each other straight in the eye. I think this might actually work.

The portrayal of race relations in *The Help*

The novel reflects the race relations of a southern city. Although Jackson comprised both black and white residents, they lived in different areas. They only came together when black Americans performed menial, subservient jobs for white people. The novel concentrates on the female white and black communities where black women were maids for rich white residents. The novel's main plot is about when the white residents realise how much their black maids know about their lives and are willing to discuss these developments in print in Skeeter's book on Nicetown, a thinly veiled description of Jackson.

Kathryn Stockett, as a white woman who had not lived in Jackson, portrayed a life she did not personally experience. In researching the novel, she said she spoke with one white employer and one black maid. She grew up in the 1970s, not the 1960s, but refers directly to the role characterised by Mammy in *Gone with the Wind* of a black American maid acting as nanny to white children to the point where the children had more knowledge and experience of the maid than they had of their own white mother. This intimacy between the two communities stood in marked contrast to the rest of the lives of the black and white community, which remained totally separate. That made the revelations contained in Skeeter's book about Nicetown so dramatic and devastating to the white, middle-class readers of Jackson who employed maids.

The Help reinforces the view that the black and white communities lived separate existences in the same city. Also, that black women, in the form of domestic servants like maids, were seen as inferior to the white, middle class who employed them. The servile life of black women, which also appears in *Gone with the Wind* of the Civil War period, had remained in the Mississippi of the 1960s.

ACTIVITY
KNOWLEDGE CHECK

Portrayal of race relations in *To Kill a Mockingbird*, *Beloved* and *The Help*
The novels *To Kill a Mockingbird*, *Beloved* and *The Help* all deal with the portrayal of black Americans within US society.

1 Produce a grid which identifies where race relations are shown to be similar between the three novels and, in a separate section, which shows where race relations are shown to be portrayed differently.

2 In pairs, write how one of the novels above reflected race relations at the time of the setting of the novel and when it was published.

THINKING HISTORICALLY   Change (8a, b & c) (II)

Judgements about change

If two professionals were asked to track a patient's health over time, one might approach this task by measuring heart rate, weight and cholesterol, while the other professional might assess the patient's mental wellbeing, relationships and ability to achieve their goals. Both are valid approaches, but result in different reports. What is true in this medical case is true in historical cases. Measuring change in something requires: (a) a concept of what that something is (e.g. What is 'health'? What is an 'economy'?); (b) judgements about how this thing should be measured; and (c) judgements about what relevant 'markers of change' are (how we distinguish a change from a temporary and insignificant fluctuation).

Historians have differed in their accounts of change and development in the black civil rights movement in 19th- and 20th-century America. Read the following quotes and then answer the questions.

'Black soldiers played a crucial role not only in winning the Civil War, but in defining the war's consequences. Their service helped transform the nation's treatment of blacks and blacks' conception of themselves. One Senator observed in 1864 "the black man is henceforth to assume a new status among us." For the first time in American history, large numbers of blacks were treated as equals before the law.'

From *Reconstruction, America's Unfinished Revolution: 1863 to 1877* by Eric Foner (1988).

'For most blacks and whites in the 1960s Martin Luther King was the movement's chief figurehead. Instantly recognisable of frequent media appearances, King's ability to operate at the interface of black and white culture contributed to his effectiveness as a communicator of black objectives to white Americans. No other civil rights leader functioned so successfully or consistently as an inter-group mediator.'

Adapted from *Sweet Land of Liberty? The African American Struggle for Civil Rights in the Twentieth Century* by Robert Cook (1998).

A Level Exam-Style Question Section C

To what extent did the portrayal of race relations in American fiction between 1850 and 2009 accurately reflect perceptions of race at the time of publication? (20 marks)

Tip

You will be required to provide a balanced, analytical answer. In your answer, you will need to explain how races were portrayed in American fiction in the years 1850–2009. You will also be expected to assess the extent to which they reflected rather than changed perceptions of race relations at the time of publication.

'Unanimously, the US Supreme Court had ruled that the Fourteenth Amendment required equal admission of all students to public schools. The decision, the Chicago Defender proclaimed, was a "second emancipation proclamation – more important to our democracy than the atom bomb or the hydrogen bomb".'

From *The Unfinished Journey* (1995) by historian William H. Chafe, writing on the *Brown* v *Board of Education* case of 1954.

1 Do all three accounts agree that improvements in black civil rights occurred in the USA in the 19th and 20th centuries?

2 Do all three accounts agree on the chronology of change? (Do they see it happening in the same time periods and at the same pace?)

3 Do all three accounts agree in characterising change as (a) rapid, (b) dramatic and (c) impacting US society as a whole?

4 Do the historians all think of black civil rights in the same way? (For example, do they all focus on the role of black Americans in achieving better civil rights in the same way?)

5 Generalising from these examples, to what extent do historians' judgements about change depend on *what* historians decide to look at and *how* they decide to measure change?

HOW FAR DID FILM AND TELEVISION INFLUENCE AND REFLECT CHANGING PERCEPTIONS OF RACE, 1850–2009?

In many ways, visual images of the portrayal of black Americans had a more striking impact on the general American public than the written word. Throughout the period 1850–2009, black Americans have been portrayed in a number of visual media. In the period 1850 to the beginning of the 20th century, the main forms of visual imagery were paintings, photographs and lithographs. All three forms of visual media were important in the portrayal of black Americans and the development of perceptions of the role of black Americans in American society. In the first half of the 20th century, going to the cinema to watch films became America's most popular pastime. Hollywood, the centre of the US film industry, dominated the world of film-making. From the end of the Second World War, film-watching was confronted with a major rival as a form of popular entertainment. This was television. In influencing and reflecting changing views on race relations, the visual media have played an important role.

Portrayal of black Americans in lithographs and photographs

Images in the period 1850–80 reflected the varied attitudes white Americans possessed towards black Americans. Lithographs appeared in newspapers, weekly magazines and as illustrations in books, and they depicted black Americans in a variety of ways. The best-selling novel *Uncle Tom's Cabin* contained lithographic illustrations that highlighted key episodes in the story which dealt with the horrors of slavery. *Harper's Weekly*, a New York-based periodical which was published between 1857 and 1916, produced depictions of black Americans regularly, particularly during the Civil War and Reconstruction periods. For instance, in July 1863, the first regular black unit of the federal army, the 54th Massachusetts Volunteer Infantry, took part in an attack on Battery Wagner on Charleston harbour. The heroic attack appeared as a lithograph in the magazine. Lithographic images also appeared which attempted to show the life of black Americans as happy and contented.

SOURCE
8
The front page of Frank Leslie's *Illustrated Newspaper* from 19 September 1874, a rival to *Harper's Weekly*, showing black Americans being killed by white supremacists in Tennessee.

SOURCE
9
A group of black slaves in Virginia listen to a man sing to the accompaniment of his banjo. In *Harper's New Monthly* magazine, this lithograph shows black Americans in 'Ole Virginny' (Virginia) looking happy and contented, in marked contrast to the image in Frank Leslie's *Illustrated Newspaper* (Source 8).

SOURCE 10

Wilson Chinn, a former slave from Louisiana, wearing the chains that slaves had to endure when punished by their white masters. The photograph was taken in 1863, at the height of the Civil War, by an anti-slavery group. It was used to depict the horrors of slavery and to encourage support for the abolition of slavery and the defeat of the Confederacy in the Civil War.

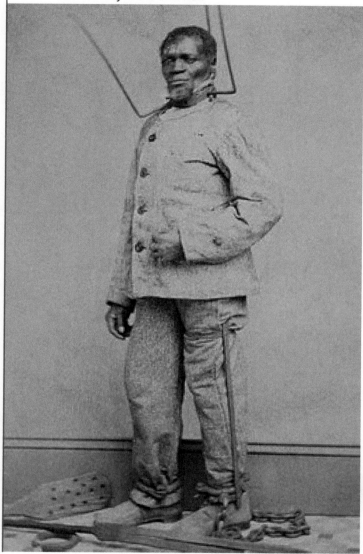

Portrayal of black Americans in paintings

Several American painters attempted to produce realistic depictions of the lives of black Americans. Probably the best-known painting of black family life under slavery was Eastman Johnson's *Negro Life at the South (Old Kentucky Home)*, which, after its exhibition in 1859 at the National Academy of Design in New York, brought the artist immediate celebrity. The critic Henry Tuckerman, writing of the work in 1867, observed that the painting was not only a masterly work of art, full of nature, truth, local

significance and character, but it was also valuable as it captured a time in American life that was altered by the Civil War.

After emancipation and the end of Civil War, the position of many black Americans did not improve economically. In 1879, painter Thomas Anshutz produced *The Way They Live*, which depicted a black woman tending a meagre cabbage patch. Paintings like this reflected the servile nature of much black American work and also reflected the perception that black Americans could only do unskilled, menial work.

These attempts at realism in American painting stood in contrast to the many illustrations, like those depicted in *Harper's Monthly* magazine, which attempted to depict a fictional idyllic life for black Americans living in the Old South.

The portrayal of race relations in *The Birth of a Nation*, 1915

The Birth of a Nation was the first full-length silent film produced by Hollywood and lasts three hours. It was a film of epic proportions covering the era of the Civil War and Reconstruction, set mainly in a town in South Carolina.

In the period just before the outbreak of Civil War, when slavery existed, black Americans are portrayed as good for nothing more than servile labour. The film then deals with epic battles of the Civil War involving a cast of thousands. The most controversial part of the film deals with the Reconstruction period (1865–77) after the Civil War. During that time, **radical Republican** white politicians from the north are seen economically exploiting the South. It also shows freed black men keen on intermarriage with white women. The heroes of that part of the film are the Ku Klux Klan, who are portrayed as defenders of all that is noble in the South, as hooded raiders who serve out 'justice'. They treated black people as inferior, denying them the right to vote and keeping them in a subservient, inferior position in society.

KEY TERM

Radical Republican
The Republican Party had been formed in 1854 to prevent the westward extension of slavery. By the end of the Civil War, radical members of that party wanted to give freed black Americans in the South full political rights and aid in economic development. They also wanted to exclude former members of the Confederate government and army from the political process.

The impact of *The Birth of a Nation*

Hollywood marketed the film as sensational. It was premiered at a grand gala screening with expensive tickets. President Woodrow Wilson had a private screening at the White House and stated that he liked the film. Black American civil rights groups, like the NAACP, protested against the film. The director, D.W. Griffith, was a southern white who remembered stories about the Reconstruction period in the South from his elderly relations.

SOURCE 11 Eastman Johnson's *Negro Life at the South (Old Kentucky Home)*, 1859. Black Americans are shown as contented farm labourers enjoying a relaxation period, singing and playing musical instruments at a dilapidated house.

SOURCE 12 A 1915 interview with the director of *The Birth of a Nation*, D.W. Griffith. In the interview, Griffith states he was not just interested in entertainment and making money.

I believe in the motion picture not only as a means of amusement, but as a moral and educational force. The time will come, and in less than ten years, when the children in the public schools will be taught practically everything by moving pictures. Certainly they will never be obliged to read history again. There will be no opinions expressed. You will merely be present at the making of history. All the work of writing, revising, collating, and reproducing will have been carefully attended to by a corps of recognized experts, and you will have received a vivid and complete expression.

The impact of Griffith's film was immense. In 1925, William Simmons, at Stone Mountain, near Atlanta, Georgia, refounded the Ku Klux Klan (KKK) and claimed that *The Birth of a Nation* was a key factor in this development. From 1915 to 1926, the KKK grew rapidly. In 1921, it reached 100,000 members, and by 1924 it had a nationwide membership of four million. Attacks on black Americans increased. The summer of 1919 became known as the Red Summer, with lynching and riots against black people taking place across the USA in cities such as Kansas City and Chicago. More than any other motion picture, *The Birth of a Nation* led to a major deterioration in race relations in the USA.

EXTRACT

A view on the issue of race relations by writer Richard Wormser, produced for the Public Broadcasting Channel of American Television, 1995.

On the evening of March 21, 1915, President Woodrow Wilson attended a special screening at the White House of THE BIRTH OF A NATION, a film directed by D.W. Griffith and based on THE CLANSMAN, a novel written by Wilson's good friend Thomas Dixon. The film presented a distorted portrait of the South after the Civil War, glorifying the Ku Klux Klan and denigrating blacks. It falsified the period of Reconstruction by presenting blacks as dominating Southern whites (almost all of whom are noble in the film) and sexually forcing themselves upon white women. The Klan was portrayed as the South's savior from this alleged tyranny. Not only was this portrayal untrue, it was the opposite of what actually happened. During Reconstruction, whites dominated blacks and assaulted black women. The Klan was primarily a white terrorist organization that carried out hundreds of murders. After seeing the film, an enthusiastic Wilson reportedly remarked: 'It is like writing history with lightning, and my only regret is that it is all so terribly true.' African-American audiences openly wept at the film's malicious portrayal of blacks, while Northern white audiences cheered. The film swept the nation. Riots broke out in major cities (Boston and Philadelphia, among others), and it was denied release in many other places (Chicago, Ohio, Denver, Pittsburgh, St. Louis, and Minneapolis). Gangs of whites roamed city streets attacking blacks. In Lafayette, Indiana, a white man killed a black teenager after seeing the movie. Thomas Dixon revelled in its triumph. 'The real purpose of my film,' he confessed gleefully, 'was to revolutionize Northern audiences that would transform every man into a Southern partisan for life.' As the NAACP fought against the film and tried unsuccessfully to get it banned, the Ku Klux Klan successfully used it to launch a massive recruiting campaign that would bring in millions of members. Griffith later regretted the racial prejudice that his film promoted. He tried to make amends by making INTOLERANCE, a film attacking race prejudice. But INTOLERANCE never approached the success of THE BIRTH OF A NATION.

SOURCE

A still from the film *The Birth of a Nation*, 1915. Colonel Cameron, a former Confederate soldier, is prevented from voting in an election by white northerners and black Americans.

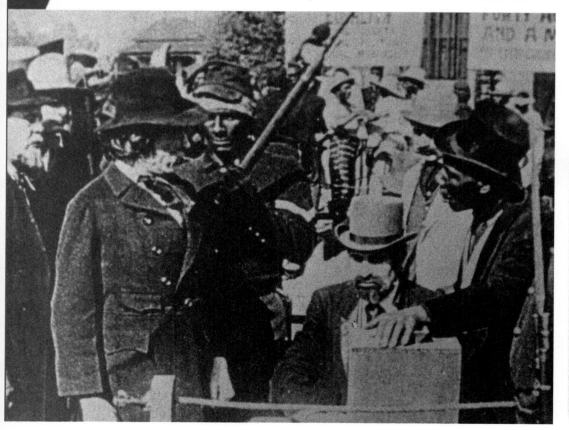

A Level Exam-Style Question Section C

How far did lithographs, paintings and film reflect changing perceptions of race relations in the USA between 1850 and 2009? (20 marks)

Tip

You are required to write a balanced answer in which you identify ways in which lithographs, paintings and films helped change perceptions of race relations and also identify ways in which they merely reflected contemporary perceptions of race relations.

How far did *In the Heat of the Night* (1967) reflect changing perceptions of the relationships between black and white Americans?

Fifty-two years after *The Birth of a Nation*, the Norman Jewison film *In the Heat of the Night* portrays race in a very different light in a very different time. It reflects the changing relations between black and white Americans, where black Americans, in particular those from the north, show greater assertion and refuse to be dominated by white people.

The film is set in the town of Sparta, Mississippi, in 1966 and is a murder mystery. The plot sets two strong characters against each other. One is a black American detective from Philadelphia, Pennsylvania, in the north. He is Virgil Tibbs, played by Oscar winner Sidney Poitier. The other is the white police chief of Sparta, Bill Gillespie, played by Rod Steiger. Tibbs is highly intelligent and a superb detective. Gillespie is an oafish redneck who dislikes outsiders in his patch, in particular black northern detectives. The film begins with animosity between the two, with Tibbs initially being arrested by the southern white police. A key moment in the film that earns its place in movie history is when Gillespie, who has been callously referring to Tibbs as 'boy', asks Tibbs what they call him in Philadelphia, and he roars back that they call him 'Mister Tibbs'.

EXTRACT

 A review of the film *In the Heat of the Night* (1967) by Tim Dirks for Filmsite, 2015. It contains direct quotes from the screenplay of the film.

After the murder of a wealthy and powerful Northern industrialist named Leslie Colbert in the town one night, a well-dressed black stranger, Virgil Tibbs (Sidney Poitier), waiting for a late night train in the deserted train station, is arrested as a prime suspect solely because of his color. Tibbs is brought before shrewd, overweight, gum-chewing, fast-talking, redneck Sheriff Bill Gillespie (Rod Steiger).

Virgil, as it turns out, is an intelligent, Philadelphia homicide detective with a badge. When Virgil confidently demonstrates his investigative skills in front of the prejudiced Sheriff and his deputies, Gillespie can't help but insult him after being embarrassed and shown up:

Gillespie: Well, you're pretty sure of yourself, ain't you, Virgil. Virgil, that's a funny name for a nigger boy to come from Philadelphia. What do they call you up there? Virgil: They call me *Mister* Tibbs.

The Sheriff tricks and challenges the smart black detective to stay and help solve the murder case using his experience in police work and forensics:

You're so damn smart! You're smarter than any white man. You're just going to stay here and show us all. You got such a big head that you could never live with yourself unless you could put us all to shame… I don't think you could let an opportunity like that pass by.

Gillespie summarizes what life is like when the Philadelphia detective visits his home:

Gillespie: You know, you know Virgil, you are among the chosen few. Virgil: How's that? Gillespie: Well I think that you're the first human being that's ever been in here. Virgil: You can't be too careful, man. Gillespie: I got no wife. I got no kids. Boy… I got a town that don't want me… I'll tell you a secret. Nobody comes here, never.

As they work together to solve the murder mystery in an atmosphere of hatred and antagonism, the central focus of the film is on the changing, unfolding relationship between the two clashing, strong-willed men as they move from inherent prejudice to grudging mutual respect and admiration for each other.

Virgil helps to solve the case amidst southern racist tensions. Suspects include wealthy citizen Eric Endicott (Larry Gates) and redneck Sheriff Bill Gillespie's bigoted deputy Sam Wood (Warren Oates), who is also accused of impregnating slutty 16 year-old Delores Purdy (Quentin Dean) in town. By the film's conclusion, it is revealed that the real murderer and 'true father' of the girl is a diner counter worker named Ralph Henshaw (Anthony James) who confesses in the Sheriff's office that he has murdered Colbert to pay for Delores' abortion.

In the final memorable scene, after the crime is solved, Virgil Tibbs and Gillespie say goodbye at the train station as Virgil leaves town. Virgil takes his suitcase, which Gillespie is carrying.

Gillespie: Well, got your ticket? Here you are. (Gillespie hands him his luggage.) Virgil: Thank you. (Gillespie offers his hand for a handshake.) Bye-bye. Gillespie: Bye. (Tibbs climbs the stairs of the train as Gillespie walks away a bit.) Virgil? (Tibbs looks back.) You take care, you hear? (A faint smile crosses both their faces.) Virgil: Yeah. (Tibbs enters the train car.)

The film sees Gillespie developing a grudging respect for Tibbs, which overcomes his racial prejudice. The portrayal of Gillespie won Rod Steiger a Best Supporting Actor Oscar.

A key incident in the film, for the portrayal of race relations, is when Detective Tibbs questions a wealthy local white plantation owner, Eric Endicott, at his mansion. Endicott is served by a servile black domestic servant. He clearly does not like being questioned by a black detective. Tibbs' questions lead to Endicott slapping Tibbs for his insolent questioning. In reply, Tibbs slaps him back, to the astonishment of Gillespie and the black servant. Endicott replies that there was a time when he could have had Tibbs shot for that action.

The 1960s saw major changes in Mississippi. In 1962, when the novel *The Help* begins, James Meredith attempted to be the first black American to enrol in the University of Mississippi. The year 1963 saw major civil rights confrontations in Birmingham, Alabama, and 1964 was the Freedom Summer in Mississippi, where attempted voter registration of black Americans led to white resistance and violence. Eventually, in 1964, the Civil Rights Act was passed, followed in 1965 by the Voting Rights Act, following a major civil rights march from Selma to Montgomery, Alabama. Even so, racial tension was high. When production began in 1966, Poitier refused to shoot in the South. He was still traumatised by the experience of being tailed by Klansmen when visiting North Carolina with Harry Belafonte in a civil rights demonstration. Poitier reluctantly agreed to a few days of tense location work in Tennessee. Plagued by whooping rednecks, much like a scene from the film itself, Poitier told Jewison that he slept with a gun under his pillow. So it was in Illinois, in the north, not Mississippi, that the film was made.

How far was *Mississippi Burning* (1988) an accurate portrayal of race relations in Mississippi in 1964?

Like *In the Heat of the Night*, *Mississippi Burning* is set in Mississippi and is based on real events. In 1964, three civil rights activists – James Cheney, a black American, and Andrew Goodman and Michael Schwerner, both white although not named in the film – were in Mississippi helping black voter registration when they disappeared in Neshoba County, which appears in the film as fictional Jessup County. They were all murdered by members of the Ku Klux Klan.

The film is a murder mystery, like *In the Heat of the Night*. This time, two white agents of the Federal Bureau of Investigation (FBI) are the main characters. One is a liberal, Agent Alan Ward, played by Willem Dafoe. The other is a rough-and-ready agent, Rupert Anderson, played by Gene Hackman. They confront a community that is led by a white supremacist mayor called Tilman. The Deputy Sheriff is Clinton Pell, a member of the Ku Klux Klan.

The film's story shows how the FBI, using unorthodox methods, uncovers the Ku Klux Klan plot and brings the main perpetrators to justice. Several scenes feature Klan brutality, including one in which several white men severely beat a young black man who was approached by the FBI for information. These scenes illustrate the dangers that black people faced for daring to speak out for racial justice in Mississippi during the mid-1960s. Towards the end of the film, the FBI agents conclude that lawful operating procedures are not going to be able to bring the activists' murderers to justice. Instead, they trick and terrorise Klan members to confess their involvement in the activists' deaths. According to the film's own logic, the threats of violence against Klan members are warranted by the Klan's own disregard for the law, and enable Ward and Anderson to find some justice for the black community.

The film, directed by Alan Parker, who is British, received a lot of criticism for what was seen as a misleading depiction of the civil rights movement. Most black characters in the film play minor roles. The key character roles are all white. The movie's focus on two renegade FBI agents displaced the key individuals and organisations who led Mississippi's civil rights movement during the 1960s. The film also excluded references to local black American citizens who challenged Mississippi's racist policies, despite threats that local white Americans made to their lives and their families. Furthermore, the FBI was not nearly as committed to civil rights as the film indicated. By focusing on fictional white FBI agents in a film about racial injustice, the film offered a whitewashed depiction of the civil rights movement. When the film was released, Martin Luther King's widow, Coretta Scott King, criticised the film for ignoring the role of both black and white civil rights activists.

Was the film *Malcolm X* (1992) an accurate reflection of race relations?

In 1992, black American director, Spike Lee, produced a film of the life of one of the civil rights movement's most controversial figures, Malcolm X. The film stars Denzel Washington playing Malcolm X and deals with Malcom X's early life, his conversion to Islam, his role as a civil rights activist, and his assassination, which occurred in 1965, 27 years before Lee's film. Much of the screenplay was based on *The Autobiography of Malcolm X*, published in 1965, the year of his death. To write the book, Malcom X collaborated with black writer Alex Haley, who also wrote *Roots* (see page 65).

Malcolm X was born Malcolm Little in 1925 in Omaha, Nebraska, a western state. He took the surname 'X' because he regarded the name 'Little' as a slave name and did not know his original African surname. Later, having converted to Islam, he adopted the name El-Hadji Malik El-Shabazz. The film tracks Malcolm X's life from a child living in poverty to a street hustler and drug taker, to his time in prison and to the pinnacle of his civil rights career as a spokesman for the Nation of Islam. He eventually fell out with the Nation of Islam, went on a pilgrimage to Mecca and returned to the USA to found his own organisation. He was assassinated by members of the Nation of Islam in New York City in 1965.

The film was released in 1992 after the Rodney King riots in south central Los Angeles (once known as the Watts district). Spike Lee flanked the story of Malcolm's life with footage from this event in his film, along with other contemporary scenes. In 2010, the Library of Congress deemed *Malcolm X* as 'culturally, historically or aesthetically significant'.

EXTRACT 4

Comments from Dr Althea Legal-Miller, a lecturer at University College London's Institute of the Americas, about the film *Malcolm X*.

[the film] *Malcolm X* emerged from an extension of conversations in the 1980s and early 1990s about Afrocentric politics. Malcom X's views and the way they were portrayed by black American director Spike Lee fitted in with contemporary views in 1992 about populist black nationalism. Malcolm X's message also appeared in hip-hop dialogues from Boogie Down Productions to Public Enemy, whose Bring the Noise starts with a recorded sample from Malcolm's influential speech 'Message to the Grass Roots'.

[Malcom X] offered black youth a blueprint for self-invention that could be fashioned out of the lived experiences of the ghetto, rising black male murder rates, urban impoverishment, neoconservative apathy and ongoing racism.

EXTRACT 5

From a review of the film *Malcolm X* by Clayborne Carson. He is a black American professor of history at Stanford University and director of the Martin Luther King Research and Education Institute. He also wrote *Malcolm X, the FBI File*.

Spike Lee frames Malcolm's life story with contemporary scenes: opening footages of Los Angeles police beating Rodney King and an epilogue showing Nelson Mandela, in front of a classroom filled with South African children, affirming Malcolm's call for liberation 'by all means necessary'. This iconic mixture gives his film a greater sense of political importance than it would otherwise have had, but its political message is ambiguous. Lee's strongest images suggest the immutability of white racism (King's beating) rather than the possibility of overcoming it (Mandela). His film ends his life resigned to his fate. Malcolm X helped create his own myth during a period when fundamental political change seemed feasible. Spike Lee revised Malcolm's myth for a time when political cynicism prevails. [The film] *Malcolm X* reflects the current tendency in African American life to express racial resentment rather than engage in collective action to achieve racial advancement.

ACTIVITY
KNOWLEDGE CHECK

Portrayal of race relations in film: *The Birth of a Nation* v. *In the Heat of the Night*

1 Write down the ways race relations are portrayed in *The Birth of a Nation* and *In the Heat of the Night*.

2 Why do you think the portrayal of race relations was shown differently?

3 Which of these two films, do you think, had a greater impact on changing perceptions of race relations in the USA?

The impact of the television miniseries *Roots* (1977)

American television in the 1950s and 1960s tended to reinforce stereotypes of black Americans. Invariably, they appeared in supporting roles, usually engaging in servile jobs such as railroad attendants, domestic servants, hotel porters or unskilled workers. The first US television series that had a black American actor as co-star was *I Spy* in the 1960s, when white American Robert Culp shared top billing with black American actor Bill Cosby. In 1976, the few shows that featured major black characters were criticised because they portrayed black Americans as poorly educated, comic characters. *Good Times*, a comedy about a poor family in an inner-city ghetto, featured a character named J.J., a teenager who regularly yelled 'Dy-No-Mite!' Another comedy, *Sanford & Son*, was a story about a junkyard operator and his tempestuous son. *The Jeffersons* was yet another comedy, which focused on a rude black bigot who owned a chain of cleaning stores. All that came to an end in 1977 with *Roots*.

Across eight evenings in 1977 and seven evenings in 1979, the miniseries *Roots* and its sequel *Roots: The Next Generation* transformed the role of black Americans on US television and played a major role in changing perceptions of race and race relations. The stars of both series were black American actors, and the two series traced the history of black Americans from slavery to the present day through the family of Alex Haley, a black writer who wrote the best-selling book *Roots*. The first series of *Roots*, which was a television adaptation of the book of the same name, published in 1976, lasted 12 hours and was shown between 23 and 30 January 1977. It was one of the most widely watched miniseries in US television history, with a television watching rating of between 45 and 66 percent. Between 18 and 23 February 1979, *Roots: The Next Generation* was shown, with a watching share of between 30 and 45 percent of the television audience. An estimated 140 million Americans saw all or part of the two series.

One of the reasons why the two *Roots* miniseries were so popular was the fact that the history of black Americans was personalised through following the life story of one family, from capture in West Africa, through slavery to emancipation in the first series. In the second series, the lives of Haley's ancestors were picked up during Reconstruction, and it went through the era of segregation up to Haley's own life as a coastguard and writer, including his collaboration with Malcolm X on the latter's biography.

Another feature of the two *Roots* miniseries was the fact that many of Hollywood's finest white actors participated in roles as slavers, slave owners and racists. Edward Asner, Lorne Greene, Lloyd Bridges and Marlon Brando all appeared, the latter in the role of Norman Rockwell, leader of the American Nazi Party, interviewed by Alex Haley in *Roots: The Next Generation*.

Some controversy surrounded Alex Haley's claim in both the book and miniseries that he could trace his African ancestor, Kunte Kinte, directly back to a village in Gambia called Juffure. However, *Roots* and its subject matter, the black American historical experience over 200 years, became a topic of national discussion and debate. College courses were established based on the miniseries, and tens of millions of white Americans had their perception of race and race relations changed forever.

The style of the *Roots* miniseries lent itself to popular discussion. The first miniseries traced a black American family tree back to West Africa and then through successive generations up to the time of the Civil War. Beginning with Kunte Kinte, who was given the slave name 'Toby', it then followed the life story of his daughter Kizzie and then her son 'Chicken George'. The following of a family tree involving the life of real black Americans brought the story of slavery to life in a way documentaries failed to do. The miniseries showed how slaves lived and what problems they faced. What added to the miniseries' power was the fact that most of the main white characters were played by leading

Hollywood actors usually known for playing 'good person' characters. In *Roots*, they appeared as villains. Lorne Greene, who played Kunte Kinte's slave owner, Chuck Connors, who raped Kizzie, and Lloyd Bridges, who played a Confederate officer in the Civil War, all made the miniseries virtually a 'must watch' experience.

The next miniseries, *Roots: The Next Generation*, brought the Haley family tree up to the present, ending with Alex Haley himself and his personal search for his own family tree, which resulted in the book *Roots*, first published in serial form in *Reader's Digest* in 1974 and then as a book in 1976.

How accurate a reflection was *The Wire* (2002–08) of the urban black American experience in the early 21st century?

The miniseries *Roots* and *Roots: The Next Generation* charted the changing world of a black American family over 200 years from slavery to the middle class. *The Wire* series, which was shown on Home Box Office (HBO) television, offered a completely different portrayal of black American life. Most of the novels and films mentioned in this chapter concentrated on black American life in the Old South. *The Wire* instead is set in a northern, urban environment in the city of Baltimore, Maryland.

The Wire is a crime drama that appeared on the HBO cable channel from 2002 to 2008. In each of the years *The Wire* appeared, it dealt with a different section of black American society: the drug wars, the docks (Baltimore is a seaport), city politics, education and the media. The whole series is seen through the eyes of the black American community in a city that had suffered considerable economic change. The collapse of the traditional jobs structure from the 1980s resulted in a growing gap between rich and poor, creating a divided society. The politicians in city hall are portrayed as incapable of anything other than self-interest. The public education system is underfunded, helping to create an unskilled underclass. The series received considerable critical acclaim. For the first time on a major cable channel, the lives of an urban black underclass were shown in detail. Scenes associated with the drugs wars and urban life were graphic and brutal.

On 2 April 2009, the British newspaper the *Daily Telegraph*, in an article entitled 'The Wire: arguably the greatest television programme ever made', stated that no other series in history has attracted such critical praise, and claimed that some critics were comparing it with the works of Dickens and Dostoevsky.

Although critically acclaimed, *The Wire* did not have the same impact on influencing race relations as *Roots* and *Roots: The Next Generation*. This is arguably because it was aired on a cable channel and did not get the huge audience of the two *Roots* miniseries.

ACTIVITY
KNOWLEDGE CHECK

Roots and *The Wire*

1 What reasons can you give to explain why *Roots* and *Roots: The Next Generation* were so popular?

2 In what ways were the lives of black Americans portrayed in *Roots* different from the portrayal of black Americans in *The Wire*?

3 Work in pairs.

   a) One person should identify reasons why *Roots* was a major development in changing perceptions of black Americans within the USA.

   b) The other person should identify reasons why *The Wire* can be regarded as giving a realistic perception of life in contemporary urban black America.

ACTIVITY
SUMMARY

Changing portrayal of civil rights issues in fiction and film

1 a) Write down the ways in which black American life was portrayed in the following:

    i) *Uncle Tom's Cabin*, *Huckleberry Finn* and *Gone with the Wind*

    ii) *To Kill a Mockingbird*, *Beloved* and *The Help*.

  b) How did the lives of black Americans change and differ between each set of novels? Give reasons for your answer.

2 a) Write down the ways in which the following helped change perceptions of race relations within the USA:

    i) *The Birth of a Nation*

    ii) *In the Heat of the Night*

    iii) *Roots*.

  b) What do you regard as the most influential film or television programme in portraying the lives of black Americans? Give reasons for your answer.

  c) Which film or television series had the most influence in bringing about changed perceptions of race relations within the USA? Give reasons for your answer.

3 Which medium had greater influence in shaping and influencing perceptions of race relations in the USA: literature or film and television?

WIDER READING

Benshoff, H.M. and Griffen, S. *America on Film*, Blackwell (2004)

Diawara, M. (ed.) *Black American Cinema*, Routledge (1993)

Graham, M. and Ward, J.W. (eds) *The Cambridge History of African American Literature*, Cambridge University Press (2011)

Lee, M. *Slavery, Philosophy and American Literature, 1830–1860*, Cambridge University Press (2005)

Mitchell, A. and Taylor, D. (eds) *The Cambridge Companion to African American Women's Literature*, Cambridge University Press (2009)

Richard, L. *African American Films Through 1959*, Mcfarland (1998)

Silk, C. and Silk, J. *Racism and Anti-racism in American Popular Culture: Portrayals of African Americans in Fiction and Film*, Manchester University Press (1990)

Young, A. *African American Literature: A Brief Introduction and Anthology*, Longman (1997)

3.3 'Free at last', 1865–77

KEY QUESTIONS

- To what extent did the Thirteenth Amendment change the position of ex-slaves?
- How far did Radical Reconstruction change the position of black Americans in the former Confederacy?
- What significance did the white backlash in the former Confederacy have on the rights of black Americans?

KEY TERMS

Secession
The process by which a state decides to leave the USA. Initially, in November 1860, South Carolina left the USA after the election of President Lincoln. Later, ten other states seceded and they jointly formed the Confederate States of America.

Electoral college
A method of electing presidents and vice presidents in the USA. Each state has electoral college votes to reflect the number of US senators and congressmen it possesses. In November of the presidential election year, voters go to the polls. In December of the same year, officials appointed to the electoral college by state legislatures cast their electoral college votes to reflect the popular vote. It is possible for a candidate to win the most popular votes, but lose in the electoral college. This occurred in 1876-77.

INTRODUCTION

In April 1865, the American Civil War came to an end. It had begun in 1861 when 11 south-eastern states seceded from the USA to form the Confederate States of America. The key issue on which **secession** took place was the preservation of the institution of slavery in the southern states. From the perspective of the rest of the USA, the war was to prevent secession and preserve the pre-war union of states. On 22 August 1862, in a letter to the editor of the *New York Tribune* Horace Greeley, President Abraham Lincoln stated if he could save the Union without freeing any slave he would do that, and if he could save it by freeing all the slaves he would do that, and if he could save it by freeing some slaves and not others he would also do that.

In the following month, September 1862, after the northern victory at the Battle of Antietam, Lincoln announced the Emancipation Proclamation, which declared that all slaves in areas held by the Confederacy were to be free from 1 January 1863. The war that began to preserve the pre-war union of states ended as a crusade to end slavery. In January 1865, in the closing months of the Civil War, slavery was abolished by constitutional amendment.

The period 1865–77 was known as the Reconstruction period, where the former Confederate states were placed under northern military occupation and new, pro-union state governments were installed. It was a new era for America's former slaves. They had been emancipated and had been given civil rights equivalent to those of white Americans. However, the period of Reconstruction saw a backlash from members of the white population of the former Confederate states. In white supremacist groups, such as the Ku Klux Klan, many white Americans attempted to reassert their dominant position within southern society that had existed before 1865.

Reconstruction came to an end as a result of the presidential election of 1876. In that year Democrat candidate, Samuel Tilden, won a majority of votes cast, but Republican candidate, Rutherford B. Hayes, won the **electoral college** by one vote. He achieved this through support from several southern states, who were willing to support him as he ended Reconstruction. The period 1865–77 seemed to offer a new beginning for black American civil rights. However, this new beginning proved to be short in duration.

1861 – April: Outbreak of the Civil War – 11 states leave the USA to form the Confederate States of America

1865 – January: General Sherman's Field Order Number 15

March: Freedmen's Bureau is created

1866 – Riots against black Americans in several southern cities

1868 – Fourteenth Amendment is ratified

| 1861 | 1862 | 1863 | 1864 | 1865 | 1866 | 1867 | 1868 | 1869 |

1863 – January: Emancipation Proclamation is implemented

1865 – April: Civil War ends

President Lincoln is assassinated; succeeded by Andrew Johnson

December: Thirteenth Amendment is ratified

Foundation of Ku Klux Klan

1867 – Beginning of Radical Republican Reconstruction

Reconstruction Acts are passed over President Johnson's veto

1869 – Ulysses Grant becomes president

The government of the USA

The US Constitution, drawn up in 1787, is the document containing the rules of American government. It can be amended only if the Congress and three-quarters of the US states agree. The USA is a federal state where political power is divided between the central, or federal, government, based in Washington DC, and state governments, such as Ohio, Virginia and Illinois. The federal government is responsible for national defence, foreign policy, interstate commerce and trade, and interstate law and order. State governments are responsible for law and order, education and welfare.

The federal government

This was and is divided into three parts:

- The **Executive** is headed by the president. The president is elected every four years and is responsible for running the government.

- The **Legislature** is the US Congress and is responsible for law-making and raising taxes. It is divided into two houses:

  - **The House of Representatives**: this has 435 members. The members of Congress are elected every two years. They are elected on the basis of population, so states such as New York and California have a large number of members of Congress, while low population states, like Vermont, have only a few.

  - **The Senate**: this contains two senators from each state, irrespective of size. They are elected for six years. All major appointments to the government have to receive Senate approval through its power of 'advice and consent'.

  Both houses have to agree to a proposal before it becomes a law. The president can veto a law, but a two-thirds majority in both houses can override his veto.

- The **Supreme Court** contains nine judges appointed by the president and approved by the Senate. They hold office for life and have the very important power of deciding whether laws conform to the US Constitution. If not, these laws are declared illegal.

TO WHAT EXTENT DID THE THIRTEENTH AMENDMENT CHANGE THE POSITION OF EX-SLAVES?

Reasons for the Thirteenth Amendment

The Civil War of 1861–65 was the most traumatic event in the history of the USA. The war had cost 620,000 American lives and had destroyed much of the Confederate economy. Under President Lincoln's leadership, the north had won the war and reunited the country. In doing so, they freed four million black American slaves. On 23 September 1862, Lincoln had issued his Emancipation Proclamation which stated that, from 1 January 1863, any slave in territory under the direct control of the Confederacy would be forever free.

1870 – Fifteenth Amendment is ratified

1873 – Slaughterhouse cases in US Supreme Court

1876 – Contested presidential election between Samuel Tilden and Rutherford B. Hayes

| 1870 | 1871 | 1872 | 1873 | 1874 | 1875 | 1876 | 1877 | 1878 |

1871 – Enforcement Acts are passed against white terror groups such as the Ku Klux Klan

1875 – Civil Rights Act is passed

1877 – End of Reconstruction

Much controversy has surrounded the Emancipation Proclamation. Was it merely a way for Lincoln to weaken the Confederacy in order to win the war? The Proclamation made no direct mention of slaves who resided in areas controlled by the northern side in the Civil War. By 1 January 1863, this comprised approximately one-third of the Confederacy and also included loyal border states such as Missouri, Kentucky, Maryland and Delaware. Also, the Proclamation was not supported by the main northern opposition party, the Democrat Party, which made several gains in the November 1862 congressional elections.

However, Lincoln had made several statements which suggested that he would abolish slavery if the opportunity arose. Before the Civil War, he had stated that the USA had to resolve the issue of slavery if it was to survive as a united nation.

From 1863, the abolition of slavery became a northern war aim. However, what would happen to the institution of slavery once the war was won by the north? Lincoln was aware that he had to ensure that slavery was abolished permanently before the war was over officially. When Lincoln was re-elected president, in November 1864, he took it as a mandate to end slavery forever. As the abolition of slavery was such an important issue, Lincoln believed it needed the support of both his own Republican Party and the opposition Democrats. Rather than waiting until a new Republican-dominated Congress was convened in March 1865, Lincoln submitted a proposal to Congress to amend the US Constitution to make slavery illegal forever. In a House of Representatives that contained a large number of Democrats, Lincoln was able to persuade sufficient Democrat congressmen to support his Republican Party members to agree to the passage of the Thirteenth Amendment to formally abolish slavery. On 31 January 1865, the proposed amendment passed by a mere two votes to ensure the necessary two-thirds majority for passage (119 votes to 56 votes). For an amendment to become officially part of the US Constitution, it also needed the support of three-quarters of the states and, by December 1865, sufficient states had supported it. In April 1865, the Civil War came to an end when Confederate general Robert E. Lee surrendered his army at Appomattox Court House, Virginia.

The importance of the Thirteenth Amendment

In one act, the Thirteenth Amendment wiped out $2 billion in property, as slaves were owned by white slave-owners. It also created four million new freemen in the USA and ended forever the division of the US population between freemen and slaves.

When the Thirteenth Amendment proposal was passed by the House of Representatives, many black Americans were allowed to attend in the public gallery, a position from which they had been barred until 1864. Also, following the adoption of the Thirteenth Amendment, Congress and many northern states passed legislation which began to break down the second-class position of black Americans. Black witnesses were now allowed in federal court cases. They could also be postmen and ride on streetcars in the capital, Washington DC.

At the annual meeting of the American Anti-Slavery Society (the abolitionist movement), William Lloyd Garrison, one of its leading members, declared that his vocation as an abolitionist had ended.

SOURCE 1   A speech by President Abraham Lincoln on Reconstruction made on 11 April 1865, three days before his assassination. He raises the issue of readmitting the Confederate state of Louisiana to the USA.

We all agree that the seceded States are out of their proper practical relation with the Union; and that the sole object of the government, civil and military, in regard to those States is to again get them into that proper practical relation. It is unsatisfactory to some that the elective franchise is not given to the colored man. I would myself prefer that it were now conferred on the very intelligent, and on those who serve our cause as soldiers.

Some twelve thousand voters in the heretofore slave-state of Louisiana have sworn allegiance to the Union, held elections, organized a State government, adopted a free-state constitution, giving the benefit of public schools equally to black and white, and empowering the Legislature to confer the elective franchise upon the colored man. Their Legislature has already voted to ratify the constitutional amendment recently passed by Congress, abolishing slavery throughout the nation. These twelve thousand persons are thus fully committed to the Union, and to perpetual freedom in the state and they ask the nation's recognition, and its assistance to make good their committal. To the blacks we say 'This cup of liberty which these, your old masters, hold to your lips, we will dash from you, and leave you to the chances of gathering the spilled and scattered contents in some vague and undefined when, where, and how.' I have been unable to perceive it. If, on the contrary, we recognize, and sustain the new government of Louisiana the converse of all this is made true. We encourage the hearts, and nerve the arms of the twelve thousand to adhere to their work, and argue for it, and proselyte for it, and fight for it, and feed it, and grow it, and ripen it to a complete success. The colored man too, in seeing all united for him, is inspired with vigilance, and energy, and daring, to the same end. Grant that he desires the elective franchise, will he not attain it sooner by saving the already advanced steps toward it, than by running backward over them? Concede that the new government of Louisiana is only to what it should be as the egg is to the fowl, we shall sooner have the fowl by hatching the egg than by smashing it?

A Level Exam-Style Question Section A

Study Source 1 before you answer this question.

Assess the value of the source for revealing the aims of Reconstruction during Abraham Lincoln's presidency.

Explain your answer, using the source, information given about its origins and your own knowledge about the historical context.
(20 marks)

Tip

It is important to consider the intended audience for the source, and the extent to which the information contained within the source provides sufficient information on the aims of Reconstruction in 1865.

SOURCE 2 A lithograph of 1872 published by federal government to show the first black American senators and congressmen.

Entered according to act of Congress in the year 1872 by Currier & Ives in the Office of the Librarian of Congress at Washington

ROBERT O. DE LARGE, M.C. of S. Carolina   JEFFERSON H. LONG, M.C. of Georgia

U.S. Senator H.R. REVELS, of Mississippi   BENJ. S. TURNER, M.C. of Alabama.   JOSIAH T. WALLS, M.C. of Florida.   JOSEPH H. RAINY, M.C. of S. Carolina.   R. BROWN ELLIOT, M.C. of S. Carolina.

THE FIRST COLORED SENATOR AND REPRESENTATIVES.

In the 41ˢᵗ and 42ⁿᵈ Congress of the United States.

NEW YORK, PUBLISHED BY CURRIER & IVES, 125 NASSAU STREET.

ACTIVITY
KNOWLEDGE CHECK

The importance of the abolition of slavery

1 What reasons can you give for why President Lincoln wished to abolish slavery during the Civil War?

2 What changes did the Thirteenth Amendment make to the lives of black Americans?

Connections

The following quotes and images reflect some aspects of slavery and attitudes towards slaves in the Roman Empire.

'Slavery in ancient Rome differed from its modern forms in that it was not based on race. But like modern slavery, it was an abusive and degrading institution. Cruelty was commonplace.'

A Roman playwright, Plautus, writing about the time of the end of the Second Punic War (201 BC), gives this picture of an inconsiderate master, and the kind of treatment his slaves were likely to get. Very probably conditions grew worse rather than better for the average slave household, for at least two centuries. As the Romans grew in wealth and the show of culture, they did not grow in humanity. In this quote, Ballio, a slave owner, is giving orders to his servants:

'Now, unless you're all attention, unless you get that sloth and drowsiness out of your breasts and eyes, I'll have your sides so thoroughly marked with thongs that you'll outvie those Campanian coverlets in color, or a regular Alexandrian tapestry, purple-broidered all over with beasts. Yesterday I gave each of you his special job, but you're so worthless, neglectful, stubborn, that I must remind you with a good basting. So you think, I guess, you'll get the better of this whip and of me – by your stout hides! Zounds! But your hides won't prove harder than my good cowhide. [He flourishes it.] Look at this, please! Give heed to this! [He flogs one slave] Well? Does it hurt?... Now stand all of you here, you race born to be thrashed! Turn your ears this way! Give heed to what I say. You, fellow! that's got the pitcher, fetch the water. Take care the kettle's full instanter. You who's got the ax, look after chopping the wood.'

Roman slaves being fed.

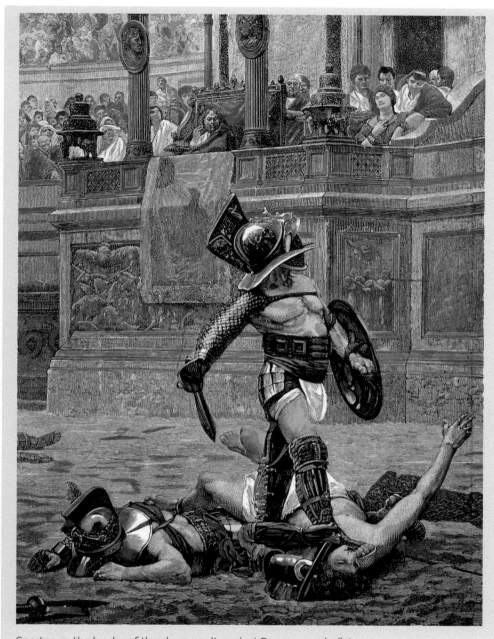

Spartacus, the leader of the slave revolt against Rome, as a gladiator.

Work in groups or individually and answer the following questions.

1 Read the first quote. How might this be seen as similar to southern white American beliefs about black Americans during slavery?

2 Read the second quote.

   a) What did southern white Americans think about racial equality?

   b) How is this similar to Roman beliefs about slavery?

3 Look at the two images. What did the white southerners learn from the experiences of the Romans about keeping slaves and fear of black revolt?

4 Make a list of other similarities between the Romans and southern white Americans during slavery. How did their understanding of the Romans affect the attitudes and actions of the southern white Americans towards black Americans?

5 Why is it important for historians to see these links across time and be able to explain how causal factors can influence situations much later in time?

The economic position of ex-slaves and the development of sharecropping

Although ex-slaves were now free in law, there was a considerable way to go before they received anything like equality. The four million freed slaves lacked education, most being illiterate. Also, as slaves they did not own property or land. Many were simple field labourers without skills to earn a living. There was an enormous amount of help and assistance required to turn ex-slaves into truly free citizens equal to white Americans. Leading black American advocate of civil rights, Frederick Douglass, declared in May 1865 that slavery would not be abolished until the black man had the right to vote.

However, one of the initial responses to freedom was considerable internal migration across the former slave-owning states. Many moved to towns in search of job opportunities, and the urban population of black Americans almost tripled after emancipation. Also ex-slaves began organising their own black churches and their own schools.

In 1865, the year of the Thirteenth Amendment, a New England-based white American visited the former slave state of South Carolina. He commented that the sole ambition of ex-slaves appeared to be to become the owner of a little land where a humble home could be erected and they could live in peace and security.

On 16 January 1865, Union general, William T. Sherman, issued Special Field Order No. 15, which confiscated as federal property a strip of coastal land extending about 30 miles inland from the Atlantic and stretching from Charleston, South Carolina, 245 miles south to Jacksonville, Florida. The order, made on General Sherman's own authority, gave most of the roughly 400,000 acres to newly emancipated slaves in 40-acre sections. Those lands became the basis for the slogan '40 acres and a mule'. Northern abolitionists and General Sherman believed that ex-slaves throughout the old Confederacy would be given the confiscated lands of former plantation owners.

EXTEND YOUR KNOWLEDGE

Frederick Douglass (1818–95)

Frederick Douglass was a prominent American abolitionist, author and public speaker. He was born a slave, but escaped at the age of 20 and went on to become a world-renowned anti-slavery activist. He wrote three autobiographies which are considered important works of the slave tradition. Douglass' work as a reformer ranged from his abolitionist activities in the early 1840s to his attacks on Jim Crow and lynching in the 1890s. For 16 years, he edited an influential black newspaper and achieved international fame as an inspiring and persuasive orator and writer. In thousands of speeches and editorials, he levied a powerful indictment against slavery and racism.

 SOURCE 3

From Special Field Order No. 15 issued by Union general, William T. Sherman, on 16 January 1865.

III. Whenever three respectable negroes, heads of families, shall desire to settle on land, and shall have selected for that purpose an island or a locality clearly defined, within the limits above designated, the Inspector of Settlements and Plantations will himself, or by such subordinate officer as he may appoint, give them a license to settle such island or district, and afford them such assistance as he can to enable them to establish a peaceable agricultural settlement. The three parties named will subdivide the land, under the supervision of the Inspector, among themselves and such others as may choose to settle near them, so that each family shall have a plot of not more than (40) forty acres of tillable ground, and when it borders on some water channel, with not more than 800 feet water front, in the possession of which land the military authorities will afford them protection, until such time as they can protect themselves, or until Congress shall regulate their title. The Quartermaster may, on the requisition of the Inspector of Settlements and Plantations, place at the disposal of the Inspector, one or more of the captured steamers, to ply between the settlements and one or more of the commercial points heretofore named in orders, to afford the settlers the opportunity to supply their necessary wants, and to sell the products of their land and labor.

IV. Whenever a negro has enlisted in the military service of the United States, he may locate his family in any one of the settlements at pleasure, and acquire a homestead, and all other rights and privileges of a settler, as though present in person. In like manner, negroes may settle their families and engage on board the gunboats, or in fishing, or in the navigation of the inland waters, without losing any claim to land or other advantages derived from this system. But no one, unless an actual settler as above defined, or unless absent on Government service, will be entitled to claim any right to land or property in any settlement by virtue of these orders.

However, large-scale land distribution did not take place in the former Confederacy, even though in 1866 the US Congress passed a law which set aside 44 million acres in five southern states for ex-slaves. By 1877, at the end of the Reconstruction period, only a small fraction of ex-slaves had created their own farms.

A number of obstacles stood in the way of ex-slaves becoming independent farmers. They lacked the experience and education to become their own 'masters'. Also, they lacked the money to buy the necessary equipment and tools to work land, and also the money to buy the land. In addition, southern white Americans were very reluctant to sell land to ex-slaves. With the loss of their property in slaves, plantation owners wanted to replace the slave system with a system of cheap black labour. As a result, many ex-slaves worked on plantations for low wages with a lifestyle not greatly dissimilar to that before emancipation.

Sharecropping

A new scheme of land rental did develop, known as sharecropping. Under this system, landowners subdivided large plantations into small farms of 30–50 acres under a rental agreement, which usually involved payment in half the crop produced on the land, hence the name sharecropping. Ex-slaves received a farm and half a crop, which was better than the arrangement under slavery. White landowners benefited because it gave them power and influence over their tenants. The move to sharecropping accelerated after the national economic depression of 1873. As the economy went into an economic downturn, sharecropping seemed to be a more economic use of land. By 1880, 80 percent of land in the cotton-producing area of the USA was farmed by sharecroppers, both ex-slaves and poor white people. In fact, white people outnumbered black people as sharecroppers.

To raise money to buy equipment and seed, sharecroppers had to use the local credit system where they borrowed money at very high interest rates. As sharecroppers possessed little or no property as capital against a loan, they were forced to offer part of their future crop if they failed to pay back their loans. This system, known as the crop lien system, forced many sharecroppers into a cycle of almost permanent debt. As most sharecroppers were illiterate, they found it difficult to operate outside such a system.

Social tensions

The end of the Civil War and emancipation of the slaves brought considerable social tensions to the former Confederacy. Four years of Civil War had severely damaged the southern economy. In Sherman's March to the Sea in 1864 from Atlanta to Savannah, Georgia, a large swathe of territory was pillaged and destroyed by marauding bands of soldiers, deserters and runaway slaves. When four million slaves were emancipated in 1865, social tensions reached new levels.

An important source of social tension was the creation of the Bureau of Refugees, Freedmen and Abandoned Lands, known as the Freedmen's Bureau. It was established in 1865 by Congress to help former black slaves and poor white people in the South in the aftermath of the Civil War. The Freedmen's Bureau provided food, housing and medical aid, established schools and offered legal assistance. It also attempted to settle former slaves on Confederate lands confiscated or abandoned during the war. However, the bureau was prevented from fully carrying out its programmes due to a shortage of funds and personnel, along with the politics of race and Reconstruction. In 1872, Congress, in part under pressure from white southerners who resented its attempt to aid the ex-slaves, shut the bureau.

White southerners, many former Confederate soldiers, engaged in violence against freed black Americans. An ex-slave, Henry Adams, claimed that over 2,000 black people were murdered in 1865 alone in east Texas. The sudden and dramatic dislocation of a former slave-owning society was clearly a factor behind the violence. An employee of the federal government agency, the Freedmen's Bureau, believed that white southerners opposed any change in the social arrangements that existed in the slavery period, when black slaves showed deference to what white people believed were their social superiors. One North Carolina white landowner told a northern army officer that a black soldier in the northern army had said good morning to him, claiming that black people should never address white people unless spoken to first.

Another major cause of social tensions occurred when ex-slaves attempted to leave plantations and set up their own farms. Black people were assaulted and murdered. A Nashville, Tennessee newspaper claimed, in 1867, that former white slave masters continued to whip, maim and kill black Americans as if slavery still existed.

The need for a political settlement

As early as 1863, President Lincoln had begun the process of reuniting the country by beginning a reconstruction programme. In December 1863, he issued the Proclamation of Amnesty and Reconstruction under which any former Confederate state could form a state government whenever a number of voters, equivalent to 10 percent of those who voted in the 1860 elections, took an oath of allegiance to the USA. Under this plan, state governments that accepted Reconstruction and the authority of the federal government were formed in the former Confederate states of Tennessee, Arkansas and Louisiana by 1865.

Several state legislatures in the former Confederacy passed what became known as Black Codes. These discriminated against ex-slaves. In Mississippi, black Americans were forbidden from owning land, and in South Carolina they could not own property in towns. Black people had to show passes when on the roads and were forbidden from carrying arms or liquor. Vagrant former slaves who had left plantations to look for work and land were punished when caught, and they faced severe fines. When these could not be paid, they were sold into private service until they worked off their fine, a position not dissimilar to their former condition of slavery.

President Lincoln hoped to restore pro-union state governments in the former Confederacy as soon as possible. However, on 14 April 1865, he was assassinated while attending a play at Ford's Theatre, Washington DC. He was succeeded by his vice president, Andrew Johnson, a southerner from the former Confederate state of Tennessee, although he remained loyal to the USA in the Civil War.

Study Source 4 before you answer this question.

Assess the value of the source for revealing how the Black Codes affected the lives of black Americans.

Explain your answer, using the source, the information given about its origins and your own knowledge about the historical context. (20 marks)

Tip

It is important to consider the intended audience for the source, and the extent to which the information contained within the source explains the impact of the Black Codes on black American ex-slaves in the former Confederacy.

SOURCE 4

From the Mississippi State Black Code, passed by the Mississippi State Legislature in November 1865. It sets out how black Americans are to be treated when found as vagrants.

Vagrancy Law

Section 1. *Be it enacted by the legislature of the state of Mississippi,* that all rogues and vagabonds, idle and dissipated persons, beggars, jugglers, or persons practising unlawful games or plays, runaways, common drunkards, common nightwalkers, pilferers, lewd, wanton, or lascivious persons, in speech or behavior, common railers and brawlers, persons who neglect their calling or employment, misspend what they earn, or do not provide for the support of themselves or their families or dependants, and all other idle and disorderly persons, including all who neglect all lawful business, or habitually misspend their time by frequenting houses of ill-fame, gaming houses, or tippling shops, shall be deemed and considered vagrants under the provisions of this act; and, on conviction thereof shall be fined not exceeding $100, with all accruing costs, and be imprisoned at the discretion of the court not exceeding ten days.

Section 2. *Be it further enacted,* that all freedmen and free Negroes in this state over the age of eighteen years found on the second Monday in January 1866, or thereafter, with no lawful employment or business, or found unlawfully assembling themselves together either in the day or night time, and all white persons so assembling with freedmen, free Negroes, or mulattoes, or usually associating with freedmen and free Negroes, on terms of equality, or living in adultery or fornication with a freedwoman and free Negro , shall be deemed vagrants; and, on conviction thereof, shall be fined in the sum of not exceeding, in the case of a freedman, and free Negro, $150, and a white man, $200, and imprisoned at the discretion of the court, the free Negro not exceeding ten days, and the white man not exceeding six months.

Section 3. *Be it further enacted,* that all justices of the peace, mayors, and aldermen of incorporated towns and cities of the several counties in this state shall have jurisdiction to try all questions of vagrancy in their respective towns, counties, and cities; and it is hereby made their duty, whenever they shall ascertain that any person or persons in their respective towns, counties, and cities are violating any of the provisions of this act, to have said party or parties arrested and brought before them and immediately investigate said charge; and, on conviction, punish said party or parties as provided for herein.

War Democrat
A member of the Democrat Party who supported the federal government against the Confederacy.

Radical Republican
A member of the Republican Party who wished to punish the South for causing the Civil War and wanted full equality for black Americans.

President Johnson's response to Reconstruction

Johnson was president of the USA from April 1865 to March 1869. He was a **War Democrat**. He had been made Lincoln's running mate as vice president in 1864 as a show of unity between Republicans and Democrats at the height of the Civil War. He was self-educated and, in his political career, he had been a mayor, a congressman and military governor of Tennessee during the Civil War, when much of that state had been conquered by the north. He was staunchly anti-Confederate and had an abiding dislike of the plantation-owning class, and he claimed to be fighting against the slave masters during the Civil War. As a southerner, he possessed the view that black Americans were inferior to white Americans. In fact, he had been a slave owner himself. Before the outbreak of the Civil War, he even stated that he wished that every family in the USA could have one slave to do the drudgery and menial tasks. When he succeeded Lincoln as president, Andrew Johnson's view towards Reconstruction tended to reflect that statement.

Johnson's statements that he wanted to punish traitors went down well with the more radical members of the Republican Party in the US Congress. When he declared that he believed that treason is a crime and that crime must be punished, one **Radical Republican** declared that God had kept President Lincoln in office as long as he was useful, and then substituted a better man to finish the job. However, Johnson's relationship with Radical Republicans in the US Congress deteriorated once his programme for Reconstruction was announced.

On 29 May 1865, President Johnson extended a general pardon to former Confederates who were willing to take the oath of allegiance to the USA. Men who had held high office in the Confederacy, or whose taxable property exceeded $20,000 in value, were excluded from the pardon but could obtain special pardons if they applied directly to President Johnson.

Johnson also decided to recognise four pro-union provisional state governments in the former Confederacy – Virginia, Louisiana, Arkansas and Tennessee, which had accepted the late President Lincoln's ten percent plan. The president then requested other former Confederate states to hold constitutional conventions to re-establish elected governments. Johnson left it up to these states to decide who should be qualified to vote, and none accepted the idea that black Americans should be enfranchised. Even worse, several states chose former senior Confederates for high office.

The newly elected governor of Mississippi had been a brigadier general in the Confederate army. Georgia went even further. They chose as a US senator Alexander Stephens, who had been vice president of the Confederate States of America. Some state governments even questioned the legality of the Thirteenth Amendment. Mississippi rejected it entirely, while other state governments **ratified** the Thirteenth Amendment with the understanding that the US Congress lacked the power to determine the future of ex-slaves. Far from admonishing these former Confederate states, Johnson did nothing.

KEY TERM

Ratified
Formally approved or sanctioned.

What made matters worse were the Black Codes introduced by several former Confederate states. These did more to undermine Johnson's programme for Reconstruction than anything else. These Codes attempted to define the ex-slaves' new rights and responsibilities. They dealt with issues such as black rights to own property, to marry, to make contracts and to appear as witnesses in courts. However, the main issue at the heart of the Black Codes was an attempt to regulate the labour market. Ex-slaves who refused to engage in work on the white man's terms would be punished. A Radical Republican in the US Congress, Benjamin Flanders, observed that the Black Codes were designed to return the situation as near to slavery as possible.

The Black Codes caused uproar across the northern states. It seemed that nothing much had changed since the days of the Confederacy. When the US Congress reassembled in December 1865, following the congressional elections, it refused to allow representatives from the former Confederacy, who were not in state governments, to take their seats. It also set up a Joint Committee on Reconstruction which decided whether or not a former Confederate state was fit to return to the Union.

At this stage in the Reconstruction period, Radical Republicans were a minority within the Republican Party. However, President Johnson's actions swelled their ranks and increased the influence of their leaders, Thaddeus Stevens and Charles Sumner. Early in 1866, Johnson attacked his Radical Republican critics as traitors. Johnson then vetoed two congressional proposals which aimed to help black Americans – the Freedmen's Bureau bill and the civil rights bill.

So great was the resentment of the US Congress that supporters of the bills to ban the Black Codes and introduce radical Republican Reconstruction were able to get the two-thirds majority required to override a **presidential veto** and both proposals became law. The Joint Committee also proposed a further amendment to the US Constitution to provide ex-slaves with equal protection of the law. Congress passed this Fourteenth Amendment, overriding Johnson's attempt to veto it.

KEY TERM

Presidential veto
In the USA, a proposal for a law change becomes an Act only when passed by both houses of Congress and signed by the president. The president can refuse to sign the proposal, preventing it becoming law. This is the veto. It can be overridden by Congress if two-thirds of each house of Congress agree to override the veto.

The congressional elections of 1866 led to a strong rise in support for Radical Republicans and they went ahead to introduce their own programme for Reconstruction. The high point of Radical Republican opposition to President Johnson came on 24 February 1868, when the House of Representatives voted 126 to 47 votes to impeach President Johnson for 'high crimes and misdemeanours in office', and to replace him with Radical Republican, Benjamin Wade. Johnson was the first president to be impeached. He was tried for impeachment by the US Senate and survived in office by one vote.

Andrew Johnson's attempt at a moderate Reconstruction programme which aimed to restore state government to the former Confederacy as soon as possible had failed. It clearly abandoned the fate of ex-slaves into the hands of white southerners, most of whom had fought for and supported the Confederacy in the Civil War. Johnson's attempt at Reconstruction gave way to a Reconstruction programme supported by the Radical Republicans.

 SOURCE 5 From an article by the black American civil rights activist, W.E.B. Du Bois, for the *Atlantic Monthly* which was published in 1901. It assesses the successes of the Freedmen's Bureau during Reconstruction.

The greatest success of the Freedmen's Bureau lay in the planting of the free school among Negroes, and the idea of free elementary education among all classes in the South. It not only called the schoolmistresses through the benevolent agencies, and built them schoolhouses, but it helped discover and support such apostles of human development as Edmund Ware, Erastus Cravath, and Samuel Armstrong. State superintendents of education were appointed, and by 1870 150,000 children were in school. The opposition to Negro education was bitter in the South, for the South believed an educated Negro to be a dangerous Negro. And the South was not wholly wrong; for education among all kinds of men always has had, and always will have, an element of danger and revolution, of dissatisfaction and discontent. Nevertheless, men strive to know. It was some inkling of this paradox, even in the unquiet days of the Bureau, that allayed an opposition to human training, which still to-day lies smouldering, but not flaming. Fisk, Atlanta, Howard, and Hampton were founded in these days, and nearly $6,000,000 was expended in five years for educational work, $750,000 of which came from the freedmen themselves. Such contributions, together with the buying of land and various other enterprises, showed that the ex-slave was handling some free capital already. The chief initial source of this was labor in the army, and his pay and bounty as a soldier. Payments to Negro soldiers were at first complicated by the ignorance of the recipients, and the fact that the quotas of colored regiments from Northern states were largely filled by recruits from the South, unknown to their fellow soldiers. Consequently, payments were accompanied by such frauds that Congress, by joint resolution in 1867, put the whole matter in the hands of the Freedmen's Bureau. In two years $6,000,000 was thus distributed to 5000 claimants, and in the end the sum exceeded $8,000,000. Even in this system fraud was frequent; but still the work put needed capital in the hands of practical paupers, and some, at least, was well spent.

ACTIVITY
KNOWLEDGE CHECK

ACTIVITY
KNOWLEDGE CHECK

Presidential reconstruction

1 Identify the ways the federal (northern) government planned to aid ex-slaves in the former Confederate states during the presidencies of Abraham Lincoln and Andrew Johnson.

2 In what ways was the Reconstruction programme of Lincoln different from that of Andrew Johnson?

3 What reasons can you identify to explain the growing rift between President Johnson and Congress over Reconstruction?

HOW FAR DID RADICAL RECONSTRUCTION CHANGE THE POSITION OF BLACK AMERICANS IN THE FORMER CONFEDERACY?

Radical Reconstruction and the impact of military rule in the south

The Republican Party had been founded in 1854, united on the specific issue of preventing the extension of slavery to the western states of the USA. They were the backbone of the northern side in the Civil War. Radical Republicans were those members of the party who wanted to use the end of the war to permanently transform southern society and bring equality between the races. Several Radical Republicans wanted to punish the former Confederacy for causing the Civil War. Following Lincoln's assassination by a southerner, John Wilkes Booth, one Radical Republican, Henry Coffin of Massachusetts, even demanded the execution of southern leaders for treason.

The key Radical Republicans in the Senate were Charles Sumner, Benjamin Wade and Henry Wilson; in the House of Representatives, they were Thaddeus Stevens, George Julian and James Ashley. The majority came from the north-east of the USA, New England in particular. That area had been the centre of the abolitionist movement. Thaddeus Stevens had been a central figure in January 1865, ensuring that the House of Representatives voted for the Thirteenth Amendment which abolished slavery. Sumner and Stevens were also advocates of giving black Americans the right to vote.

The Reconstruction programme of President Andrew Johnson fell far short of the expectations of the radicals in the Republican Party. Their growing disillusionment with Johnson's failure to transform southern society and give adequate support to the ex-slaves led to a growing rift between president and Congress. A tipping point came in the congressional elections of 1866, when Radical Republicans made a large number of gains in seats to both the House of Representatives and Congress. From that time on, the Radical Republicans began to set the agenda for reconstruction of the former Confederacy. The impetus for rapid change had come in part from events in the South. In May 1866, white crowds in Memphis, Tennessee, attacked black Americans who had fought in the northern army in the Civil War. Forty-six people were killed. In July 1866, in New Orleans, Louisiana, white people attacked black Americans on their way to a political meeting, leaving 40 people dead.

On 2 March 1867, two days before the old Congress came to an end and before the new members elected in the 1866 elections took their seats, Congress passed three important laws, which passed over President Johnson's veto – the Military Reconstruction Act, the Command of the Army Act and the Tenure of Office Act.

The Military Reconstruction Act invalidated the state administrations approved by President Johnson. Instead, it divided the former Confederate states, except Tennessee, into five military districts, under commanders empowered to employ the army to protect life and property. Tennessee had already accepted the terms of congressional Reconstruction. Although the Act did not replace President Johnson's state administrations, it set out the way new state governments could be created and recognised by Congress. If a former Confederate state wished to be recognised by Congress, its written constitution had to provide for the same right to vote for all adult males. The state legislature also had to support the Fourteenth Amendment to the Constitution, which gave all Americans equal protection of the law; and before the end of 1867, all the former Confederate states, except Texas, had to hold new elections. To reinforce this Act, Congress passed the Habeas Corpus Act, which increased the possibility of southern citizens having their cases heard in federal rather than state courts.

On 27 March 1868, Congress went further and removed the power of the US Supreme Court to review cases which arose from the application of the Military Reconstruction Act, ensuring that Congress had the ultimate say. In the 1869 Supreme Court case *Texas* v *White*, the US Supreme Court confirmed the idea that Congress had the power to decide on the organisation of state governments, endorsing the Radical Republican views on Reconstruction.

The Command of the Army Act required that all orders to the army from President Johnson, as commander-in-chief, had to go through the headquarters of the army, which was under the command of Ulysses S. Grant, a keen supporter of the Republican Party. Finally, the Tenure of Office Act required the consent of the Republican-dominated Senate for the president to remove any office-holder.

The impact of these changes, in particular the Military Reconstruction Act, was immense. Radical Reconstruction in 1867 required the former Confederate states to accept that black people had the right to vote. It also forced them to accept the Fourteenth Amendment, which gave all US citizens equal protection of the law. The military government directly ruled the former Confederate states which did not have state governments. Their task was to implement the wishes of the federal government and the US Congress. They implemented the changes required by the Freedmen's Bureau. They also had the responsibility of protecting ex-slaves, **scalawags** and **carpetbaggers** from violence and intimidation by southern white Americans, and in particular those white people who had joined white supremacist groups, such as the Ku Klux Klan and the Knights of the White Camellia. To former slaves and supporters of the federal government and Reconstruction, the military governments were seen as protectors. To other southern white Americans, they were seen as a northern army of occupation. When Democrat-controlled governments were elected across the South in the last years of Reconstruction, they were termed 'redeemer' governments, because many white people saw these Democrat governments as ridding them of changes in racial, social and political relations which had been forced on them by the victorious north. It reinforced the southern white idea that the Civil War was about state rights versus the federal government.

The Reconstruction Acts of 1867 transformed the southern electorate by temporarily disenfranchising 15 percent of potential white voters, who had been office-holders under the Confederacy. These Acts also led to the enfranchisement of 703,000 ex-slaves. As a result, black voters outnumbered white voters by almost 100,000, with black voting majorities in five states: South Carolina, Mississippi, Louisiana, Florida and Alabama.

Given these major electoral changes, many northerners moved south to exploit the new political environment. Many were former soldiers who had fought for the north. Known as carpetbaggers, they encouraged black voters to join the Union League, which urged black people to vote for carpetbagger candidates in elections. In addition, some white southerners, mainly small farmers who had not owned slaves before 1865, supported the new Republican system of government in the South. Known as scalawags, this group held many political offices in the former Confederacy under Radical Reconstruction.

KEY TERMS

Scalawag
Southern white person who was willing to work with the Reconstruction state governments created by the north.

Carpetbagger
Northern white person who went south to make money and exploit the economic dislocation of the former Confederacy after the Civil War. They allegedly carried bags made of carpet, which contained their belongings. Carpetbaggers were accused of using newly enfranchised black voters to gain state government contracts. A Union League was created which encouraged black people to vote for carpetbagger candidates for state elections.

SOURCE 6

From 'An Act to provide for the more efficient Government of the Rebel States (Passed over President Johnson's veto March 2, 1867)', also known as the first Reconstruction Act, which was passed by the Radical Republicans.

Whereas no legal State governments or adequate protection for life or property now exists in the rebel States of Virginia, North Carolina, South Carolina, Georgia, Mississippi, Alabama, Louisiana, Florida, Texas and Arkansas; and whereas it is necessary that peace and good order should be enforced in said States until loyal and republican State governments can be legally established: Therefore,

Be it enacted by the Senate and House of Representatives of the United States of America in Congress assembled, That said rebel States shall be divided into military districts and made subject to the military authority of the United States as hereinafter prescribed, and for that purpose Virginia shall constitute the first district; North Carolina and South Carolina the second district; Georgia, Alabama and Florida the third district; Mississippi and Arkansas the fourth district; and Louisiana and Texas the fifth district.

Sec. 2 And be it further enacted, That it shall be the duty of the President to assign to the command of each of the said districts an officer of the army, not below the rank of brigadier-general, and to detail a sufficient military force to enable such officer to perform his duties and enforce his authority within the district to which he is assigned.

Sec. 3 And be it further enacted, That it shall be the duty of each officer assigned as aforesaid, to protect all persons in their rights of person and property, to suppress insurrection, disorder, and violence, and to punish, or cause to be punished, all disturbers of the public peace and criminals; and to this end he may allow local civil tribunals to take jurisdiction of and to try offenders, or, when in his judgment it may be necessary for the trial of offenders, he shall have power to organize military commissions or tribunals for that purpose, and all interference under color of State authority with the exercise of military authority under this act, shall be null and void.

The Fourteenth and Fifteenth Amendments to the US Constitution

In 1868 and 1870, the Fourteenth and Fifteenth Amendments were added to the US Constitution. With the Thirteenth Amendment of 1865, which abolished slavery, these amendments are referred to as the Civil War Amendments and aimed to give black Americans full civil equality. The Fourteenth Amendment, first proposed in 1866 but not ratified into law until 1868, gave all US citizens equal protection of the law.

It was a proposal that united the Radical Republicans and was a key feature of their programme for Reconstruction. It contained three major provisions. Firstly, it excluded former Confederate leaders from politics. Secondly, it established that all US citizens were entitled to equal protection of the law, and finally, it defined what constituted a US citizen. After the ratification of the Fourteenth Amendment in 1868, anyone was a citizen who was born or naturalised in the USA and subject to its jurisdiction. This reversed the US Supreme Court decision of 1857, known as the **Dred Scott case**. As a result, all ex-slaves became citizens of the USA. As these changes were made by Constitutional Amendment, President Johnson could not veto them.

The proposal of the Fourteenth Amendment helped to unite Republicans in 1866, acted as an important platform for their campaign to win seats in the 1866 congressional elections, and helped to form the basis for the removal of Johnson's state governments and their replacement with state governments acceptable to the Radical Republicans. A key provision for the readmission of a former Confederate state to the USA was acceptance of the Fourteenth Amendment.

KEY TERM

Dred Scott **case**
A US Supreme Court case where the court declared that black Americans may not be citizens of the USA. It caused uproar at the time and was a factor behind the growing conflict between free and slave states that resulted in the Civil War in 1861.

SOURCE 7

The Fourteenth Amendment to the US Constitution. It was passed by Congress on 13 June 1866 and ratified on 9 July 1868.

Section 1. All persons born or naturalized in the United States, and subject to the jurisdiction thereof, are citizens of the United States and of the State wherein they reside. No State shall make or enforce any law which shall abridge the privileges or immunities of citizens of the United States; nor shall any State deprive any person of life, liberty, or property, without due process of law; nor deny to any person within its jurisdiction the equal protection of the laws.

Section 2. Representatives shall be apportioned among the several States according to their respective numbers, counting the whole number of persons in each State, excluding Indians not taxed. But when the right to vote at any election for the choice of electors for President and Vice-President of the United States, Representatives in Congress, the Executive and Judicial officers of a State, or the members of the Legislature thereof, is denied to any of the male inhabitants of such State, being twenty-one years of age, and citizens of the United States, or in any way abridged, except for participation in rebellion, or other crime, the basis of representation therein shall be reduced in the proportion which the number of such male citizens shall bear to the whole number of male citizens twenty-one years of age in such State.

Section 3. No person shall be a Senator or Representative in Congress, or elector of President and Vice-President, or hold any office, civil or military, under the United States, or under any State, who, having previously taken an oath, as a member of Congress, or as an officer of the United States, or as a member of any State legislature, or as an executive or judicial officer of any State, to support the Constitution of the United States, shall have engaged in insurrection or rebellion against the same, or given aid or comfort to the enemies thereof. But Congress may by a vote of two-thirds of each House, remove such disability.

> **A Level Exam-Style Question Section A**
>
> *Study Source 7 before you answer this question.*
>
> Assess the value of the source for revealing how the Reconstruction policies of the federal government attempted to radically improve the lives of black American ex-slaves in the former Confederacy.
>
> Explain your answer, using the source, information given about its origins and your own knowledge about the historical context. (20 marks)
>
> **Tip**
>
> *It is important to consider the intended audience for the source, and the extent to which the information contained within the source provides sufficient information on the changing position of ex-slaves during Reconstruction.*

In February 1869, the US Congress approved the Fifteenth Amendment. This prohibited any federal or state government from depriving any US citizen of the right to vote on racial grounds. To the Democrats in Congress, the Fifteenth Amendment was a revolutionary measure and was seen as the central feature of Radical Reconstruction.

However, the Fifteenth Amendment made no reference to the right of ex-slaves to hold political office and failed to make the requirements to vote uniform across the USA. For instance, one Radical Republican, Henry Wilson, criticised the proposal because it did not forbid literacy, property or educational tests. This gave future state governments the opportunity to discriminate against potential black voters on these grounds. Also, supporters of women's suffrage attempted to include female voters in the proposal, but this was not accepted. However, Radical Republicans hailed the Fifteenth Amendment as a triumph. Before the Amendment, in California Chinese people had been barred from voting and, as late as 1868, only eight northern states had allowed black Americans to vote. States used a variety of restrictions on registration to vote, even after the Fifteenth Amendment, to prevent certain ethnic groups from voting.

Future US president, James Garfield, who was a congressman in 1869, declared that the Fifteenth Amendment gave black Americans control of their own destiny and placed their fortunes in their own hands. It was ratified in 1870. Taken together, the Fourteenth and Fifteenth Amendments conferred on freed slaves the full rights of citizenship.

The Civil Rights Act 1875

By 1875, Radical Reconstruction was on the wane. In the 1874 congressional elections, the Democrats made sweeping gains. However, the Republicans still maintained a majority in both houses of Congress. In 1875, the last act of Reconstruction in favour of black Americans was passed in the form of the Civil Rights Act. It proclaimed many of the aims of the Radical Republicans, such as supporting equality before the law for all citizens, and justice for all regardless of race or colour, and the full enjoyment by all citizens of 'inns, public conveyances on land and water, theatres, and other places of public amusement'. However, the Act failed to mention public schools.

Of greater significance were the actions of the US Supreme Court. In 1873, in what was known as the Slaughterhouse decision, the Court ruled that the Fourteenth Amendment protected the rights of national citizenship, such as the right to interstate travel, but it did not protect the civil rights that individual Americans received from state citizenship. This meant that the federal government could not safeguard the rights of black citizens against any violation by the states. This negated much of the impact of the Fourteenth Amendment on the rights of black citizens.

In 1876, the US Supreme Court, in the *United States* v *Reese* case, threw out an **indictment** against a Kentucky official who had prevented black Americans from voting. The Court judgment stated that the Fifteenth Amendment did not give the right to vote to anyone. In 1883, the US Supreme Court invalidated the 1875 Civil Rights Act and confirmed the decision made in *United States* v *Reese* of 1876. As a result, many of the landmark changes made by the Radical Republicans in the years after 1866 were negated by the US Supreme Court. In 1877, following the election of Rutherford B. Hayes as president, Reconstruction came to an end in the South and the last northern troops were withdrawn. By that date, both major Radical Republican leaders, Thaddeus Stevens and Charles Sumner, had died.

> **KEY TERM**
>
> Indictment
> A formal charge or accusation of a serious crime.

SOURCE

8 From the Civil Rights Act, passed by Congress on 1 March 1875.

Be it enacted, That all persons within the jurisdiction of the United States shall be entitled to the full and equal enjoyment of the accommodations, advantages, facilities, and privileges of inns, public conveyances on land or water, theaters, and other places of public amusement; subject only to the conditions and limitations established by law, and applicable alike to citizens of every race and color, regardless of any previous condition of servitude.

Sec. 2. That any person who shall violate the foregoing section by denying to any citizen, except for reasons by law applicable to citizens of every race and color, and regardless of any previous condition of servitude, the full enjoyment of any of the accommodations, advantages, facilities, or privileges in said section enumerated, or by aiding or inciting such denial, shall, for every such offense, forfeit and pay the sum of five hundred dollars to the person aggrieved thereby, ... and shall also, for every such offense, be deemed guilty of a misdemeanor, and, upon conviction thereof, shall be fined not less than five hundred nor more than one thousand dollars, or shall be imprisoned not less than thirty days nor more than one year...

Sec. 3. That the district and circuit courts of the United States shall have, exclusively of the courts of the several States, cognizance of all crimes and offenses against, and violations of, the provisions of this act; and actions for the penalty given by the preceding section may be prosecuted in the territorial, district, or circuit courts of the United States wherever the defendant may be found, without regard to the other party; and the district attorneys, marshals, and deputy marshals of the United States, and commissioners appointed by the circuit and territorial courts of the United States, with powers of arresting and imprisoning or bailing offenders against the laws of the United States, are hereby specially authorized and required to institute proceedings against every person who shall violate the provisions of this act, and cause him to be arrested and imprisoned or bailed, as the case may be, for trial before such court of the United States, or territorial court, as by law has cognizance of the offense, except in respect of the right of action accruing to the person aggrieved; and such district attorneys shall cause such proceedings to be prosecuted to their termination as in other cases.

The significance of the presence of black American representatives in federal and state legislatures

In 1868, a black American delegate to a political convention said in a statement to his fellow delegates that he believed they were not prepared for suffrage, but that they could learn. He likened the vote to giving a man tools to use and that in time he would learn a trade.

Hundreds of ex-slaves took part in state political conventions and others joined Union Leagues to aid the Republican Party. By 1867, black Americans were beginning to participate in politics and gaining political influence. However, only one state political convention, in South Carolina, had a majority of black delegates.

Overall, in state government, approximately 600 black people, most ex-slaves, served as legislators. However, no black person was elected governor of a state. In Louisiana, Pickney Pinchback, a northern black American and former northern soldier in the Civil War, won election as lieutenant (deputy) governor and did serve for a short time as acting governor. In other states, black Americans were elected as state treasurers and secretaries of state. Only two black people served as senators in the US Congress, Hiram Revels and Blanche B. Bruce, both from Mississippi, and 14 black Americans served as congressmen in the House of Representatives. Given their political inexperience, black representatives were accused of being under the control and influence of carpetbaggers and scalawags.

The new reconstructed state governments embarked on radical reform, such as the creation of state-wide educational systems, but these reforms cost millions of dollars and the government was accused of financial incompetence by southern white people, who placed much of the blame on the black representatives. These accusations fuelled the idea among southern white people that the Reconstruction period was a failure, and that part of that failure was allowing black Americans to participate in the political process.

ACTIVITY
KNOWLEDGE CHECK

Radical Reconstruction

1 What were the aims of Radical Republicans in the Reconstruction period?

2 Why did the Radical Republicans clash with President Andrew Johnson on the issue of Reconstruction?

3 How significant were the changes made during Radical Reconstruction to the lives of white and black Americans in the former Confederacy?

WHAT SIGNIFICANCE DID THE WHITE BACKLASH IN THE FORMER CONFEDERACY HAVE ON THE RIGHTS OF BLACK AMERICANS?

The end of the Civil War saw the former Confederacy face serious problems. The four years of war resulted in the deaths of 25 percent of the white adult male population. Large sections of the South had been devastated by war, most notably Virginia, Tennessee and Georgia. The economy was in ruins and the abolition of slavery had cost slave owners the loss of $2 billion of property. In addition, the Civil War Amendment and other federal legislation had led to a revolution in civil rights and race relations.

To ensure the former Confederacy accepted these dramatic changes, the area suffered military occupation from 1867. In such circumstances, some form of southern white backlash was almost inevitable. White opposition took many forms. Random attacks on, and the lynching of, black Americans, and the implementation of the Black Codes by many provisional state governments attempted to ensure that ex-slaves were forced to accept an inferior position in southern society. Fear of black domination and exploitation by northern carpetbaggers led to vitriolic attacks by southern white newspapers.

The Ku Klux Klan and the White League

Ku Klux Klan

On 24 December 1865, a group of former Confederate soldiers got together in Pulaski, Tennessee, to form an organisation to protect the southern white populaton and to intimidate southern black people. It was called the Ku Klux Klan (KKK), derived from the Greek for circle (Kuklos). It claimed to maintain chivalry, humanity, mercy and patriotism.

In the spring of 1867 at a convention in Nashville, Tennessee, the Ku Klux Klan elected former Confederate general, Nathan Bedford Forrest, as Grand Wizard. Forrest was one of the most successful cavalry generals of the war and one of the most feared and respected Confederate generals. Another senior Confederate general, John C. Gordon, also became a prominent member. It began as a group of pranksters dressing up and engaging in light-hearted intimidation of black Americans. However, the KKK soon changed into a major terror organisation. Members aimed to keep their anonymity by wearing hoods and robes. Elaborate rituals and names of officials such as Grand Cyclops became a feature of the KKK. It was one of a variety of southern white vigilante organisations. The Knights of the White Camellia operated in Louisiana, the Red Shirts in South Carolina, the Knights of the Rising Sun in Texas, the White Line in Mississippi and the White League in other states. These all had the same general aim of enforcing the social system that had existed before the end of the Civil War, where black Americans were treated as inferior to white people.

Colonel de Blanc of the Knights of the White Camellia, in 1868, summed up the ideas behind these white terror groups when he stated that he believed that black Americans were guilty of crimes against white people, such as arson, attacking white women and even murder of white Americans.

SOURCE 9

A warning issued by the Ku Klux Klan in the *Independent Monitor* newspaper, Tuscaloosa, Alabama, on 1 September 1868. The two hanged figures are white carpetbaggers.

[From the Independent Monitor, Tuscaloosa, Alabama, September 1, 1868.]
A PROSPECTIVE SCENE IN THE CITY OF OAKS, 4TH OF MARCH, 1869.

"Hang, curs, hang! * * * * * *Their* complexion is perfect gallows. Stand fast, good fate, to *their* hanging! * * * * * If they be not born to be hanged, our case is miserable."
The above cut represents the fate in store for those great pests of Southern society— the carpet-bagger and scalawag—if found in Dixie's land after the break of day on the 4th of March next.

A Facsimile put in Evidence before the Congressional Committee.

The targets for these white terror groups were black Americans, carpetbaggers, members of the Republican Party and officials of the federal government. For instance, Emanuel Fortune was driven out of Jackson County, Florida, by the KKK and claimed that the object of the organisation was to kill all of the leading men of the Republican Party who had taken a prominent stand against the unfair treatment of black Americans.

Klansmen also murdered three scalawag members of the Georgia legislature in 1870 and drove a further ten scalawags from their homes. Also in 1870, an armed mob of white men attacked a Republican Party rally, killing four black people and wounding 54 others.

However, the main recipients of KKK violence were black Americans. The height of KKK violence came in 1869–71. Any black institution was open to attack. In the autumn of 1870, after the ratification of the Fifteenth Amendment which gave black adult males the vote, nearly every black church and black schoolhouse in Tuskegee, Alabama, was burned down. In 1871, 500 masked men laid siege to the Union County Gaol and lynched eight black prisoners.

Beatings, arson and murder were constant fears for black people across the former Confederacy. Lynching of black Americans at random increased after 1865 and became a regular feature of the Reconstruction years. The first major period of lynching was between 1865 and 1871. It began as a purge of black Americans who had joined the Republican Party. In their bid to prevent the ratification of new constitutions for southern states, white terror groups attacked and lynched black Americans, particularly during the 1868 elections, where 1,300 potential voters, both black and white Republicans, were murdered.

This incidence of lynching black Americans declined rapidly after the federal government passed the Ku Klux Klan Act of 1871, which allowed southern governments to introduce martial law in counties where they deemed white terror groups were active. In the years 1868 to 1876, the incidence of lynching stood at 50–100 per year.

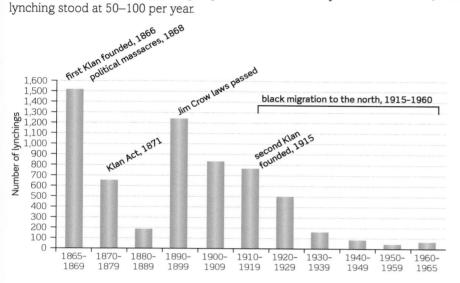

Figure 3.1 The incidence of lynching of black Americans from 1865 to 1965.

SOURCE 10

From an account by Ben Johnson, who was born a slave in 1848. He was interviewed about his experiences of the Ku Klux Klan by members of the federal Writers' Project during the New Deal, 65 years after the events he describes here.

I was born in Orange County [North Carolina] and I belong to Mr. Gilbert Gregg near Hillsboro. I don't know nothin' 'bout my mammy and daddy, but I had a brother Jim who was sold to dress young misses fer her weddin'. The tree is still standing where I set under an' watch them sell Jim. I set dar an' I cry an' cry, especially when they puts the chains on him an' carries him off, an' I ain't never felt so lonesome in my whole life. I ain't never hear from Jim since an' I wonder now sometimes if 'en he's still living.

I knows that the master was good to us an' he fed an' clothed us good. We had our own garden an' we was gitten' long all right.

I seed a whole heap of Yankees when they comed to Hillsboro an' most of them ain't got no respect for God, man, nor the devil. I can't remember so much about them though cause we lives in town... an' we has a guard.

The most that I can tell you 'bout is the Ku Klux. I never will forget when they hung Cy Guy. They hung him for a scandalous insult to a white woman an' they comed after him a hundred strong.

They tries him there in the woods, an' they scratches Cy's arm to get some blood, an' with that blood they writes that he shall hang 'tween the heavens and the earth till he is dead, dead, dead, and that any nigger what takes down the body shall be hanged too.

Well sir, the next morning there he hung, right over the road an' the sentence hanging over his head. Nobody would bother with that body for four days an' there it hung, swinging in the wind, but the fourth day the sheriff comes an' takes it down.

There was Ed an' Cindy, who before the war belonged to Mr Lynch an' after the war he told them to move. He gives them a month and they ain't gone, so the Ku Kluxes gets them.

It was on a cold night when they came and dragged the niggers out of bed. They carried them down in the woods an' whup them, then they throes them in the pond, their bodies breakin' the ice. Ed comes out an' come to our house, but Cindy ain't been seen since.

The White League

Another important white supremacist, paramilitary group was the White League. This was formed in March 1874 in Louisiana. It was seen as the military arm of the Democrat Party while Louisiana was under federal military occupation. Perhaps the most notorious act attributed to the White League was the Coushatta massacre, which occurred in August 1874. It was sparked off by a dispute between the White League and Marshall Twitchell, a northern carpetbagger who had become a Louisiana state senator. Members of the White League forced six Republican Party officials to resign and then murdered them, along with five black Americans.

A month later, on 14 September 1874, the White League achieved its greatest triumph in what became known as the Battle of Liberty Place. The opportunity arose when President Grant removed most of the federal troops from Louisiana because of an outbreak of yellow fever. The White League assembled in Louisiana's largest city, New Orleans, and demanded the resignation of the governor, William Kellogg, and his replacement by John McEnery, the unsuccessful Democrat Party candidate for the position of governor in what was a disputed gubernatorial election in 1872. In a fracas, 5,000 members of the White League routed 3,500 members of the New Orleans Metropolitan Police and ousted the Republican governor. President Grant responded with the dispatch of federal troops to restore order and reinstate the Republican governor. Although the White League had overthrown the city government of New Orleans for three days, no charges were brought against any member of the group. Both white and black voters of Louisiana were denied the right to vote until the Compromise of 1877, with Louisiana remaining under federal military rule.

Other activities of white supremacist groups

Another incident, attributed to the Knights of the White Camellia, led to the single biggest loss of life of black Americans during Reconstruction. In 1873, in Colfax, Louisiana, black people began drilling with weapons in fear of attack by white terror groups. On Easter Sunday, armed with a small cannon and rifles, white men slaughtered 50 black Americans. When the black Americans offered to surrender under a flag of truce, the massacre continued. In total, 280 black Americans were killed.

Faced with such widespread violence and murder, the US Congress replied with attempts to protect black Americans and their white supporters. The 1870 Enforcement Act placed penalties against anyone who interfered with a citizen, either black or white. A second Enforcement Act placed the election of congressmen under the surveillance of federal election officials, and the 1871 Third Enforcement Act (also known as the Ku Klux Klan Act) gave federal troops the power to suspend **habeas corpus** and arrest suspected KKK members. It also outlawed activities closely associated with KKK activity, such as forming secret conspiracies, wearing disguises and intimidating officials. President Ulysses Grant used the Act, in October 1871, to declare martial law in nine counties of western South Carolina, which led to mass prosecutions. These acts helped to break the back of most of the terror activities of the KKK and other white supremacist groups.

> **KEY TERM**
>
> **Habeas corpus**
> A writ requiring a person to be brought before a judge or court, especially for investigation of a restraint of the person's liberty, used as a protection against illegal imprisonment.

The restoration of Democrat control in the South

White terror group activity had the effect of undermining Republican Party organisation in the Deep South. In the 1875 elections in Mississippi, local Democrat Party rifle clubs paraded in black areas and provoked riots in which hundreds of black people were killed. Historian Kenneth Stampp, who wrote on Reconstruction, noted that on election day many black Americans stayed hidden away.

Also, resentment of military occupation and the impact of black participation in elections and local politics alienated many white voters. By 1875, only Louisiana, Florida and South Carolina had Republican-controlled state government. All the other former Confederate states were controlled by the Democrat Party, which opposed Reconstruction.

Former Confederate states	Readmission to Union under Radical Republican Party Reconstruction	Date Democrat Party takes control	Duration of Republican rule (years)
Alabama	25 June 1868	14 November 1874	6.5
Arkansas	22 June 1868	10 November 1874	6.5
Florida	25 June 1868	2 January 1877	8.5
Georgia	15 June 1870	1 November 1871	1.0
Louisiana	25 June 1868	2 January 1877	8.5
Mississippi	23 February 1870	3 November 1875	5.5
North Carolina	25 June 1868	3 November 1870	2.0
South Carolina	25 June 1868	12 November 1876	8.0
Tennessee	24 July 1866*	4 October 1869	3.0
Texas	25 June 1868	14 January 1873	3.0
Virginia	26 January 1870	5 October 1869	0.0

* Tennessee readmitted before Radical Republican Reconstruction as they had ratified the Fourteenth Amendment.

Figure 3.2 The duration of Republican Party rule in the former Confederate states.

A Level Exam-Style Question Section B

To what extent did the lives of black Americans change for the better during the Reconstruction period of 1865–77? (20 marks)

Tip

You need to provide a balanced analytical account in which you are able to identify important positive changes to the lives of black Americans, such as the impact of the Thirteenth, Fourteenth and Fifteenth Amendments and the acquisition of land, against negative aspects, such as the rise in intimidation and violence by white supremacist groups such as the KKK.

The end of Reconstruction, 1877

Officially, Reconstruction came to an end in March 1877, with the inauguration of Rutherford B. Hayes as president. However, the reassertion of southern white rule had begun much earlier. A turning point was the election of Ulysses Grant as president in 1868. As early as 1869, Congress refused to provide extra funding for the Freedmen's Bureau. Grant took a far less radical approach to dealing with the former Confederacy than the Radical Republicans in the US Congress. An example was the Amnesty Act of 1872, which pardoned all but the most senior officers and officials of the former Confederate states. When the Republican governor of Mississippi appealed to President Grant for federal troops to suppress white terror groups who were disrupting the 1875 state elections, Grant replied that the public were tired of annual autumnal outbreaks in the South. As a result, no federal troops were provided. However, Grant admitted after the Democrats won the election in 1875 that they had done so using fraud and violence.

Also in 1873, a major economic depression had affected the US economy. As a result, northern businessmen were pressuring the federal government to normalise relations with the former Confederate states as a way of stimulating economic activity that would aid the end of the economic depression.

The violence associated with the Ku Klux Klan and other white terror groups had disrupted Republican Party rule in the South. The decline in violence after 1871 was due in part to the Enforcement Acts, but also to the fact that the Democrat Party, which opposed Reconstruction, had taken control of most southern states by 1875. To the white southerners, these states had been 'redeemed'.

However, Reconstruction came to an end following the 1876 presidential and congressional elections. The Democrat Party nominated Samuel Tilden, the governor of New York state, as their candidate. The Republicans faced a major row over who should represent them. President Grant's Republican administrations of 1869 to 1876 had been badly affected by major corruption scandals. As a result, the party chose the reforming governor of Ohio, Rutherford B. Hayes, as their candidate. In a private letter in 1875, Hayes had expressed a view on Reconstruction when he stated that leaving the South alone seemed to be the most appropriate course of action. Hayes deliberately sought southern support in the election.

In the election in November 1876, Samuel Tilden won the most votes. He won states such as New York, New Jersey, Connecticut and Indiana. However, in presidential elections it is not the popular vote that determines victory but the electoral college vote. Tilden received 184 electoral college votes, one short of victory. Although Hayes received fewer popular votes, he won the electoral college votes in the southern states of Louisiana, Florida and South Carolina. This meant that Hayes won 185 electoral college votes overall, beating Tilden by one electoral college vote. Although the Democrat Party protested, Hayes was inaugurated as president in March 1877. With Hayes' presidency, Reconstruction was officially at an end. In April 1877, the last Republican Party governor in the South, in South Carolina, left office. He attacked Hayes' southern policy, saying it consisted of the abandonment of southern Republicans, and especially black Americans, to the control and rule of not only the Democratic Party, but also those in the South who viewed slavery as a divine institution.

Reconstruction began with the aim of reuniting a divided nation after a bitter four-year civil war. To Radical Republicans, it was an opportunity to change permanently the social and political framework of the USA, and the South in particular. Full civil rights and racial equality were their aim. However, Reconstruction failed in its main aim. It led to a southern white backlash and considerable racial strife and violence. Films like *The Birth of a Nation* (see Chapter 2), released in 1915, reflect the continuing bitterness of southern white Americans towards the period. White carpetbaggers and scalawags became figures of contempt in the white south. To black Americans, the Reconstruction period was viewed differently. W.E.B. Du Bois, a leading black civil rights activist, saw Reconstruction as an era when slaves were freed and for a brief moment stood in the sun, but then moved back towards slavery.

ACTIVITY
KNOWLEDGE CHECK

The white backlash and the end of Reconstruction

1 Describe how white terror groups, such as the Ku Klux Klan, affected the lives of black Americans during Reconstruction.

2 Give reasons why violence and intimidation by white terror groups, such as the Ku Klux Klan, declined after 1872.

3 What evidence is there in Figure 3.1 about the way in which Reconstruction gradually came to an end in the former Confederacy?

THINKING HISTORICALLY   Cause and consequence (7c)

The value of historical explanations

Historical explanations derive from the historian who is investigating the past. Differences in explanations are usually about what the historians think is significant. Historians bring their own attitudes and perspectives to historical questions and see history in the light of these. It is therefore perfectly acceptable to have very different explanations of the same historical phenomenon. The way we judge historical accounts is by looking at how well argued they are and how well evidence has been deployed to support the argument.

Here are three approaches to Reconstruction:

Approach A	Approach B	Approach C
Reconstruction was caused by decisions taken by politicians, in particular the president of the USA. It was imposed from the top by great men, such as Abraham Lincoln. Ordinary people then fell into line and did whatever they were told.	Reconstruction was a movement of similar people in the northern states with similar ideas. They were generally in agreement about the need to reconstruct the South following the Civil War.	The unifying of the USA following the Civil War of people who shared a common language and common history until 1861 was inevitable. The great movements of history point us to this fact.

Work in groups of between three and five. (You will need an even number of groups in the class.)

1 In your groups, devise a brief explanation of Reconstruction of 200–300 words that matches one of the approaches above. Present your explanation to another group, who will decide on two things:

  a) Which of the approaches is each explanation trying to demonstrate?

  b) Considering the structure and the quality of the argument and use of evidence, which is the best of the three explanations?

2 If you choose a 'best' explanation, should you discount the other two? Explain your answer.

ACTIVITY
SUMMARY

'Free at last', 1865–77

1 Create a table summarising the key features of the Reconstruction programmes of President Lincoln, President Johnson and the Radical Republicans.

2 Whose Reconstruction programme did more to aid and assist ex-slaves?

 WIDER READING

Books

Farmer, A. *The American Civil War: Causes, Course and Consequences: 1803-1977,* Hodder Access to History (2008)

Kelley, R. (ed.) *To Make Our World Anew,* Oxford University Press (2005)

Paterson, D., Willoughby, S. and Willoughby, D. *Civil Rights in the USA, 1863-1980,* Heinemann (2001)

Film

Lincoln, directed by Stephen Spielberg (2012)

3.4

The triumph of 'Jim Crow', 1883–c1900

KEY QUESTIONS

- How significant for black Americans were the civil rights cases of 1883 in the US Supreme Court?
- To what extent did the spread of Jim Crow Laws change race relations in the South and how were black people excluded from voting?
- To what extent did the Supreme Court cases of 1896–99 alter the lives of black Americans?

INTRODUCTION

During the Reconstruction period from 1865 to 1877, a new dawn seemed to have arrived for black Americans and race relations in the USA. The Civil War Amendments (Thirteenth, Fourteenth and Fifteenth), ratified between 1865 and 1870, gave black Americans civil and political equality with white Americans. Slavery was abolished, black Americans became citizens of the USA with equal protection of the law and, in 1870, adult males received the right to vote. In addition, the US Congress passed Civil Rights Acts, in 1866 and 1875, which banned discrimination against black Americans on public transportation and in entertainment venues.

However, the new dawn did not last. By 1877, Reconstruction had come to an end. 'Redeemed' Democrat state government, dominated by white people, had gained control of the former Confederate states of the Old South. From 1883 to the turn of the century, all the civil and political gains made by black Americans in the Old South were effectively removed. A new dark age in race relations had arrived. It was the age of Jim Crow, a term which came from the name of a popular 19th-century minstrel – a white entertainer who 'blacked up' to look like and impersonate a black American.

Jim Crow Laws was a term used to describe a series of laws passed by former Confederate states from the 1880s, which introduced legal segregation into race relations. Separate facilities in education, public transportation and entertainment were introduced for black and white citizens. In addition, other Jim Crow Laws effectively disenfranchised much of the adult male black population. By the turn of the 20th century, black and white Americans in the South were living separate lives. All the gains in civil rights for black Americans, in the years 1865–77, had effectively disappeared.

1877 – The end of Reconstruction: last federal troops leave the former Confederacy

1887 – Florida introduces legal segregation in railway carriages between black and white citizens

1890 – Mississippi changes state constitution in a plan to exclude black Americans from voting

| 1875 | 1880 | 1885 | 1890 |

1883 – Civil rights cases in US Supreme Court

Civil Rights Act of 1875 declared unconstitutional

1888 – Mississippi follows Florida's lead and introduces legal segregation on the railways

1892 – New voting regulations involving poll tax and literacy tests in Mississippi

HOW SIGNIFICANT FOR BLACK AMERICANS WERE THE CIVIL RIGHTS CASES OF 1883 IN THE US SUPREME COURT?

The role of the US Supreme Court in American government

An important national institution that helped to deny black Americans their civil rights was the US Supreme Court. This institution was not expressly mentioned in the original US Constitution of 1787, but it was created under the Judiciary Act of 1789 as a final court of appeal in both **civil law** and **criminal law**, for both the national and state governments.

A major increase in the US Supreme Court's power and influence came with the appointment of John Marshall as the fourth **chief justice**. In his period in that role from 1801 to 1835, Marshall ensured that the US Supreme Court acquired the right to interpret the meaning of the US Constitution. This meant that the US Supreme Court could decide whether or not laws and actions by politicians were unconstitutional. In 1883, a series of cases was decided by the US Supreme Court that had an enormous impact on black Americans' civil rights.

KEY TERMS

Civil law
A court case between two individuals or two private organisations. It usually involves the request for monetary damages caused by an action of the accused party.

Criminal law
A court case involving the federal government, state government or local government against an individual or organisation that has broken the criminal law or federal, state or local law.

Chief justice
The presiding judge of the US Supreme Court.

The civil rights cases of 1883

In 1883, the US Supreme Court comprised nine justices. The chief justice was Morrison P. Waite of Ohio. Each Supreme Court judge was nominated to that office by the president, but only became a justice when two-thirds of the US Senate provided its 'advice and consent'. Decisions by the Supreme Court were determined by majority voting. In the civil rights cases of 1883, the justices voted 8 to 1 in favour of declaring much of the civil rights legislation of the USA unconstitutional. Only Justice John M. Harlan voted against.

SOURCE 1

The majority judgment of the US Supreme Court written by Justice Bradley. It is the view of the Supreme Court in the civil rights cases of 1883. Justice Bradley sets out what he and the majority of the US Supreme Court regard as the major differences between the Thirteenth and Fourteenth Amendments to the US Constitution.

We must not forget that the province and scope of the Thirteenth and Fourteenth amendments are different: the former simply abolished slavery; the latter prohibited the States from abridging the privileges or immunities of citizens of the United States, from depriving them of life, liberty, or property without due process of law, and from denying to any the equal protection of the laws. The amendments are different, and the powers of Congress under them are different. What Congress has power to do under one it may not have power to do under the other. Under the Thirteenth Amendment, it has only to do with slavery and its incidents. Under the Fourteenth Amendment, it has power to counteract and render nugatory all State laws and proceedings which have the effect to abridge any of the privileges or immunities of citizens of the United States, or to deprive them of life, liberty or property without due process of law, or to deny to any of them the equal protection of the laws. Under the Thirteenth Amendment, the legislation, so far as necessary or proper to eradicate all forms and incidents of slavery and involuntary servitude, may be direct and primary, operating upon the acts of individuals, whether sanctioned by State legislation or not; under the Fourteenth, as we have already shown, it must necessarily be, and can only be, corrective in its character, addressed to counteract and afford relief against State regulations or proceedings.

1896 – *Plessy* v *Ferguson* Supreme Court case accepts 'separate but equal' interpretation of the Fourteenth Amendment

1899 – *Cumming* v *Richmond County Board of Education* endorses legal segregation in public schools

1900 – Ida Wells-Barnett pamphlet is published on violence against black Americans

| 1895 | 1900 | 1905 | 1910 |

1898 – Louisiana introduces the Grandfather Clause to its voting regulations, which excludes vast majority of black voters

Williams v *Mississippi Supreme Court* case endorses changes in voting rules in Mississippi

The issues decided by the civil rights cases of 1883

The cases were brought by black Americans against actions by governments and institutions which they felt were denying them their civil rights. Five cases, which were dealt with as a group in the US Supreme Court judgment came before the Court in November 1882. These were: *United States* v *Stanley*, *United States* v *Ryan*, *United States* v *Nichols*, *United States* v *Singleton* and *Robinson et ux.* v *Memphis and Charleston Railroad*. The Court issued its judgment in 1883. Two of the cases involved racial discrimination in hotels in Missouri, two concerned racial discrimination in theatres in San Francisco, California and New York City, and a fifth involved racial discrimination on a railway. It should be noted that several of the cases occurred in states that were never part of the Confederacy, so the denial of equal civil rights for black Americans took place across the country.

In *Robinson et ux.* v *Memphis and Charleston Railroad*, a husband and wife sued the railroad because the train conductor refused to allow the wife into the women's only carriage because she was a dark-skinned black American. Her husband, also a black American, was light-skinned and the conductor thought he was white. The conductor concluded that the black woman was an improper person because she was married to a white man. In the New York City case, William Davis, a black American and his female friend (who was one-eighth black) were denied entry to an opera house because of their racial origin. When Davis refused to leave, he was arrested, which led him to sue the opera house.

Collectively, the five cases asserted that the complainants, all black Americans, were denied their civil rights which had been guaranteed by the Civil Rights Act, passed by Congress in 1875. They also claimed that their civil rights were denied because these acts of racial discrimination were contrary to the Fourteenth Amendment of the US Constitution. This amendment guaranteed all Americans the equal protection of the law. It was also argued that racial discrimination was an example of inferior treatment and a badge of servitude. As a result, the actions highlighted in the cases were contrary to the Thirteenth Amendment, which had abolished slavery.

However, the white Americans who were defending their actions claimed that the US Congress had no power to tell individual Americans how they ran their businesses. They also claimed that the Fourteenth Amendment merely banned some actions by state governments, not individuals.

The Supreme Court decision of 15 October 1883

The Court ruling of 15 October 1883 caused an uproar among the black American community. Justice Joseph Bradley was given the task of explaining the 8 to 1 majority decision. He declared that the Civil Rights Act of 1875 was unconstitutional. To support that view, Justice Bradley claimed that the Thirteenth Amendment did not give the US Congress power to make laws on the issue. As the cases involved individual acts of racial discrimination, they did not contravene the Thirteenth Amendment. As far as breaking the Fourteenth Amendment, the Court declared that it outlawed specific actions by state governments only, such as the right to vote or to sit on a jury, not individual acts of discrimination.

Only one justice dissented from this view, Justice John Harlan. He was the only member of the Supreme Court who had owned slaves before 1865. He declared that the Civil Rights Act of 1875 had extended to black Americans civil rights held by white Americans and was therefore constitutional. He also believed the Fourteenth Amendment had granted equal protection of the law to all Americans, black and white, and that the US Congress did have the right to pass legislation to protect the civil rights of black Americans in areas of life such as theatres, railways and hotels.

As a result of the decision, most of the gains made by black Americans during Reconstruction were removed. Black Americans were now open to racial discrimination by individuals and businesses across the USA.

SOURCE

 2

From a pamphlet entitled *The Barbarous Decision of the United States Supreme Court Declaring the Civil Rights Act Unconstitutional and Disrobing the Colored Race of All Civil Protection. The Most Cruel and Inhuman Verdict Against a Loyal People in the History of the World*. It was compiled and published by Bishop H.M. Turner in 1893 in Atlanta, Georgia. It was a major criticism by a senior black American clergyman of the decision of the US Supreme Court in the civil rights cases of 1883.

The reason I have gone to the United States Supreme Court library at Washington, D. C., and procured a true and correct copy of the revolting decision, which declared the Civil Rights bill unconstitutional, and entails upon the colored people of the United States every species of indignities known to proscription, persecution and even death itself, and will culminate in their leaving the United States or occupying the status of free slaves, until extermination follows, is because the great mass of our people in this country, including black and white, appear to be so profoundly ignorant of the cruel, disgraceful and inhuman condition of things affecting the colored race, and sustaining the brutal laws, which are degrading and goring their very lives out; I have met hundreds of persons, who, in their stupid ignorance, have attempted to justify the action of the Supreme Court in fettering the arms of justice and disgracing the nation by transforming it into a savage country. The world has never witnessed such barbarous laws entailed upon a free people as have grown out of the decision of the United States Supreme Court, issued October 15, 1883. For that decision alone authorized and now sustains all the unjust discriminations, proscriptions and robberies perpetrated by public carriers upon millions of the nation's most loyal defenders. It fathers all the 'Jim-Crow cars' into which colored people are huddled and compelled to pay as much as the whites, who are given the finest accommodations. It has made the ballot of the black man a parody, his citizenship a nullity and his freedom a burlesque. It has ingendered the bitterest feeling between the whites and blacks, and resulted in the deaths of thousands, who would have been living and enjoying life today. And as long as the accompanying decision remains the verdict of the nation, it can never be accepted as a civil, much less a Christian, country.

If this is not now a free government, if citizens cannot now be protected, if the three amendments have been undermined by the Supreme Court we must have another, and if that fails, then another; and we must neither stop nor pause until the Constitution shall become a perfect shield for every right of every human being beneath our flag.

A Level Exam-Style Question Section A

Study Source 2 before you answer this question.

Assess the value of the source for revealing the impact of the civil rights cases of 1883 on black Americans.

Explain your answer, using the source, information given about its origins and your own knowledge about the historical context. (20 marks)

Tip

It is important to consider the intended audience for the source, and the extent to which the information contained within the source provides sufficient information on black American reaction to the civil rights cases.

A Level Exam-Style Question Section B

'The civil rights cases of 1883 showed that the gains in civil and political equality achieved by black Americans during Reconstruction (1865–77) were short-lived.'

How far do you agree with this statement? (20 marks)

Tip

This type of question requires a balanced, analytical response. You will be expected to provide evidence to suggest that the civil rights cases of 1883 brought to an end the political and civil rights acquired by black Americans in the Reconstruction era. For instance, you should refer to the nullification of the changes made by the Civil Rights Act of 1875. However, this should be balanced with evidence to state that even after the civil rights cases of 1883, black Americans still possessed the right to vote and did possess some protection under the law for their civil rights, particularly outside the southern states.

The reaction of black Americans to the Court's judgment

To many black Americans, the civil rights cases of 1883 legalised racial segregation. The black American civil rights activist, Frederick Douglass, who had campaigned for the abolition of slavery before the Civil War, spoke to a large gathering at the Lincoln Hall, Washington DC, on 22 October 1883, shortly after the Court's judgment was announced.

The *Cleveland Gazette*'s Washington DC correspondent reported that the hall was crowded to capacity, with many members of the public being turned away due to lack of space. Although the audience was urged by Douglass to respect court decisions, he compared the civil rights cases of 1883 to the decisions before the Civil War to force the prospect of slavery on the Kansas Territory and to the Fugitive Slave Law of 1850, and stated that the decision stood against the principles of liberty.

The reaction outside Washington DC was similar. Thomas Fortune, editor of the *New York Globe*, reported that black Americans across the country were discussing the US Supreme Court decision in the civil rights cases of 1883. On 20 November 1883, the Washington DC correspondent to the *Arkansas Mansion* newspaper wrote that the civil rights cases caused great anger among black Americans. A mass meeting in Birmingham, Alabama, produced a series of resolutions condemning the

decision and declaring that it deprived black Americans of the enjoyment of the right to equal accommodations. This meeting appointed five men to a committee to present grievances to the railroads in Alabama and to request a plan to ensure that black Americans should enjoy as good accommodations as any other race when paying the same fare.

The civil rights cases of 1883 opened the door to legal segregation and the implementation of Jim Crow Laws.

ACTIVITY
KNOWLEDGE CHECK

The civil rights cases of 1883

1 What arguments were put forward by the US Supreme Court in declaring the Civil Rights Act of 1875 unconstitutional?

2 How important were the civil rights cases of 1883 in increasing racial inequality in the USA?

TO WHAT EXTENT DID THE SPREAD OF JIM CROW LAWS CHANGE RACE RELATIONS IN THE SOUTH AND HOW WERE BLACK PEOPLE EXCLUDED FROM VOTING?

The spread of Jim Crow Laws

After the re-establishment of white rule in the southern states following the end of Reconstruction in 1877, the civil rights of black Americans were eroded by a number of laws passed by various southern state legislatures. These laws, collectively called Jim Crow Laws, introduced a system of legal segregation of the black and white races in education, public transportation and public facilities. In addition, some Jim Crow Laws introduced new regulations on the registration of voting, which removed the right of the vast majority of black Americans to vote in these southern states.

Changes to rail travel in Florida, 1887

The civil rights cases of 1882–83 brought to the US Supreme Court were the result of individuals and private organisations engaging in racial discrimination against black Americans. Once the US Supreme Court declared that the provisions of the 1875 Civil Rights Act were no longer lawful, it gave state governments the opportunity to introduce legal segregation of the races. In 1887, Florida became the first state to introduce legal segregation in railway carriages (in the USA known as railroad cars). The Florida state law of 1887 declared that black and white passengers had to occupy separate railway carriages. Any black person who was convicted of violating this new legal segregation faced a fine of $500, a considerable sum in the late 19th century.

Although Florida was the first state to legally segregate black and white people on railways, it was quickly followed by other states introducing similar laws. Legislation was introduced by Mississippi in 1888, by Texas in 1889, by Louisiana in 1890 and by Alabama, Kentucky, Arkansas and Georgia in 1891.

SOURCE 3 A British postcard of 1905 advertising Cook's Lightning Soap. It shows perceptions held at the time about race relations and the role of Jim Crow Laws in the USA. The term 'nigger' to describe a black American is now regarded as a term of abuse. However, in the 19th and early 20th centuries, it was used to describe black Americans. Other terms to describe black Americans at that time were negro, colored and Afro-American.

Finally, in 1898 and 1899, the other former Confederate states followed suit, with South Carolina, North Carolina and Virginia introducing legal segregation in railway travel. In 1900, the first non-Confederate state, Maryland, introduced legal segregation, with the western state of Oklahoma following when it became a state in 1907. The details of the Jim Crow Laws regarding railroads are very nearly the same in all these states. They required white people, on the one hand, and 'negroes', 'persons of color', 'persons of African descent', etc., on the other, to occupy separate seats, compartments or coaches.

SOURCE

4

A letter by Frederick Douglass, a leading black American civil rights activist, writing about the Jim Crow Laws, 23 November 1887. The original letter raised the issue of the introduction of segregation in public schools in the southern states, in particular the states of Kentucky and Virginia.

My Dear Sir:

Pardon delay – answer to your letter made careful enquiry necessary. From all I can learn colored Lawyers are admitted to practice in Southern Courts, and I am very glad to admit the fact – for it implies a wonderful revolution in the public sentiment of the Southern States. I have not yet learned what are the inequalities between the races as to school privileges in the South. In some of the states the time allotted to colored schools is less than that allowed to whites. And I have heard and believe that in none of the states are the teachers of colored Schools as well paid as the teachers of White schools. My own observation has been that white teachers of Colored Schools in the southern states, show but little interest in their pupils. This is not strange, since they have been selected as teachers more because of their necessities, than from any interests they have shown in the progress and elevation of the colored race. I say this not of all, but of those in Virginia for instance who have come under my observation.

In Kentucky I believe so far as the law is concerned equal advantages are extended to colored children for Education, and the Same may be true of other states. I think the Bureau of Education will give you all the information you may require on this branch of the subject of your enquiries. Our wrongs are not so much now in written laws which all may see – but the hidden practices of a people who have not yet abandoned the idea of Mastery and dominion over their fellow man.

With great Respect Yours truly Fred^k Douglass

Cedar Hill Anacostia

Washington DC

The extension of segregation to other social areas and other states

Legal segregation of black and white Americans was extended across a wide variety of social and recreational areas in the years from 1887 to the beginning of the 20th century. On the railway system, legal segregation was expanded to having separate black and white waiting rooms. This process was begun in Mississippi in 1888 by the local railroad commission and was later introduced in Arkansas and Louisiana. In 1893, a challenge to this practice was made by black Americans in South Carolina, but it was held to be constitutional by the courts. In 1906, South Carolina extended legal segregation to all restaurants and eating houses at railway stations.

Another area where legal segregation affected public transportation was in street cars, known as trams in the UK. Legal separation of the races occurred in Georgia in 1891, followed by Louisiana in 1902, Mississippi in 1904, and Florida and Tennessee in 1905.

By the early 20th century, much of the former Confederacy had two separate societies living side by side, one black and one white. As well as legal segregation on public transportation, other public facilities were racially separated, including hospitals, hotels, restaurants, public houses, prisons, theatres and even cemeteries.

In addition to legal segregation, enacted by state law, *de facto* segregation also developed. This was segregation done by individuals. Even prostitution was segregated in some areas. The city of New Orleans in Louisiana had separate areas for black and white prostitutes. Racially segregated regulations also affected private organisations. Only white people could use the new pavilion at Nashville's Glendale Park, used for baseball, and the swimming pool at Raleigh's Brookside Park. A new zoo in Atlanta's Grant Park opened in 1890 and featured cages in the middle of the building, with an aisle on one side for white people and an aisle on the other side for black people. However, some parks in the 1880s were open to both black and white people, such as Nashville's Watkins Park,

Atlanta's Grant Park and Piedmont Park, where the Atlanta *Constitution* reported that black and white Americans watched a Negro militia company drill.

These segregation laws were introduced for a variety of reasons. Among them were claims of the scientific proof of the inferiority of the black race, known as social Darwinism. Also, some northerners saw segregation as a way of ending the sectional divisions between north and south that existed during the Civil War and Reconstruction. These northerners were concerned that the Civil War and Reconstruction had increased divisions within the USA, and they were willing to see a reduction in civil rights for black Americans if it led to improved relations between northern and southern white Americans.

Even prominent members of the southern black community accepted the onset of segregation. On 12 September 1895, Booker T. Washington, a leading black American civil rights leader, delivered a speech in Atlanta, Georgia, in front of a segregated audience of black and white Americans, and with reporters from national newspapers present. In his speech, known as the Atlanta Compromise, Booker T. Washington put forward his view of race relations. He stated that he was willing to accept racial segregation in the South if it still allowed black Americans to acquire education and skills to improve their standard of living.

EXTEND YOUR KNOWLEDGE

Booker T. Washington (1856–1915)

Booker T. Washington was one of the most famous and influential black Americans in the 1890s. He was America's foremost black educator and the leading black American civil rights leader of his day after the death of Frederick Douglass in 1895.

He was born a slave in Virginia and had worked as a child in salt furnaces and coal mines in West Virginia. He decided to educate himself and enrolled at the Hampton Institute. In 1881, he founded Tuskegee College to educate black American men. The college grew to accommodate 200 black university students. He insisted that the route to black advancement was through industrial education, gaining skills that would provide black Americans with a route out of economic poverty. His efforts to improve black American education attracted financial support from such white benefactors as Andrew Carnegie and John D. Rockefeller, both multimillionaires.

In 1895, in his 'Atlanta Compromise' speech, Booker T. Washington accepted social segregation and disenfranchisement as long as white people allowed black Americans to advance economically within society.

He published his autobiography *Up from Slavery* in 1901, and also founded the National Negro Business League in 1900. Both President Theodore (Teddy) Roosevelt (1901–09) and President William Howard Taft (1909–13) used Booker T. Washington as an adviser on black American affairs.

Booker T. Washington's views were attacked by fellow black American academic, W.E.B. Du Bois in 1903. Du Bois demanded full civil rights for black Americans.

SOURCE

From 'The separation of the races in public conveyances', an article about the impact of Jim Crow Laws on public transportation, published in *American Political Science Review*, May 1909. It was written by Gilbert Thomas Stephenson, a white American lawyer.

There is perhaps no phase of the American race problem which has been discussed quite so much within the last decade as the Jim Crow laws; that is, the statutes requiring separate accommodations for white and colored passengers in public conveyances. This has been the case largely because these legislative enactments are of general concern, while the other legal distinctions have directly affected only certain classes of either race. For instance, the laws prohibiting intermarriage concern only those of marriageable age; the suffrage qualifications apply only to males of voting age: the statutes requiring separate schools immediately affect only children and youths. But the laws requiring white and colored passengers to occupy separate seats of compartments or coaches concern every man, woman, and child, who travels, the country over. They affect not only those living in the States where the laws are in force, but the entire traveling public. The white man or the colored man in Massachusetts may not care anything about the suffrage restrictions of South Carolina, but, if he travels through the South, he must experience the requirements of the Jim Crow laws.

Inasmuch, then, as these statutes are of such general concern, it is proper that the people should know where they are, what they are, and the means of their execution. It is not the purpose of this article to take sides and discuss the justice or injustice of the laws, or the partiality or the impartiality of their execution, but rather to examine the provisions of the laws, and, so far as may be, to summarize the court decisions upon the different sections of the laws.

The spread of Jim Crow Laws

1 How useful is Source 4 in telling us about racial attitudes towards black people at the beginning of the 20th century?

2 How does Source 5 provide useful information on the impact of Jim Crow Laws on public transportation?

3 Describe the various Jim Crow Laws introduced to ensure the separation of the black and white races.

Excluding black voters

The period of Reconstruction saw a revolution in the electorate of the former Confederate states. The Fifteenth Amendment extended the right to vote to all adult black Americans. As a result, 700,000 ex-slaves were enfranchised. Black voters outnumbered white voters in five of the former Confederate states. During the Reconstruction era, many black Americans were elected to office both at state and national level. In Texas, 42 black Americans were elected to the state legislature, with 50 in South Carolina, 127 in Louisiana and 99 in Alabama. Black Americans also became US senators and congressmen.

However, following the end of Reconstruction, southern state governments, which were dominated by the Democrat Party, began a process which effectively removed most black Americans from the voting and political system of the southern states. The impact was to reverse the political gains of black Americans achieved during Reconstruction and to ensure, into the 1970s, the dominance of the white-dominated Democrat Party in the South.

Discrimination in Mississippi from 1890

A major attempt to exclude black Americans from voting took place in the state of Mississippi in 1890. In that year, a delegation was appointed by the state legislature to adopt a new state constitution. According to a delegate quoted in the local state capital newspaper, *The Jackson Clarion-Ledger*, the state legislature wanted a new constitution for one reason – to deprive black Americans of the right to vote. Before 1890, the constitution and laws of Mississippi provided that all male citizens who were 21 years of age and over could register to vote if they had lived in the state for six months and in the county for one month. The exceptions were those who were insane or who had committed crimes that disqualified them.

In 1890, Mississippi's population was 55 percent black American. However, of the 134 delegates appointed to draw up a new state constitution, only one delegate was black.

Article 12 of the new state constitution made major changes to the voting system. Its main way of reducing the black vote was to demand a poll tax of $2 for voter registration. As poverty among black Mississippians was very high, the poll tax disproportionately affected black voters, who could not afford to pay it.

Another method of reducing the black vote was to introduce a literacy test for all voter registration. This involved the ability to recite and explain parts of the Mississippi State Constitution. As 60 percent of Mississippi's black population were illiterate in 1890, this also had a profound effect on the number of black Americans able to vote.

The impact of these changes radically affected the number of registered voters. Before 1890, 67 percent of those people of voting age were black Americans. By 1 January 1892, when the new constitution came into effect, this proportion had dropped to 5.7 percent, a proportion that lasted until the 1960s. By 1899, approximately 122,000 white males were registered to vote, 82 percent of the potential white voting population.

To add to the exclusion of black Americans from the electoral process, all primary elections of the Democrat Party were exclusively white. As these were organised by political parties as private organisations, they were not covered in the state constitution. Also, as the Democrat candidate almost always won, it made it virtually irrelevant if the remaining registered black voters participated in a federal or state election.

A Level Exam-Style Question Section A

Study Source 6 before you answer this question.

Assess the value of the source for revealing how white Mississippians planned to exclude black Americans from voting.

Explain your answer, using the source, information given about its origins and your own knowledge about the historical context. (20 marks)

Tip

It is important to consider the intended audience for the source, and the extent to which the information contained within the source provides sufficient information about the exclusion of black voters from the electorate.

SOURCE

From the Mississippi State Constitution, Article 12, which dealt with election law within the state. The State Constitution was adopted in 1890 and was operational from 1892.

ARTICLE 12 – FRANCHISE

Sec. 242. The legislature shall provide by law for the registration of all persons entitled to vote at any election, and all persons offering to register shall take the following oath or affirmation: 'I_____, do solemnly swear (or affirm) that I am twenty-one years old, (or I will be before the next election in this county) and that I will have resided in this State two years, and _____election district of _____county one year next preceding the ensuing election [or if it be stated in the oath that the person proposing to register is a minister of the gospel in charge of an organized church, then it will be sufficient to aver therein, two years residence in the State and six months in said election district], and am now in good faith a resident of the same, and that I am not disqualified from voting by reason of having been convicted of any crime named in the constitution of this State as a disqualification to be an elector; that I will truly answer all questions propounded to me concerning my antecedents so far as they relate to my right to vote, and also as to my residence before my citizenship in this district; that I will faithfully support the constitution of the United States and of the State of Mississippi, and will bear true faith and allegiance to the same. So help me God.' In registering voters in cities and towns, not wholly in one election district, the name of such city or town may be substituted in the oath for the election district. Any willful and corrupt false statements in said affidavit, or in answer to any material question propounded as herein authorized, shall be perjury.

Sec. 243. A uniform poll tax of two dollars, to be used in aid of the common schools, and for no other purpose, is hereby imposed on every male inhabitant of this State between the ages of twenty-one and sixty years, except persons who are deaf and dumb or blind, or who are maimed by loss of hand or foot; said tax to be a lien only upon taxable property.

Louisiana's Grandfather Clause, 1898

Other southern states decided to use different methods to deny black Americans the right to register to vote. On 8 February 1898, the Louisiana Constitutional Convention met for the first time. It had a similar aim to the Mississippi Constitutional Convention of 1890. The president of the convention made clear what the convention hoped to achieve when he said it aimed to remove from the electorate illiterate voters, the vast majority of whom were black Americans.

The convention delegates included a provision requiring that potential voters pass a literacy test or own a certain amount of property in order to register. Since many white men were neither literate nor property owners, they also included a new Section 5 to the state constitution. This was known as the Grandfather Clause. This section stated that no man who had been eligible to vote on 1 January 1867 would be required to meet literacy or property-ownership requirements in order to register to vote; neither would his son or grandson be required to meet those requirements. Since black men were not granted the right to vote until the Fifteenth Amendment in 1870, they were excluded from this exemption. Louisiana's law was different to some, in that voters had to register under the Grandfather Clause by 1 September 1898.

This change, which effectively removed the vast majority of black voters from the electoral roll, was passed by 96 votes to 28. One state legislator, L.J. Dossman, voted in favour of the change because it would remove every black American from the electoral roll.

Like the constitutional changes in Mississippi, the Grandfather Clause had a profound impact on the black vote in Louisiana. In 1896, the estimated number of black Americans registered to vote in Louisiana was 130,000; in 1904, the estimated number was 1,342.

However, in 1915, an NAACP legal challenge to the Grandfather Clause was upheld by the US Supreme Court and it was declared unconstitutional. This was one of the first legal victories achieved by black Americans against Jim Crow Laws.

W.E.B. Du Bois (1868–1963)

W.E.B. Du Bois was a leading black American academic and civil rights activist. In 1895, he became the first black American to receive a doctorate degree (PhD) from Harvard University, the most prestigious university in the USA. He then studied in Germany. He engaged in sociological studies of black Americans. In 1899, he published *The Philadelphia Negro: A Social Study*. This established his national reputation among black Americans. From 1898 to 1910, he taught sociology at Atlanta University.

Du Bois was a forthright opponent of racial segregation and challenged Booker T. Washington's view that economic advancement was preferable to full civil equality for black Americans. In 1903, he published *Souls of the Black Folk*, which highlighted the plight of black Americans living under Jim Crow Laws. In 1909, he was the key figure in founding the Niagara Movement for civil rights equality for black Americans. In the following year, he helped to found the National Association for the Advancement of Colored People (NAACP), which fought, mainly through court cases, for black civil equality. He was also the editor and regular contributor to the NAACP magazine, *The Crisis*.

Impact on voter numbers in the South in the 1890s

As mentioned above, the changes made in Mississippi and Louisiana had a major negative impact on the size of the black electorate, which shrank considerably. In Louisiana, the reduction was 90 percent. In the 1890s, each southern state passed constitutional amendments placing stipulations on voting that hit black Americans hardest.

There were three main ways of doing this: poll taxes, property tests and literacy tests. Property tests made it illegal to vote unless you owned property. The poll tax simply put a tax on voting. Poll taxes, now illegal, clearly had a discouraging effect on voting by poor people, both white and black. Poll taxes and property tests reduced the level of poor white participation in voting considerably, though not as much as they reduced black American voting. Together with literacy tests, the impact on black American voting in the southern states was to see a drop of 65 percent, and on white voting by a drop of 26 percent. The Grandfather Clause, which was adopted in a number of states following Louisiana's example, was aimed exclusively at black Americans and helped to cement the racial divide between poor white Americans and poor black Americans where it was introduced.

SOURCE

From a speech by Booker T. Washington, a leading black American activist, entitled 'A New Heaven and a New Earth', delivered at the States and International Exposition in Atlanta, Georgia, on 18 September 1895. It was delivered in front of a mixed-race audience, which was segregated. Also present were journalists from national newspapers.

Our greatest danger is that in the great leap forward from slavery to freedom we may overlook the fact that the masses of us are to live by the production of our hands, and fail to keep in mind that we shall prosper in proportion as we learn to dignify and glorify common labor, and put brains and skill into the common occupations of life; shall prosper in proportion as we learn to draw a line between the superficial and the substantial, the ornamental gewgaws [cheap show jewellery] of life and the useful. No race can prosper till it learns that there is as much dignity in tilling a field as in writing a poem. It is at the bottom of life we must begin, and not at the top. Nor should we permit our grievances to overshadow our opportunities.

The wisest among my race understand that the agitation of questions of social equality is the extreme folly, and that progress in the enjoyment of all the privileges that will come to us must be the result of severe and constant struggle rather than artificial forcing. No race that has anything to contribute to the markets of the world is long in any degree ostracised. It is important and right that all privileges of the law be ours, but it is vastly more important that we be prepared for the exercise of those privileges. The opportunity to earn a dollar in a factory just now is worth infinitely more than the opportunity to spend a dollar in an opera house.

The exclusion of black voters

What methods were used by state governments to ensure the exclusion of large numbers of black voters?

EXTRACT

1 From *Sweet Land of Liberty?: The African American Struggle for Civil Rights in the Twentieth Century* by Robert Cook (1998).

Although Jim Crow was in part a product of the unique political and socio-economic circumstances of the late 19th century it did not represent a major break with the southern past.

EXTRACT

2 From *Black Leadership in America from Booker T Washington to Jesse Jackson* by John White (1994).

Socially, Southern race relations were marked by the increasing separation of the races – in public accommodations, hospitals, prisons, schools and places of entertainment. It marked a decisive change from the South's earlier and almost total exclusion of blacks from medical, welfare, educational and other facilities.

EXTRACT

3 From *Reconstruction: America's Unfinished Revolution* by Eric Foner (1988).

Black office holding did not entirely cease with Redemption (end of Reconstruction). Small numbers of blacks continued to sit in Southern legislatures, and a few even won election to Congress. (The last Southern black member of the House of Representatives until the modern era was North Carolina's George H White, who served from 1897 to 1901.) Blacks still held seats on city councils and minor posts in some plantation counties and enclaves of genuine black power persisted, from the 'black second' Congressional district of eastern North Carolina to South Carolina's low country and the Texas black belt.

THINKING HISTORICALLY   Evidence (6b)

The strength of argument

Read Extracts 1, 2 and 3 from historians and then answer the questions below.

1 Read Extract 1.

   a) What is weak about this claim?

   b) What could be added to it to make it stronger?

2 Read Extract 2.

   a) Is this an argument? If yes, what makes it one?

   b) How might this argument be strengthened?

3 Read Extract 3.

   a) How have they expanded their explanation to make the claim stronger?

   b) Can you explain why this is the strongest claim of the three sources?

4 What elements make a historian's claims strong?

TO WHAT EXTENT DID THE SUPREME COURT CASES OF 1896–99 ALTER THE LIVES OF BLACK AMERICANS?

In 1890, the black American leader, Booker T. Washington, gave the distinct impression, in his Atlanta Compromise speech, that he was willing to accept a racially segregated south. However, his views were not shared by other black Americans. Several cases against the segregation and voting laws of southern state governments were submitted to state and federal courts. However, the US Supreme Court reinforced the new reality of legal segregation and ensured that a segregated society between black and white persisted into the middle of the 20th century.

Plessy v Ferguson, 1896

One of the most important cases to be decided by the US Supreme Court was *Plessy* v *Ferguson*. The case challenged the Louisiana law of 1890 which demanded 'separate but equal' accommodation on railroads for black and non-white people. It was decided by black and Creole Americans (people of mixed race) to challenge this law. They formed the Citizens Committee to Test the Constitutionality of the Separate Car Law. This group arranged a test case along with the railroad company that opposed the law due to the expense of supplying another railway carriage just for non-white people. However, the Court upheld the legal segregation of black and white people, claiming that both races received 'separate but equal protection of the law', so the practice did not contravene the Fourteenth Amendment.

The case is interesting because the complainant, Homer Plessy, was only one-eighth black; he looked like a white man. Plessy was a civil rights activist. He was an educated man who had been chosen for the case in part because he did not look black, but considered himself to be, and was considered in his community to be a 'black' man. Plessy deliberately broke the segregated streetcar law and was arrested. His lawyer hoped to prove, by pointing to Plessy's mixed background, how absurd it was to segregate facilities by colour. As he was of mixed race, in which part of the street car should he sit?

The Supreme Court simply ignored this argument, stating only that Plessy was known to be black, so he was black and would have to sit in the back of the train. The Court went on to argue that segregating facilities posed no problem, as long as the facilities were equal. Justice Henry Billings Brown, who wrote the Supreme Court explanation of its decision, said that the state government was powerless to stop individual views on racial discrimination and the belief of many southern white people that black Americans were socially inferior. *Plessy* v *Ferguson* gave US Supreme Court support for legal segregation, and state laws establishing separate facilities for black and white people across the South quickly followed .

Reaction to the decision was mixed. The Rochester, New York state, newspaper, the *Union Advertiser*, saw the decision as a victory for states' rights; the Richmond, Virginia, *Dispatch* alleged that the real culprit in this case was Homer Plessy, who was simply causing trouble. However, public opposition to the *Plessy* v *Ferguson* decision came from both white and black Americans. The *New York Tribune* found that it was unfortunate that the Supreme Court supported racial discrimination. The black American-owned *A.M.E. Church Review* stated, in an editorial in June 1896, that the US Supreme Court had taken away basic civil rights from black Americans. The National Federation of Afro-American Women condemned the Court's decision in a resolution that foretold future boycotts by black Americans of segregated facilities on public transportation.

Plessy v *Ferguson* proved to be a landmark US Supreme Court decision. It supported legal segregation and this remained the Supreme Court view until the 1954 case of *Brown* v *Board of Education, Topeka, Kansas*.

'The "Jim Crow" Car', by black American the Reverend Walter H. Brooks, about the legal segregation of races on the railways. It was published in the *Richmond Planet* newspaper, Virginia, on 15 September 1900.

This too is done to crush us,
But naught can keep us back;
'My place', foorsooth a section,
Twixt smoker, front and back,
While others sit in coaches,
Full large and filled with light,
And this our Southern Christians,
Insist is just and right.

We're singled out from others,
A mark of shafts of scorn,
Here huddled like tamed cattle,
From early night till morn;
The golden rule's rejected,
Who cares for such a thing?
Who cares whose prejudiced o'er race,
Inflict this bitter thing?

The insult almost kills me,
God, help and bear the wrong,
Well, mine is the story of the weak,
Who fails before the strong;
Who falls – to ride in triumph,
When God his sword shall gird,
And the proudest evil doer,
Shall tremble at his Word.

The importance of *Williams* v *Mississippi*, 1898

Two years after the Supreme Court decision in *Plessy* v *Ferguson*, another blow to black American civil rights occurred in the Court decision of *Williams* v *Mississippi*, which dealt with the issue of the changes made to the Mississippi State Constitution in 1890, which disenfranchised large numbers of black voters. The key issues were the introduction of a $2 poll tax to register to vote, and literacy tests.

From a November 1904 article in *Appeal*, a national black American newspaper. It gives the views of a black American lawyer about the ways black Americans can campaign successfully against Jim Crow Laws. The Interstate Commerce Act of 1887 stated that there should be no discrimination, including racial discrimination, in interstate commerce (commerce included railroad transportation between two or more states).

Prof. William H H Hart, the Afro-American lawyer arrested some time ago at Elkton, Maryland, under the Maryland 'Jim Crow' law, and whose case is now under the courts of that state, addressed a large assemblage of Afro-American people at Lincoln Temple. He declared that he had found in the instate commerce act the method by which he would breakdown the barriers raised against Afro-Americans by state laws by providing for separate accommodation in railroad trains for the white and colored races.

'There is no sense in looking for redress upon the 14th Amendment of the Constitution. The Supreme court of the United States doesn't like it, and the white people of this country do not. Some day the 14th Amendment will come into its heritage and grow. We must consider the interstate commerce act. Everything goes down before it:- religion, morality, state authority, race and color. I tell you, here and now, that you have found the man who will free you from this contemptible "Jim Crow" law.'

Cumming v *Richmond County Board of Education*, 1899

A third case that involved black American challenges to actions which they claimed denied them 'equal protection of the law' involved education. In 1880, in Richmond County, Georgia, a school was created for black American students called Ware High School. To attend the school, all students had to pay $10 a year. However, on 10 July 1897, the Richmond County Board of Education levied a tax of $45,000 for that year for the support of primary, intermediate, grammar and high schools in the county, which was then due and being collected. This change still allowed the existence of some black schools, but the black American complainants alleged that this tax was used for the purpose of providing education in schools where 'non-whites' were refused admission.

The Supreme Court, in a unanimous 9–0 decision, upheld the decision of the Board of Education. It claimed that to close a high school for 60 black students and replace it with four elementary (junior) schools for 300 black students was not unconstitutional. The Board of Education had not been racially motivated in its decision because it replaced one black Americans-only school with four black Americans-only schools. The Court claimed that as the Ware High School students were paying $10 a year, they could get an education privately.

The case extended the idea of 'separate but equal protection of the law' to education. It allowed all states to set up racially segregated public school education systems. This arrangement lasted until the 1950s.

Collectively, the US Supreme Court decisions of *Plessy* v *Ferguson*, *Williams* v *Mississippi* and *Cumming* v *Richmond County Board of Education* upheld actions by state governments to create a racially segregated society in which black Americans were treated differently. In addition, *Williams* v *Mississippi* ensured that large numbers of black Americans were denied the right to register to vote, thereby consolidating white domination of southern state governments.

ACTIVITY
KNOWLEDGE CHECK

The impact of US Supreme Court decisions in the 1890s
Describe and explain how the following Supreme Court judgments ensured that black Americans were treated as second-class citizens:

a) *Plessy* v *Ferguson*, 1896

b) *Williams* v *Mississippi*, 1898

c) *Cumming* v *Richmond County Board of Education*, 1899.

The use of violence

Underpinning all the attempts by southern governments and private organisations to impose racial discrimination was the ever present fear for black Americans of violence. All-white terror groups, such as the Ku Klux Klan, had declined following the end of Reconstruction, but random violence by white Americans against black Americans occurred well into the 20th century.

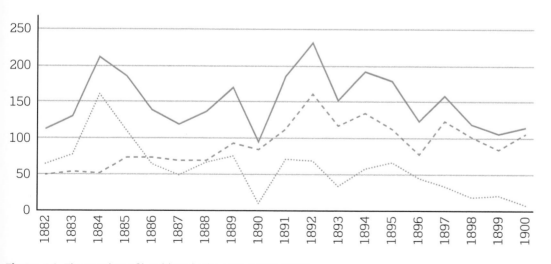

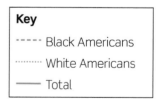

Key
----- Black Americans
.... White Americans
——— Total

Figure 4.1 The number of lynchings in the USA, 1882–1900.

SOURCE
10 The use of violence against black Americans, from a lithograph of 1890. It appeared in the magazine *National Police Gazette*.

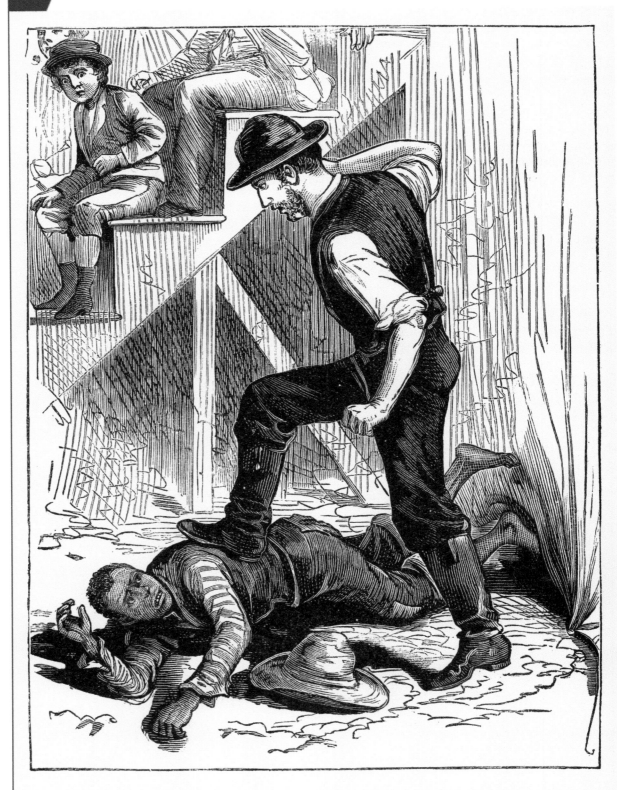

STAMPED TO DEATH BY A CIRCUS HAND—A NEGRO BOY AT NORFOLK, VA., KILLED FOR CRAWLING UNDER A CIRCUS TENT.

In the 1890s, an average of 187 lynchings of black Americans took place every year, mainly in the South. That works out at an average of over three per week. These lynchings were not just the random hanging of black people at night by a few violent white supremacists. Typically, hundreds of white Americans would gather to watch. At that time, a black American from Mississippi declared that white Americans had to have a licence to kill anything but a black person – they were always 'in season'. Ida Wells-Barnett, a female black American civil rights activist, made a study of violence against black Americans in the 1890s, in particular lynchings. She concluded that reasons for lynchings included talking disrespectfully to a white person, slapping a white boy, writing an insulting letter, being too prosperous and having a personal debt to a white person. The biggest excuse for a lynching was the rumour that a black man had raped a white woman.

In Texas in 1893, 10,000 white people gathered to watch the lynching of black American, Henry Smith. He had been accused of murdering a white girl. He was tied to a chair and driven around town. The murdered girl's father tortured Smith with hot irons, burning off his skin, then poked his eyes out. Photographs were taken of the event and publicised.

The constant fear of violence and random murder made it extremely difficult for black Americans to stand up to the introduction of legal racial segregation and acts of racial discrimination.

SOURCE

11 From a pamphlet entitled *Mob Rule in New Orleans: Robert Charles and His Fight to Death, the Story of His Life, Burning Human Beings Alive, Other Lynching Statistics.* It was written by Ida Wells-Barnett, a leading female black American civil rights campaigner, in 1900.

Immediately after the awful barbarism which disgraced the State of Georgia in April of last year, during which time more than a dozen colored people were put to death with unspeakable barbarity, I published a full report showing that Sam Hose, who was burned to death during that time, never committed a criminal assault, and that he killed his employer in self-defense.

Since that time I have been engaged on a work not yet finished, which I interrupt now to tell the story of the mob in New Orleans, which, despising all law, roamed the streets day and night, searching for colored men and women, whom they beat, shot and killed at will.

In the account of the New Orleans mob I have used freely the graphic reports of the *New Orleans Times-Democrat* and the *New Orleans Picayune.* Both papers gave the most minute details of the week's disorder. In their editorial comment they were at all times most urgent in their defense of law and in the strongest terms they condemned the infamous work of the mob.

It is no doubt owing to the determined stand for law and order taken by these great dailies and the courageous action taken by the best citizens of New Orleans, who rallied to the support of the civic authorities, that prevented a massacre of colored people awful to contemplate.

For the accounts and illustrations taken from the above-named journals, sincere thanks are hereby expressed.

The publisher hereof does not attempt to moralize over the deplorable condition of affairs shown in this publication, but simply presents the facts in a plain, unvarnished, connected way, so that he who runs may read. We do not believe that the American people who have encouraged such scenes by their indifference will read unmoved these accounts of brutality, injustice and oppression. We do not believe that the moral conscience of the nation—that which is highest and best among us—will always remain silent in face of such outrages, for God is not dead, and His Spirit is not entirely driven from men's hearts.

When this conscience wakes and speaks out in thunder tones, as it must, it will need facts to use as a weapon against injustice, barbarism and wrong. It is for this reason that I carefully compile, print and send forth these facts. If the reader can do no more, he can pass this pamphlet on to another, or send to the bureau addresses of those to whom he can order copies mailed.

Besides the New Orleans case, a history of burnings in this country is given, together with a table of lynchings for the past eighteen years. Those who would like to assist in the work of disseminating these facts, can do so by ordering copies, which are furnished at greatly reduced rates for gratuitous distribution. The bureau has no funds and is entirely dependent upon contributions from friends and members in carrying on the work.

Ida B. Wells-Barnett Chicago, Sept. 1, 1900

SOURCE 12

From a French magazine, published in 1892. It shows the lynching of four black Americans in Florida who were accused of murdering a white person. A white mob stormed the gaol and lynched the men before a trial took place. It is an imagined depiction of what took place.

QUATRE NÈGRES « LYNCHÉS » POUR AVOIR ASSASSINÉ UN CHEF DE TRAVAUX

Dessin de Henri MEYER. — Gravure de MÉAULLE. — Voir l'article, page 395.

A Level Exam-Style Question Section B

'The introduction of Jim Crow Laws by state governments was the most important reason for the denial of civil and political equality for black Americans.'

How far do you agree? (20 marks)

Tip

In your answer, you need to provide evidence in favour of the proposition in the question. The answer should include evidence of specific acts of state governments to limit the black American right to vote and the introduction of legal segregation in areas such as education, public transportation and public facilities. This should be balanced with coverage of other factors, such as the role of the US Supreme Court and the use of violence.

ACTIVITY
KNOWLEDGE CHECK

The use of violence

How useful are Sources 10 and 12 for revealing the extent of violence against black Americans in the last decade of the 19th century?

ACTIVITY
SUMMARY

The Triumph of Jim Crow

1 How useful are Sources 4 and 7 and Figure 4.1 in explaining why black Americans faced increasing racial discrimination in the period 1883–c1900?

2 How were the gains achieved by black Americans in the Reconstruction era of 1865–77 removed in the period 1883–c1900?

3 What do you regard as the most effective method of ensuring that black Americans were reduced to the position of second-class citizens in the period 1883–c1900?

 WIDER READING

Chafe, W.H., Gavins, R. and Korstad, R. (eds) *Remembering Jim Crow*, The New Press (2004)

Kelley, R. *To Make Our World Anew*, Oxford University Press (2005)

Tuck, S. *The Black Freedom Struggle from Emancipation to Obama*, Harvard University Press (2010)

3.5

The New Deal and race relations, 1933–41

INTRODUCTION

The New Deal period of 1933–41 saw considerable political, social and economic change in the USA. From 1929 to 1933, the USA had been plunged into a major economic depression. By the time Franklin D. Roosevelt was inaugurated as the new president, in March 1933, 25 percent of the workforce was unemployed and the country was on the brink of economic collapse. The economic depression had occurred when the Republican Party was the dominant force in the US Congress and also held the presidency. The major downturn in the economy swept the Republicans from office in the presidential, congressional and state elections of November 1932. They were replaced as the dominant political party by the Democrats. From 1933 to 1941, the Democrats held the presidency. Franklin D. Roosevelt became the first and only US president to be elected on three successive occasions, in 1932, 1936 and 1940 (he was elected for a fourth time in 1944 as well).

The election of Franklin D. Roosevelt (FDR) not only caused a political revolution in US politics, but his domestic policy, the New Deal, brought about major social and economic change. The New Deal aimed to get America out of economic depression and back to work. FDR planned on 'relief, recovery and reform'. His first priority was to bring welfare relief to those Americans out of work and suffering poverty. He also planned to introduce legislation to aid economic recovery. Finally, he planned to reform the US economic system to prevent a recurrence of economic depression.

When he died, in April 1945, FDR was regarded as one of the great reforming presidents. His New Deal reforms transformed the USA. However, black Americans, unlike their white counterparts, did not always benefit from the changes made during the New Deal years of 1933–41. A major black American grievance was the need for a federal law against lynching, and the F.D. Roosevelt administration and Congress failed to prevent this. Also, although New Deal agencies provided work and welfare support for most workers, black Americans were not always treated equally with other Americans. The New Deal may have been significant in terms of programmes to end economic depression and its effects, but it did not offer similar advances in black Americans' civil rights.

1933 – March: Franklin D. Roosevelt is sworn in as president

March to June: First 100 days of the New Deal, which includes the creation of the National Recovery Administration, Civilian Conservation Corps and Agricultural Adjustment Administration

1929 – Beginning of economic depression; by 1933, 25 percent of workforce is unemployed

| 1929 | 1930 | 1931 | 1932 | 1933 | 1934 |

1932 – Democrat Franklin D. Roosevelt wins presidential election

1934 – Beginning of NAACP anti-lynching campaign

HOW IMPORTANT WERE SOUTHERN DEMOCRATS AT HINDERING BLACK CIVIL RIGHTS?

Party organisation in the USA

The USA has a federal system of government. This means political power is shared between a central, or federal, government based in Washington DC and state governments, of which there were 48 between 1933 and 1941. The federal government is responsible for foreign policy, national defence, interstate crime prevention, and interstate commerce and trade. State governments are responsible for such activities as education and law and order. The party system in the USA reflected this division of power. Each state had its own party organisation. This applied to both the Democrat and Republican parties. These state-based party organisations got together only once every four years to elect a president and vice president.

The Democratic Party, which dominated US politics during the New Deal years, had a wide variety of political views. In the north-east of the USA, in states such as New York and Massachusetts, the main influences in the party were Irish, Italian and German Americans. It adopted a liberal policy towards social reform and race relations. In the southern states, the main influences in the Democrat state parties were white Americans. They were in favour of legal racial segregation. What united the Democrat Party, in the years before 1933, was support for strong local state government. The Democrat Party had dominated southern state governments since the end of Reconstruction in 1877. Every election year since that time, Democrats held control of southern state governments and sent Democrat congressmen and senators to Washington DC. In the November 1932 congressional elections, the Democrat Party won all the seats to the House of Representatives in all the former Confederate states and every Senate seat that was up for election. All former Confederate states had Democrat-controlled state governments.

The Democrats controlled southern politics for a number of reasons. Firstly, the Republican Party was associated with the northern side in the Civil War, had freed the slaves in 1865 and was responsible for the military occupation of the South under Reconstruction. Secondly, Democrat state governments after 1887 began introducing laws that discriminated against black Americans and by 1933 had disenfranchised large numbers of potential black voters. Finally, Democrat-controlled state governments ensured that they kept power through gerrymandering, a process whereby state governments decided the boundaries of state government constituencies and congressional district boundaries. These were drawn in a way to ensure that they maximised the possibility of Democrats winning as many seats as possible.

1935 – Beginning of Second New Deal, which includes Wagner Act and Social Security Act

1937 – President Roosevelt fails in his attempt to reform US Supreme Court

Conservative Coalition of Republicans and southern Democrats is formed

1941 – USA joins the Second World War

| 1935 | 1936 | 1937 | 1939 | 1940 | 1941 |

1936 – Franklin D. Roosevelt wins landslide victory in presidential election

1940 – Franklin Roosevelt becomes only president to be elected on three occasions

Party organisation in the US Congress

The US Congress is dominated by the committee system. Each major branch of government, such as foreign relations, commerce, judiciary, finance and defence, has a relevant committee in both the House of Representatives and the Senate, which scrutinises the working of government departments. In addition, each of these congressional committees discusses proposals for legislation, known as bills, which are linked to their relevant government departments. The chairpersons of these committees have enormous power over what is discussed and what laws will be passed. In addition, two congressional committees in the House of Representatives had considerable power. The House Ways and Means Committee decided which bill ought to go to which committee and the House Rules Committee decided on procedure. Between them, these committees determined how the overall committee system operated.

The allocation of committee chairpersons is made under the seniority principle. This means that those members of Congress and senators with the longest continuous service are chosen as chairpersons. With the Democrat Party, the members with the longest continuous service were usually from the southern states. As a result, from 1933, the committee system of Congress was dominated by southern Democrats. For instance, the chair of the House Judiciary Committee in 1937, Hatton Towers of Texas, was an implacable opponent of any attempt to introduce an anti-lynching law and used his authority to thwart most attempts. It took the non-southern Democrats on the Judiciary Committee to allow an anti-lynching bill to be discussed in the House of Representatives in 1937–38.

1 Introducing a bill to Congress
Any member of Congress can introduce a bill. Usually a bill is submitted to the Senate and House of Representatives at the same time, so is 'co-sponsored'. Most federal laws have a double-barrelled title, one name is the Senate sponsor and the other is the House sponsor.

2 Referral to a committee
When a bill is introduced, it is given a number. The bill is then referred to a committee with jurisdiction over the primary issue of the legislation. Sometimes, a bill will be referred to multiple committees.

The committee that decides which bill is sent to which committee is the House Ways and Means Committee. In the 1930s, the Committee was dominated by southern white Democrats.

3 Committee action
The chairperson of the committee determines whether there will be a hearing on the bill. The committee chairperson could 'kill' the bill at this stage. Most committee chairpersons during the New Deal, in both House and Senate, were southern white Democrats.

4 Committee report
The committee chairperson's staff write a report of the bill, describing the intent of legislation.

5 Floor debate and votes
The Speaker of the House and the majority leader of the Senate determine if and when a bill comes before the full body for debate and amendment and final passage. Both these posts were held by southern white Democrats during the New Deal.

6 Referral to the other chamber
When the House or the Senate passes a bill, it is referred to the other chamber, where it usually follows the same route through committee and floor action. This chamber may approve the bill as received, reject it, ignore it or amend it before passing it.

7 Conference on a bill
If only minor changes are made to a bill by the other chamber, usually the legislation goes back to the originating chamber for a concurring vote. However, when the House and Senate versions of the bill contain significant and/or numerous differences, a conference committee is officially appointed to reconcile the differences between the two different versions into a single bill. If the conferees are unable to reach agreement, the legislation dies. If agreement is reached, a conference report is prepared describing the committee members' recommendations for changes. Both the House and the Senate must approve of the conference report. If either chamber rejects the conference report, the bill dies.

8 Action by the president
After the conference report has been approved by both the House and Senate, the final bill is sent to the president. If the president approves of the legislation, he signs it and it becomes law. If the president does not take action for ten days while Congress is in session, the bill automatically becomes law. If the president opposes the bill, he can veto it, or, if he takes no action after the Congress has adjourned its second session, it is a 'pocket veto' and the legislation dies.

9 Overriding a veto
If the president vetoes a bill, Congress may decide to attempt to override the veto. This requires a two-thirds roll-call vote of the members who are present in sufficient numbers for a quorum.

10 Role of the US Supreme Court
Even after a bill becomes a federal Act, the US Supreme Court could declare it unconstitutional, which means it can no longer be regarded as a law.

Figure 5.1 How a proposal for change (a bill) becomes a federal (national) law within the USA. The flow chart shows those parts of the process where southern white Democrat politicians in the US Congress had the power to influence the process. (See Chapter 3 for the structure of the federal government.)

The impact of southern Democrats during the New Deal, 1933–41

In the November 1932 presidential election, Franklin D. Roosevelt won by a substantial margin. He won 57.4 percent of the popular vote, gaining 22.8 million votes compared to his Republican opponent, Herbert Hoover, who won 15 million votes. The electoral college vote (see Chapter 3) widened the margin of victory. FDR won 472 electoral college votes compared to Hoover's 59 votes.

However, within the US system of government, the president had limits to his political power. To pass legislation, he had to gain support in both the House of Representatives and the Senate. Powerful committee chairpersons could damage the president's programme by either rejecting, amending or slowing down the passage of his proposals. Ultimately, the president's most important skill was the ability to persuade those in Congress to support him.

When running for the office of president in 1932, Franklin Roosevelt chose as his vice-presidential running mate John Nance Garner of Texas, a southern Democrat. The aim was to secure southern Democrat support for his bid for power. Garner had been elected Speaker of the House of Representatives in 1931, the most powerful job in Congress. Garner proved to be a valuable ally of Franklin D. Roosevelt in ensuring his New Deal legislation passed through Congress. In the 1936 presidential election, which FDR won by a landslide, winning the support of 46 of the 48 states, Garner was again his vice-presidential candidate. Throughout the period, Garner worked closely with Roosevelt in bringing about major social and economic reforms associated with the New Deal. However, Garner also ensured that Franklin Roosevelt would not try to upset the southern white dominance of the southern states. This included the use of **white primaries** in the Texas Democrat Party. As the Democrats dominated the state elections, whoever was chosen in the Democrat primary election would invariably win in the main election against other parties.

The rapid increase in federal government power as a result of New Deal programmes, such as the National Recovery Administration (NRA), the Public Works Administration (PWA) and federal banking laws, caused disquiet among many Democrats. The Party had traditionally supported state government and was opposed to big federal government. In 1935, the Democrat presidential candidate of 1928, Al Smith of New York state, actually joined the Liberty League, an organisation opposed to the New Deal.

The concern over the increase in federal and, in particular, presidential power, led to the growth of opposition among some southern Democrats. The attempts by FDR to change the composition of the US Supreme Court through the judicial procedures reform bill of 1937 (later known as the Court Packing Plan of 1937) led to a major change in the Democrat Party. Franklin Roosevelt's efforts to change the composition of the Supreme Court failed and led to the publication of what was known in the media as the Conservative Manifesto in December 1937.

EXTEND YOUR KNOWLEDGE

Court Packing Plan, 1937
In the First New Deal, the US Supreme Court declared some key legislation unconstitutional because the Court decided it gave the federal government too much power. The most important were the National Recovery Act and Agricultural Adjustment Act. Following his landslide victory in 1936, F.D. Roosevelt announced a plan that would have given the president the power to add one justice for every Supreme Court justice over the age of 70, up to a total of six. FDR explained that the older justices were not able to handle the increasing workload, so the additional justices would improve the Court's efficiency. Much of the nation saw through FDR's explanation. Newspaper editors, Republicans, southern and moderate Democrats, and even the three liberals on the Supreme Court condemned the plan as a blatant effort to politicise the Court to make it more favourable to the president. The measure was eventually allowed to die in committee, following some Court support for his policies and an opportunity for a Supreme Court appointment.

The major politician behind the Conservative Manifesto was Democrat senator for North Carolina, Josiah W. Bailey. It was entitled 'An Address to the People of the United States' and demanded a limitation to high federal spending on New Deal programmes. It also led to an informal union of southern Democrats and Republicans to oppose any further major social and economic reform. It supported limited federal government, a completely independent Supreme Court and state government. The Conservative Manifesto was able to get support from Republican and southern Democrat politicians because 1937–38 saw a return to economic recession, coined the Roosevelt Recession by historians, which Bailey blamed on the federal government's excessive spending on social programmes. From 1937 to 1941, southern Democrats and their Republican allies helped to limit any further major New Deal programmes.

Southern Democrats, throughout the 1930s, used racism to win the support of the white vote. In 1935, a former governor of Mississippi, Theodore Bilbo, was elected to the US Senate. His support for racism towards black Americans went so far as to lead him to introduce an amendment to a bill to help relieve unemployment and distress for all Americans so that federal funds would be made available to deport all black Americans to Liberia in West Africa.

Southern Democrats ensured that New Deal programmes benefited white Americans. They also ensured that no attempt was made by the federal government to interfere with Jim Crow Laws. Franklin Roosevelt's need for southern Democrat support for his New Deal measures, in the years 1933–37, ensured that the great social and economic reforms of the New Deal did not lead to any extension of civil rights for black Americans. Southern Democrat politicians in the US Congress were able to do this because they controlled most of the committees of Congress. The House Ways and Means Committee and the House Rules Committee both decided whether or not a bill could be debated in the House of Representatives. From 1937 to 1941, the informal Conservative coalition of southern Democrats and Republicans ensured that the radicalism of the early New Deal of 1933 to 1937 came to an end.

EXTRACT

1   From *Freedom from Fear, The American People in Depression and War, 1929 to 1945* by historian David M. Kennedy, published in 1999.

Since Reconstruction days, the solid South had been the foundational constituency of the Democratic Party. The South's peculiar racial sensitivities provided the occasion in 1938 for a stunning demonstration of the power of that region's elected representatives to stymie the legislative process and to write finis to the New Deal chapter in American history. Southern Democrats had reluctantly agreed at their party's convention in the summer of 1936 to give up the two-thirds majority rule for electing presidential nominees. [This] device traditionally granted the South an effective veto over any candidate judged unsafe on the race issue. (South Carolina's Senator Ellison 'Cotton Ed' Smith had walked out of the convention when a black clergyman delivered the invocation. 'By God, he's as black as melted midnight!' Smith exploded. 'Get outa my way. This mongrel meeting ain't no place for a white man!' he announced as he departed. 'I don't want any blue gummed, slew footed Senegambian praying for me politically.' Smith exited a second time when Chicagoan Arthur Mitchell, the first black Democrat ever elected to Congress seconded Roosevelt's nomination.) Later that year Roosevelt's overwhelming victory margin dramatized the unsettling truth that a Democratic president could be elected without a single southern electoral vote.

ACTIVITY
KNOWLEDGE CHECK

The influence of southern white politicians in the Democrat Party
Explain why southern Democrat politicians in the US Congress sought to block legislation proposed by a Democrat president.

TO WHAT EXTENT DID PRESIDENT FRANKLIN D. ROOSEVELT FAIL TO IMPROVE RACE RELATIONS?

When Franklin D. Roosevelt was elected president, he brought a ray of hope to a USA gripped by economic depression. When he was inaugurated president on 4 March 1933, he claimed the only thing Americans had to fear was fear itself. Unlike any previous president, Franklin Roosevelt spoke directly to the American people through the medium of radio. His 'Fireside Chats' were directed at the American people in their own homes, and he spelled out how he was going to get the USA out of economic depression. His campaign song for the 1932 election was 'Happy Days are Here Again'. However, the feeling of hope and the desire for change did not have an impact on all Americans. Black Americans also hoped that F.D. Roosevelt would help improve their lives and deal with their civil rights grievances. The majority of black Americans, however, lived in the southern states of the former Confederacy and still faced racial discrimination, disenfranchisement and random violence and intimidation.

Continuation of Jim Crow Laws

Although black and white Americans lived in the same country, to all intents and purposes they lived separate lives. By the 1930s, racial segregation had become a dominant feature of American life, not just in the southern states. Racial segregation took two distinct forms:

- *De jure* segregation referred to specific laws passed by state and city government which created separate facilities for black Americans.

- *De facto* segregation referred to the provision of separate facilities for black Americans by private organisations or citizens in areas such as housing.

Legal (*de jure*) racial segregation

At the national level, the US armed forces were racially segregated. In the US army, separate black American units existed with white American officers. This situation lasted until 1948. In federally administered national parks in southern states, legal segregation in the form of separate catering, camping and hotel accommodation was provided for black Americans.

At state level, the doctrine of 'separate but equal' pervaded nearly all aspects of life. Separate public schools existed for black and white children, not just in the southern states. In 1954, a US Supreme Court decision ended this racial segregation. The school district cited in that case was in Topeka, Kansas, a state which had never allowed slavery and had fought against the Confederacy in the US Civil War of 1861–65.

However, it was in the former Confederate states where Jim Crow Laws enforcing racial segregation were most pervasive. The state of Alabama, in the heart of the former Confederacy, gives an indication of the divisive way in which race relations were organised. Under Alabama state law at that time, no white female nurses were allowed to nurse in wards or rooms in hospitals where black American men were placed. Also, in railway stations, separate waiting rooms had to be provided for black and white railway travellers. Even on the trains, separate railways carriages had to be provided for black and white passengers.

In the neighbouring state of Georgia, similar restrictions were placed on all black Americans. In restaurants, black and white Americans could not be served with food in the same room. At amateur baseball matches, black and white baseball teams not only could not play each other, but were forbidden from playing near each other's neighbourhoods. Even public parks were racially segregated, with black and white park areas.

Even outside the former Confederate states, black Americans faced racial discrimination. The mountain state of Wyoming, which called itself 'The Equality State', outlawed intermarriage between black and white Americans. In Oklahoma, which did not become a state until 1907, black Americans suffered discrimination where public recreational facilities, such as fishing, boating and bathing were racially segregated. There were even separate telephone booths.

In addition to legal racial segregation across the USA, black Americans found restrictions on what houses and flats they could buy or rent and which clubs and social organisations they could join. The most popular sports game in the 1930s was baseball. The national professional baseball leagues were all white. There was a separate Negro Baseball League.

A Level Exam-Style Question Section A

Study Source 1 before you answer this question.

Assess the value of the source for revealing the impact of legal segregation under Jim Crow Laws on black Americans.

Explain your answer, using the source, information given about its origins and your own knowledge about the historical context. (20 marks)

Tip

It is important to consider the intended audience for the source, and the extent to which the information contained within the source provides sufficient information about the impact on black Americans of Jim Crow Laws, as it only refers to one state.

SOURCE 1

From the Code of the state of Alabama, 1923, which sets out the Jim Crow Laws of that state on the issue of racial segregation which were in operation in the 1930s.

1901.—Sections 101-103

Sec. 102. The legislature shall never pass any law to authorize or legalize any marriage between any white person and a negro, or descendant of a negro.

Sec. 194. The poll tax mentioned in this article shall be one dollar and fifty cents upon each male inhabitant of the state, over the age of twenty-one years, and under the age of fifty-five years, who would not now be exempt by law; but the legislature is authorized to increase the maximum age fixed in this section to not more than sixty years. Such poll tax shall become due and payable on the first day of October in each year, and become delinquent on the first day of the next succeeding February, but no legal process, nor any fee or commission shall be allowed for the collection thereof. The tax collector shall make returns of poll tax collections separate from other collections.

Sec. 195. Any person who shall pay the poll tax of another, or advance him money for that purpose in order to influence his vote, shall be guilty of bribery, and upon conviction therefor shall be imprisoned in the penitentiary for not less than one nor more than five years.

1901 ARTICLE XIV. EDUCATION

Sec. 256. The legislature shall establish, organize, and maintain a liberal system of public schools throughout the state for the benefit of the children thereof between the ages of seven and twenty-one years. The public school fund shall be apportioned to the several counties in proportion to the number of school children of school age therein, and shall be so apportioned to the schools in the districts or townships in the counties as to provide, as nearly as practicable, school terms of equal duration in such school districts or townships. Separate schools shall be provided for white and colored children, and no child of either race shall be permitted to attend a school of the other race.

1875 ARTICLE XIII. EDUCATION.

Sec. 1. The general assembly shall establish, organize, and maintain a system of public schools throughout the state, for the equal benefit of the children thereof between the ages of seven and twenty-one years; but separate schools shall be provided for the children of citizens of African descent.

A Level Exam-Style Question Section B

'In the 1930s, legal (*de jure*) racial segregation was a bigger problem for black Americans than *de facto* racial segregation.'

How far do you agree with this statement? (20 marks)

Tip

This type of question requires a balanced, analytical response. You will be expected to provide evidence that legal segregation made black Americans second-class citizens in the southern states. However, this should be balanced with evidence to state that black Americans faced de facto segregation across the USA in housing and jobs, and that racial discrimination was not limited to the southern states.

Exclusion of black voters

The introduction of registration to vote restrictions in the 1890s (see Chapter 4) led to a major reduction in the number of black Americans entitled to vote. Poll taxes disproportionately affected black voters as they were invariably much poorer than white Americans in southern states. In addition, literacy tests helped to exclude black Americans, with as much as 60 percent of the black American population in southern states being illiterate. In states where the Democrat Party was dominant, such as the southern states, all-white primary elections ensured that, even when black Americans had an opportunity to vote in state and federal elections, they were effectively excluded from the democratic process.

The attempt in Louisiana to restrict black voting through the introduction of the Grandfather Clause in 1898 (see Chapter 4) was overturned by the US Supreme Court in 1915 as unconstitutional. However, this had a very limited impact on encouraging higher black participation in voter registration. Legal restrictions on black voting were reinforced by the threat of violence and intimidation. The Ku Klux Klan had seen a rapid rise in support across the USA in the 1920s. Lynching of black Americans continued to be a major social problem.

EXTRACT

 The impact of white primary elections in the south on black disenfranchisement at elections. From *The Shaping of Southern Politics: Suffrage Restriction and the Establishment of the One-Party South, 1880–1910* by J. Morgan Kousser (1974).

Disenfranchisement brought about one-party rule in the Southern states. This meant that the Democratic nominee for any office was assured of victory in the general election, shifting the real electoral contest to the party primary. This fact provided yet another opportunity to disenfranchise blacks. Texas passed a law forbidding blacks from participating in Democratic primary elections. The Supreme Court struck down this law as a plain violation of the 14th and 15th Amendments in *Nixon* v *Herndon*, 273 U.S. 536 (1927). So Texas passed another law providing for each party's state executive committee to determine who could vote in its primaries. Accordingly, the Texas Democratic Party Executive Committee resolved to permit only white Democrats to participate in its primary. The idea was that, as a private association, the party executive committee was not subject to the 14th and 15th Amendments, which applied only to the states. [The US Supreme Court] resolved in *Smith* v *Allwright*, 321 U.S. 649 (1944), which found that primary elections were so pervasively regulated by the state that, in doing their part to run primaries, political parties were state actors and thus subject to the 14th and 15th Amendments. Texas Democrats evaded this ruling by arrangement with the all-white Jaybird Democratic Association (a leadership caucus within the party), which held elections unregulated by the state. The winner of the Jaybird Party election would enter the Democratic party primary, and the Democratic party would put up no opposition, thus ensuring victory to the Jaybird Party candidate. The Supreme Court saw through this ruse in *Terry* v *Adams*, 345 U.S. 461 (1953), finally putting an end to the white primary after 9 years of acquiescence and 26 years of litigation.

The history of black disenfranchisement demonstrates that it was a product not simply of the actions of Southern states and individuals, but of a failure to uphold and exercise federal power. Congress failed to fully exercise its powers under the 14th amendment (for example, it never reduced Southern states' congressional representation in proportion to its illegal disenfranchisement, as it was authorized to do). The Supreme Court actively undermined federal executive powers to protect black voting rights, refused to acknowledge racial discrimination even when it was obvious, and acquiesced in blatant constitutional violations by resorting to specious reasoning.

The defeat of federal attempts at anti-lynching legislation

The 1930s saw several attempts to end lynching. The campaign was spearheaded by the National Association for the Advancement of Colored People (NAACP), formed in 1909, and the Association of Southern Women for the Prevention of Lynching (ASWPL), established in 1930. The idea that unelected vigilantes could murder a person, whether black or white, was a feature of American life. It contravened two key aspects of the US Constitution: the right to life and the right to due process of law under the Fifth Amendment of the Constitution. Although a feature of American life since the creation of the USA in the late 18th century, lynching of black Americans began to increase in the years after 1882. There were 4,608 victims of lynching in the USA between 1882 and 1932, and more than seven out of ten were black Americans.

With the highest annual figure of 230 in 1892, the number of victims steadily decreased during the 20th century, dropping below double figures for the first time in 1932. The next year, the first year of Franklin D. Roosevelt's administration, the number of lynchings rose to 28, with the rise possibly aggravated by the economic turmoil of the Depression.

Several attempts to declare lynching a criminal offence had been made before 1933. In 1922, a congressional bill, the Dyer bill, had been introduced into the US Congress but failed to pass. In the 1930s, several further attempts were made, culminating in the Gavagan bill, which passed the House of Representatives in 1937 but failed to become law as it was defeated in the US Senate. As with all attempts to pass anti-lynching laws through the US Congress, **filibusters** led by southern Democrats ensured that they were defeated.

KEY TERM

Filibuster
The deliberate use of extensive speech-making in order to prevent a vote on a proposal. In the US Senate, there is a policy of complete freedom of speech. A senator can speak on any topic they like for as long as they like. They do not necessarily have to limit their speech to the topic of debate. A vote on a proposal cannot take place until all senators have had their say. Filibustering was used extensively by southern Democrat senators to prevent a vote on issues such as black American civil rights. On occasion, beds were brought into the Senate chamber so southern senators could speak in relays for days on end. If a vote had not taken place by the end of a session of the US Senate, it had to be reintroduced at a future date.

SOURCE

2

From Walter White's letter to Senator Edward Costigan, 27 November 1933. Walter White was executive secretary of the NAACP. Senator Costigan subsequently co-sponsored a federal anti-lynching bill in the US Senate.

My dear Senator Costigan:

I am writing to inquire if you would be willing to introduce in the coming session of Congress a federal anti-lynching bill.

As you doubtless know, a bill which was drafted by our Legal Committee was introduced in Congress some years ago by Congressman L. C. Dyer of Missouri. This bill passed the lower house in 1922 but was defeated by a filibuster in the Senate led by senators from states which had the worst lynching record. The publicity on the bill played a very important part in the stirring public sentiment against lynching and there has been a steady decrease in the number of lynchings since the Dyer Bill passed the House. This year, however, there has been a most alarming recrudescence. On November 17 the twenty-third lynching since January 1 occurred, against ten during all of 1932. One of the worst of these was the burning of George Armwood at Princess Anne, Maryland. Attorney General Preston Lane sent the names of nine of the lynchers, with evidence against them, to the prosecuting attorney at Princess Anne who refused point blank even to arrest these men. His refusal was based on the belief, so he asserted that if he arrested the men a mob would come and free them.

It is our conviction that only a federal law will be effective in reaching lynchers in those states and those sections of states where no state authority will be effective. Under separate cover I am sending you a copy of the Dyer Bill and copies of briefs sustaining its constitutionality. I send you also copy of 'Lynching and the Law' by J.H. Chadbourn, published by the University of North Carolina Press and of 'Rope and Faggot', a study of lynching made by myself under a fellowship from the Guggenheim Foundation.

There are, of course, lawyers who have doubts as to the constitutionality of a federal bill against lynching. It is our conviction, however, that only the United States Supreme Court can determine whether a bill is constitutional or not. It is our further conviction that the situation is so grave that it is the duty of Congress to pass such a bill and let the United States Supreme Court determine is constitutionality. It is also our feeling that the contention of some of the defenders of lynching or of the opponents of federal legislation that lynching is nothing but murder is not altogether a sound argument. Lynching is more than murder. It is anarchy when a mob sets itself up as a judge, jury and executioner. In doing so it not only violates whatever rights the lynched person has as a citizen of the state in which he is lynched but also deprives him of his rights as a citizen of the federal government...

P.S. – Since this letter was dictated there have occurred at San Jose, California, two lynchings: Thomas H. Thurmond and John Holmes, confessed kidnapper-slayers of Brooke Hart, were taken from jail and hanged on November 26. It is reported in the press that when Governor James Rolph, Jr., was advised of these lynchings he said, 'This is the best lesson that California has ever given the country. We show the country that the state is not going to tolerate kidnapping.'

Later dispatches declare that Governor Rolph has stated that he will pardon any person convicted for this lynching. No one can question the horribleness of the kidnapping and murder with which these two lynched men were charged. At the same time, Governor Rolph's attitude can lead to nothing but a complete breaking down of our whole system of law enforcement. His attitude and that of the District Attorney in Maryland are glaring examples of the need of federal legislation against lynching.

Before 1933, attempts had been made in the southern states to campaign against lynching. A Commission on Interracial Cooperation (CIC) had been created in 1919 to promote better relations between black and white Americans and, in particular, to bring an end to lynching. The CIC's study of lynching entitled 'The Tragedy of Lynching', by Arthur Raper, was published in 1933. That year also offered a new opportunity, as Franklin Roosevelt's government promised a social and economic transformation of the USA. The NAACP saw the issue of introducing an anti-lynching law, as well as ending a major denial of black American civil rights, as a way of raising funds for the organisation. They proposed two anti-lynching bills in 1933.

However, Franklin Roosevelt was extremely reluctant to deal with the subject. For instance, in his presidential message to Congress, in January 1934, he made no proposal to introduce a federal anti-lynching law. In May 1934, he told the secretary of the NAACP, Walter White, that he was unwilling to challenge the power of southern Democrat congressmen and senators as he feared that an anti-lynching law would alienate them, saying he needed their support for other New Deal legislation that would provide work and social welfare for poor and unemployed Americans, including black Americans. Therefore, throughout the years 1933–41, the president remained silent in public on the issue of lynching.

EXTEND YOUR KNOWLEDGE

Walter White (1893–1955)

Walter White was one of the most important civil rights leaders of the first half of the 20th century. As executive secretary of the National Association for the Advancement of Colored People (NAACP), White spearheaded a national effort to achieve political, economic and social rights for black Americans. White, whose blond, blue-eyed looks belied his black American ancestry, was born in Atlanta, Georgia.

Following graduation from Atlanta University in 1916, he worked for an insurance company. His civil rights career began when he organised a protest against the Atlanta Board of Education's plan to drop seventh grade for black students in order to finance the building of a new white high school. After founding the Atlanta branch of the NAACP, he moved on to become assistant secretary for the organisation's national staff in 1918. By 1931, he had become executive secretary, the highest position in the organisation. During this period, White also wrote several books, including two novels, *The Fire in the Flint* (1924) and *Flight* (1926), as well as a study of the factors behind lynching, *Rope and Faggot: A Biography of Judge Lynch* (1929).

As leader of the NAACP, White led the fight for anti-lynching legislation – a cause he was intimately familiar with, having investigated more than 40 such deaths. During his tenure, the NAACP also launched major legal campaigns to end white primaries, poll taxes and segregated housing and education.

Although White primarily focused on improving conditions for black Americans, he recognised the international implications of the race issue and devoted time and effort to them. He was a delegate to the Second Pan-African Congress in 1921 and a member of the Advisory Council for the Government of the Virgin Islands in 1934–35. He was also an adviser to the USA delegation at the founding conference of the United Nations.

Lack of presidential support does not explain fully Roosevelt's failure to address key aspects of race relations like lynching. It was southern opposition, primarily in the US Senate, that prevented legislation from passing. Towards the end of 1933, the NAACP had recruited two leading liberal Democrat senators to support an anti-lynching proposal. These were Robert Wagner of New York and Edward Costigan of Colorado. Costigan introduced an anti-lynching bill in the Senate on 4 January 1934. The key provision was to punish state government officials who failed to apprehend a mob engaged in lynching. A mob was defined as three or more people acting 'without authority of law', with the aim of killing or injuring any person suspected, charged or convicted of a crime. Those state government officials found guilty would face a $5,000 fine and/or a five-year gaol term. In addition, if found guilty of lynching or attempted lynching, the victim or their family would receive $10,000.

The bill went to the Senate Judiciary Committee, which was dominated by northern Democrats, who submitted it for debate in the Senate. There it faced a two-month filibuster. Senate majority leader, a southern Democrat, Joseph Robinson of Arkansas, in particular, tried to kill the proposal, and in June 1934 the Senate adjourned with no vote on the issue. The bill was reintroduced in 1935 and failed to go to a vote due to another southern Democrat filibuster. Northern Democrats refused to push the issue, for fear of splitting the Democrat Party in the middle of passing important New Deal social and economic reform legislation.

In 1937 and 1938, another attempt was made to introduce anti-lynching legislation. The bill was introduced into the House of Representatives by Democrat congressman Joseph A. Gavagan, who represented the black American area of Harlem in New York City. At the time of the introduction of the anti-lynching bill, a high-profile lynching case appeared in the national media. Two black Americans were seized by a white mob in Duck Hill, Mississippi. They tortured their victims by searing their flesh with blasts from gasoline blow torches. The white mob then burnt the bodies. The story was read out in the chamber of the House of Representatives when the Gavagan bill was being debated. Two days later, the Gavagan anti-lynching bill was passed by the House and then sent to the Senate for debate; it was defeated. By that time, the USA was facing another economic recession and the president faced a backlash from southern Democrats and Republicans over his attempts to reform the membership of the US Supreme Court. Southern Democrat senators engaged in a filibuster, which again killed any prospect of the anti-lynching bill passing. In the Congressional debates on the anti-lynching proposal, several southern Democrats made their views clear. John Rankin of Mississippi claimed the bill would encourage black men to think that they could rape white women, and Edward Cox of Georgia claimed the bill was an attempt to break the spirit of the white south and introduce social equality. In 1940, another attempt was made to pass the Gavagan anti-lynching bill. It passed through the House of Representatives in January 1940, but again failed to pass through the Senate because of a southern Democrat filibuster. The NAACP became resigned to the fact that a federal anti-lynching law was unlikely to become law. Walter White, the executive secretary of the NAACP, in a personal letter to a colleague, explained the organisation's limited support, saying there was a growing feeling among NAACP members that a disproportionate amount of time and money was being put into the anti-lynching fight, to the neglect of their other work.

Faced with such opposition within Congress, the attempt by the NAACP and Democrats sympathetic to federal anti-lynching legislation failed during the New Deal years.

SOURCE

3 From an article in the black American magazine *The Crisis*, published in January 1934. It was written by W.E.B. Du Bois. Du Bois was the founder of *The Crisis* and a major force in the creation of the NAACP in 1909. The article was entitled 'Segregation' and Du Bois caused controversy by supporting it. Although a founder of the NAACP, by 1934, Du Bois's views were at variance with those held by the head of the NAACP at that time, Walter White.

The thinking colored people of the United States must stop being stampeded by the word segregation. The opposition to racial segregation is not and should not be any distaste or unwillingness of colored people to work with each other, to cooperate with each other, to live with each other. The opposition to segregation is an opposition to discrimination. The experience in the United States has been that usually when there is racial segregation, there is also racial discrimination.

But two things do not necessarily go together, and there should never be an opposition to segregation pure and simple unless segregation does involve discrimination. Not only is there no objection to colored people living beside colored people if the surroundings and treatment involve no discrimination, if streets are well lighted, if there is water, sewerage and police protection, and if anybody of any color who wishes, can live in the neighbourhood.

The NAACP have never officially opposed separate Negro organizations - such as churches, schools and business and cultural organizations. It has never denied the recurrent necessity of united separate action on the part of Negroes for self-defence and self-development; but it has insistently and continually pointed out that such action is in any case a necessary evil involving often a recognition from within the very color line which we are fighting without. That race pride and race loyalty, Negro ideals and Negro unity, have a place and function today, the NAACP never has denied and never can deny.

But all this simply touches the whole question of racial organization and initiative. No matter what we wish or say, the vast majority of Negroes are born in colored homes, educated in separate colored schools, attend separate colored churches, marry colored mates. Here is segregation with a vengeance, and its problems must be met and its course guided. It would be idiotic simply to sit on the side lines and yell, 'No segregation' in an increasingly segregated world.

ACTIVITY
KNOWLEDGE CHECK

The failure to address black grievances

1 Draw a spider diagram identifying what you regard as the three most important grievances that black Americans had during the New Deal years.

2 Compare your answers with those of a partner and decide on your combined top three answers.

3 What reasons can you give for the failure of anti-lynching laws in the USA during the New Deal years?

HOW FAR DID THE NEW DEAL BENEFIT BLACK AMERICANS?

The New Deal aimed to bring about a social and economic transformation in the USA. Franklin D. Roosevelt had been elected president at the height of the economic depression. However, although the New Deal brought many social and economic changes and helped to prevent the US economy from collapsing, it had a limited impact on improving the civil rights of black Americans.

The effect of the Agricultural Adjustment Administration (AAA) on black farmers

The 1920s was known as an era of economic prosperity as the US economy experienced unprecedented economic growth. However, American agriculture did not share in this prosperity. A fall in agricultural prices affected many farmers. This was due in part to over-production. When FDR came to power, he aimed to rectify the situation. Of all the New Deal issues facing the Democrat administration of F.D. Roosevelt, agriculture took up more time than any other problem. One of the first acts of Roosevelt during his first 100 days in office was the passage of the Agricultural Adjustment Act on 12 May 1933. The Act provided a plan to compensate farmers for voluntary cutbacks in agricultural production. Congress put aside $100 million to compensate farmers who slaughtered surplus pigs or ploughed up surplus corn and grain in a bid to stabilise farm prices. To supervise the agricultural reforms, the Agricultural Adjustment Administration (AAA) was created under Henry Wallace. To assist the process of reducing agricultural production, the Farm Credit Administration (FCA) helped farmers to pay their mortgages and the Consumer Credit Administration gave loans to farmers. By the end of 1934, Wallace announced that there had been significant declines in wheat, cotton and corn production, which helped to stabilise agricultural prices and, with it, farm incomes. Between 1932 and 1935, farm incomes rose by 58 percent. Unfortunately, this did not lead to lower prices for consumers.

However, although the New Deal helped to stabilise US agriculture, black American farmers did not always benefit. In the southern states, sharecropping predominated among black farmers, and small groups of rich white farmers dominated agriculture. Nearly 40 percent of all black American workers in the USA in the New Deal years made their living as sharecroppers and tenant farmers. The rich white farmers dominated the county committees set up to administer AAA funds. Although 700,000 farms existed in the cotton-growing area of the USA, the vast majority of the money received for farmer subsistence went to the large farms owned by white Americans. Between 1933 and 1934, 100,000 black tenant farmers and sharecroppers were forced off their land, as white landlords reduced their acreage in order to qualify for AAA financial payments. By 1940, approximately 200,000 black farmers had been driven off their land.

In an attempt to gain some AAA financial assistance and to stop evictions from farms, many black farmers organised themselves into lobby groups, such as the Alabama Sharecroppers Union and the Southern Tenant Farmers Union. Unfortunately, these groups had only very limited success in trying to prevent evictions.

In 1936, the US Supreme Court declared the AAA unconstitutional, stating that the federal government had exceeded its powers. In 1937, the Roosevelt administration set up the Farm Security Administration (FSA), which aimed to help tenant farmers. It made efforts to give black farmers a voice in the allocation of financial assistance by appointing them to agency committees throughout the southern states. However, opposition from southern Democrats in Congress and white-dominated southern state governments forced the Roosevelt administration to withdraw black American representation on FSA committees. In 1938, a second Agricultural Adjustment Act was passed by Congress but, like the first Act, it gave little support to black farmers.

Segregation in the Civilian Conservation Corps (CCC)

An important aspect of the New Deal was to address the high level of unemployment caused by the economic depression. When FDR became president, 13 million people, 25 percent of the workforce, were idle. On 31 March 1933, the Emergency Conservation Work Act created the Civilian Conservation Corps (CCC). Its aim was to provide work experience, initially for young men aged 17 to 25 years. They were to be housed in camps organised and run by the US army, but under the general direction of the Department of the Interior. They received $30 a month, of which $25 was to be sent home to the workers' families. By August 1933, 275,000 young men were housed in 1,300 CCC camps across the USA. By 1942, when the CCC came to an end during the Second World War, over three million young men had gone through the programme. The CCC workers engaged in conservation projects, such as improving accommodation and road access to national parks and building state parks. They planted trees, fought forest fires and built bridges and roads. They also had job training opportunities to learn new skills.

SOURCE 4 Black American young men at a segregated Civilian Conservation Corps camp in New Jersey in 1933.

SOURCE 5 A letter from the head of the Civilian Conservation Corps, Robert Fechner, to the president of the NAACP, Thomas L. Griffith, outlining why the Civilian Conservation Corps was introducing racially segregated CCC camps.

21 September 1935

Mr. Thomas L. Griffith, Jr., President National Association for the Advancement of Colored People, 1105 E. Vernon Avenue, Los Angeles, California

Dear Mr. Griffith:

The President has called my attention to the letter you addressed to him on September 14, 1935, in which you ask for information relating to the policy of segregation in CCC camps.

The law enacted by Congress setting up Emergency Conservation Work specifically indicated that there should be no discrimination because of color. I have faithfully endeavoured to obey the spirit and letter of this, as well as all other provisions of the law.

At the very beginning of this work, I consulted with many representative individuals and groups who were interested in the work, and the decision to segregate white enrollees, negro enrollees, and war veterans, was generally approved. I believe that the record of the past thirty months will sustain the wisdom of our decision.

While segregation has been the general policy, it has not been inflexible, and we have a number of companies containing a small number of negro enrollees. I am satisfied that the negro enrollees themselves prefer to be in companies composed exclusively of their own race.

This segregation is not discrimination and cannot be so construed. The negro companies are assigned to the same types of work, have identical equipment, are served the same food, and have the same quarters as white enrollees. I have personally visited many negro CCC companies and have talked with the enrollees and have never received one single complaint. I want to assure you that I am just as sincerely interested as anyone in making this work of the greatest possible value to all who have a part in it.

Sincerely yours, (Sgn) ROBERT FECHNER Director

A Level Exam-Style Question Section A

Study Source 5 before you answer this question.

Assess the value of the source for revealing the impact of the Civilian Conservation Corps on black Americans.

Explain your answer, using the source, information given about its origins and your own knowledge about the historical context. (20 marks)

Tip

It is important to consider the intended audience for the sources, and the extent to which the information contained within the sources provides sufficient information on black Americans in the CCC.

Ten percent of places in the CCC were reserved for black Americans, and between 1933 and 1942, 275,000 young black men went through the CCC programme. However, black Americans faced racial discrimination. In Clarke County, Georgia, about 60 miles north-east of Atlanta, not one black

American resident was chosen to attend CCC camps, even though black Americans comprised 60 percent of the population. Black Americans in Georgia eventually received CCC places only when the federal government threatened to withhold all CCC funding from that state. The white state governor, Eugene Talmadge, had opposed black involvement. In Mississippi, where black Americans comprised 50 percent of the state's population, only 46 black Americans were recruited by the CCC, which was only 1.7 percent of the state's black population.

In the early years of the CCC, camps were racially integrated. It even stated in the act of Congress that established the CCC that there should be no racial discrimination in the CCC. However, these integrated camps were disbanded in July 1935, when CCC director, Robert Fechner, issued a directive ordering the complete segregation of black and white enrolees. Fechner acted in response to complaints from local white communities and politicians in the South, who wanted Jim Crow Laws extended to the CCC. Yet opposition was not limited to the South. Opposition was also against all-black CCC camps. In Pennsylvania, a local white community petitioned the CCC to cancel the creation of a black CCC camp on the grounds that local white girls might want to go out with young black men.

SOURCE

From an article entitled 'A Negro in the CCC' by black American, Luther C. Wandall. It was published in the black American magazine *The Crisis* in August 1935. The author was a New Yorker and here gives a first-hand picture of CCC life.

During the two years of its previous existence I had heard many conflicting reports concerning the Civilian Conservation Corps, President Roosevelt's pet project. One boy told me that he almost froze to death one night out in Washington. Some said that the colored got all the leftovers. Others said that everything was all right. But my brother, who is a World War veteran, advised me emphatically: 'I wouldn't be in anything connected with the Army.'

So it was with some apprehension that I surveyed the postal card instructing me to see Miss A. at the Home Relief Bureau the following Friday. At this Bureau I signed a paper, of which I kept two copies, and the Bureau one. This paper asserted that I was 'accepted for enrollment' and should report the following Monday 'to U.S. Army authorities for further registration.'

One thing I saw at the Bureau increased my apprehension. So many of the boys who appeared in answer to cards were excused because they had been 'dishonorably discharged' in a previous enlistment. It was impossible to tell whether they were disappointed or not, but they were not always discreditable-looking persons.

According to instructions, I went Monday morning at 8 o'clock to Pier I, North River. There were, I suppose, more than 1,000 boys standing about the pier. And here I got another shock. Many of the boys carried suitcases. I had not been instructed that we would leave that day. But still, I reasoned, we would be given time to go home and tell our folks goodbye.

The colored boys were a goodly sprinkling of the whole. A few middle-aged men were in evidence. These, it turned out, were going as cooks. A good many Spaniards and Italians were about. A good-natured, lively, crowd, typical of New York.

At eight o'clock we were rapidly admitted to the pier, given papers and herded into the warehouse, out on the water. And here the 'fun' began. A few boys were being admitted from time to time to a lower platform through a small gate in the center. And of course, everyone in that mob was anxious to get there.

At first there was a semblance of order. The men in charge of us formed us into companies of fifty as we came up. But suddenly a U.S. Army officer in full uniform entered the door. A mighty roar went up from the boys, who surged forward, evidently thinking that they could follow him. But the officer, a tall handsome fellow, moving with easy grace, completely ignored them, and passed on through.

With some effort we were finally forced back into a so-called line. But a newspaper photographer appeared. The line broke again, and after that confusion reigned for the most part.

There were no seats where we were. So I stood about until two o'clock before I finally got through that little gate. We answered questions, and signed papers, and then a group of us marched over to U.S. Army headquarters on Whitehall Street in charge of an Army officer.

Here we stripped for a complete physical examination. Then we were grouped into busloads. Each busload of 35 ate a meal at South Ferry before boarding the bus. This meal consisted of beans, pickles, bread, coffee and butter, and was eaten out of Army mess-kits.

So there I was, on a bus bound for Camp Dix, New Jersey, without having prepared or told anyone goodbye. Our bus was comfortable, and equipped with a radio, so the ride was a very enjoyable one.

A Level Exam-Style Question Section B

'New Deal programmes introduced during the presidency of F.D. Roosevelt failed black Americans.'

How far do you agree with this statement? (20 marks)

Tip

This type of question requires a balanced, analytical response. You will be expected to provide evidence that New Deal programmes treated black Americans as second-class citizens in the southern states. However, this should be balanced with evidence to state that black Americans did receive help and assistance, but not as much as white Americans.

Differential wages in the National Recovery Administration (NRA)

When the New Deal began in 1933, the organisation that was seen as its centrepiece was the National Recovery Administration (NRA), created by the National Industrial Recovery Act (NIRA) of June 1933. The NIRA created two administrations. The Public Works Administration (PWA) was allocated $3.3 billion to fund the construction of highways, public buildings, bridges, tunnels and military equipment, such as naval ships. The PWA was meant to offer immediate work for the large numbers of unemployed. The other part of the Act created the NRA. This was placed under the leadership of General Hugh Johnson. It also hoped to create jobs and raise wages. It aimed to set codes of fair practice, including a basic wage and safety standards. The NRA codes included a 40-hour working week, a minimum wage of $13 a week ($12 in the South) and a prohibition on using child labour, which was defined as employing anyone under the age of 16 years. Those businesses willing to participate in the scheme were awarded a Blue Eagle logo.

However, black Americans faced considerable racial discrimination under the NRA codes. The first approved NRA code was for the cotton textile industry. Although large numbers of black Americans worked in the industry, they tended to occupy unskilled jobs such as cleaners and manual workers. When industry codes were drawn up, Congress deliberately excluded these types of jobs. In other NRA codes, workers received a flat percentage increase in their wages. For instance, in the hotel industry code, a 20 percent increase was agreed for all workers, but whereas bellboys, who were predominantly black Americans, were given a 20 percent increase on $51 a month wages, white hotel clerks received a 20 percent increase on their monthly salaries of $100.

An area of work where black American women predominated was in domestic service and household work. In 1934, a group named the National Association for Domestic Workers announced itself from its headquarters in Jackson, Mississippi. The group complained that the so-called average wage for domestic workers of $3.50 per week was far too low and requested a much higher wage.

Racial discrimination in other New Deal legislation

One of the landmark changes brought about during the New Deal years was the recognition of trade union rights to collectively bargain for better wages and conditions for their members. Section 7(a) of the National Industrial Recovery Act of 1933 and the Wagner Act of 1935 gave trade unions this important right. However, black Americans were under-represented in trade unions. In 1930, 19 major trade unions excluded black Americans from membership because of racism. It was estimated by the NAACP that in 1930 total black American union membership was 50,000 out of a national total of 3.4 million. Half of the 50,000 were in one union: the all-black American Brotherhood of Sleeping Car Porters on the railways. By increasing job security for union members under Section 7(a) and the Wagner Act, black American workers were disadvantaged. When it was proposed that Section 7(a) allowed one union to represent all workers in a particular factory (including women workers), known as a closed shop, the NAACP stated that it was not a closed shop that was in the offing, but a white shop.

Another landmark reform of the New Deal was the Social Security Act of 1935. For the first time, federal funding was provided for old-age pensions. However, the law excluded domestic servants and agricultural workers, areas which provided 65 percent of the work available for black Americans. Thomas Arnold Hill, a black American civil rights activist, who was a leader of the Urban League, stated in 1936 that he felt the New Deal legislation benefited white workers and left black workers in an inferior position, largely ignored or excluded.

How the New Deal aided black Americans, including welfare benefits and relief

However, the New Deal also opened up opportunities for black Americans in the federal government.

- In 1934, a black American, Robert Weaver, was appointed as President Roosevelt's special adviser on the Economic Status of the Negro. His rise was due in large part to Harold Ickes, the Secretary of the Interior from 1933 to 1946. Ickes had been a former president of the Chicago branch of the NAACP, and in his role in the PWA, in particular its housing division, Ickes directly aided black Americans. The housing division, which became the US Housing Authority, introduced **racial quotas** for its construction projects, and by 1940, black Americans occupied one-third of its housing units.

- The biggest relief agency set up by the New Deal was the Works Progress Administration (WPA), under Harry Hopkins. Between 1936 and 1940, the WPA provided work for 350,000 black Americans every year. Its educational programmes employed over 5,000 black American teachers and taught 250,000 black Americans how to read and write. In the National Youth Administration, the head of the Negro Affairs Department, black American Mary McLeod Bethune, provided skills training for 500,000 young black Americans.

- The one area where black Americans did benefit from the New Deal was through the creation of the Resettlement Administration in 1935. It was later renamed the Farm Security Administration. The Administration aimed to co-ordinate the various New Deal programmes designed to help the rural poor. It was placed under the direction of Rexford Tugwell, a close adviser to the president. Tugwell genuinely tried to run a 'colour blind' administration. Of its 150 rural projects, 115 were all white, nine all black and 26 were mixed-race projects. In Gee's Bend, Alabama, an all-black community received financial aid and assistance. The Administration gave the community cattle, seeds and fertiliser to help them become self-sufficient. In 1937, the Administration purchased land worth $122,000 and subdivided this among the community's black farming population. However, the Administration's life was short-lived, and it closed down in 1938 because it lost its federal government funding.

KEY TERM

Racial quota
As black Americans comprised ten percent of the US population, ten percent of jobs created by federal programmes were to be allocated to them.

ACTIVITY
KNOWLEDGE CHECK

The impact of the New Deal on black Americans
From the information above on New Deal legislation, draw a grid with the names of New Deal laws as headings. Underneath each heading, write down whether or not the legislation benefited black Americans, explaining the reasons for your choice.

EXTRACT

3 From Vivienne Sanders, *Race Relations in the USA since 1900* (2003).

New Deal programmes helped blacks by providing one million jobs, nearly 50,000 public housing units, and financial assistance and skilled occupations training for half a million black youths.

EXTRACT

4 From Michael Hiltzik, *The New Deal: A Modern History* (2011).

Issues of race and racial justice had no place in the Democratic platform [of 1932] and no part in candidates' speeches. A questionnaire prepared by the NAACP seeking candidates' views on racial issues went unanswered by Franklin D Roosevelt.

EXTRACT

5 From Michael Parrish, *The Anxious Decades, America in Prosperity and Depression, 1920–41* (1992).

The New Deal did much in one decade to challenge social status but with respect to black Americans critics complained that it did not do nearly enough to attack historic patterns of bigotry and discrimination... Roosevelt did not attempt to alter the two most obvious forms of oppression afflicting the majority of black citizens in the South: segregation and disenfranchisement.

EXTRACT 6

From Joshua Freeman, American Social History Project, *Who Built America? Working People and the Nation's Economy, Politics, Culture and Society*, Volume 2 (1992).

Blacks suffered more deeply than other Americans the ravages of poverty in the Depression. New Deal public works programs did alleviate some African-American destitution... Yet racism continued in... public works and housing programs. President Roosevelt and his cabinet officers received hundreds of letters complaining of the discriminatory actions of local relief officials.

THINKING HISTORICALLY Evidence (6c)

Comparing and evaluating historians' arguments

The New Deal of 1933–41 was seen as a significant period of US history. It involved the active involvement of the federal government in trying to get the economy out of economic depression. By March 1933, when Franklin D. Roosevelt became president, 25 percent of the US workforce was unemployed. The New Deal saw a major increase in the role and scope of the federal government and the beginnings of a welfare state of federal social welfare support for US citizens.

Read Extracts 3–6 from historians and then answer the following questions.

1 Compare the four accounts and identify factual statements or claims that they agree upon. Make a list of these points.

2 Look carefully at how the historians use language. Do they use equally cautious language in making their claims or is one more confident and assertive than the other? Which of the historians is over-claiming?

The work of Eleanor Roosevelt

The president's wife, known as the First Lady, has always played an important role in the USA. Up to 1933, this role was overwhelmingly ceremonial and social. First Ladies supported their husbands during social functions and trips around the country. In 1933, things changed. For the first time, the First Lady played an important role in deciding policy. This was Eleanor Roosevelt. More than any other First Lady, before or since, Eleanor helped to forge the direction of national policy. Her intelligence, powerful personality and social and political links gave her influence. Eleanor Roosevelt regularly advised her husband on aspects of federal policy and championed the position of women and ethnic minorities. She became an unofficial member of F.D. Roosevelt's advisory team.

Eleanor Roosevelt's impact was almost immediate. Two days after FDR was inaugurated president, she held her first press conference. During the New Deal years, she held 348 such conferences, explaining to the press what she felt ought to be done. In particular, she highlighted the plight of young people faced with extreme poverty and lack of opportunity. Her link to the American public was also enhanced through letter-writing. She encouraged Americans, mainly young Americans, to write to her at the White House. Over 300,000 letters were received by her from 1933 onwards, during the time her husband was president. By January 1934, she had received thousands of letters describing racial violence, poverty and homelessness created by racial discrimination, and pleading for some type of assistance. She frequently forwarded some of these letters to Harry Hopkins, cabinet member responsible for much of the New Deal relief programmes. She also pressured National Recovery administrator Donald Richberg to investigate the race-based wage differentials implemented by southern industries, and asked Navy secretary Claude Swanson why black Americans were confined to mess hall assignments. Her efforts achieved very limited success. In the US Navy, black Americans remained in servile positions on board American warships.

Eleanor Roosevelt lent her support to the NAACP campaign to introduce an anti-lynching law. This brought her into conflict with her husband, President Franklin Roosevelt, who believed he could not openly support such legislation as it would alienate the southern white Democrats.

One of the most prominent black Americans to participate in the administration of the New Deal was Mary McLeod Bethune. On the insistence of Eleanor Roosevelt, President Roosevelt made Mary his special adviser on minority affairs in 1935, the year she founded her own civil rights organisation, the National Council of Negro Women. The following year, she became the chairperson of an informal 'Black Cabinet', a group of federally appointed black American officials, to help plan priorities for the black American community. It was occasionally referred to in the press as the 'Black Brains Trust', to mirror an informal set of white advisers to the president called the 'Brains Trust'. The most important members of the 'Black Cabinet' were: Mary McLeod Bethune; William Hastie, assistant solicitor in the Department of the Interior; Robert Weaver, adviser on Negro Affairs in the Public Works Administration; and Robert Vann, assistant to the US Attorney General. They provided information and advice to Eleanor Roosevelt. In 1936, Mary McLeod Bethune achieved national prominence through her appointment as director of the Negro Affairs Division of the National Youth Administration (NYA).

However, the ability of Eleanor Roosevelt to improve the position of black Americans in New Deal programmes proved limited. For instance, the Tennessee Valley Authority helped bring electricity to the impoverished Upper South region, which aided both black and white Americans. However, black American workers were not allowed to live next to white workers at the TVA camp at Norris, Tennessee. In fact, almost every work relief camp and construction crew working on New Deal projects was divided on a racial basis.

Nevertheless, Eleanor Roosevelt was associated with one of the most high-profile symbolic gestures in favour of black Americans during the New Deal years. In early 1939, the prominent black American opera singer, Marion Anderson, was invited to sing in Washington DC on Easter Sunday as part of a national celebration. She was scheduled to sing at Constitution Hall, near the White House. However, Constitution Hall was owned by an all-white organisation, the Daughters of the American Revolution. They refused to allow a black American to sing in their hall. As a result, on 27 February 1939, Eleanor Roosevelt made a public display of resigning from the Daughters of the American Revolution. Instead, she arranged for Marion Anderson to sing on the steps of the Lincoln Memorial in central Washington DC. She got President F.D. Roosevelt to give public support and, on Easter Sunday, 75,000 people turned up to see Marion Anderson sing. Even though they were invited, Vice President John Nance Garner of Texas and all but one of the US Supreme Court failed to appear. The event attracted the biggest crowd to hear a black American until Martin Luther King made his 'I have a dream' speech in August 1963.

SOURCE

7

A letter from Eleanor Roosevelt to Walter White, the executive secretary of the NAACP, who was leading a nationwide campaign for a federal anti-lynching law. The letter is dated 19 March 1936. Senator Van Nuys was supporting an anti-lynching bill. Senator Byrnes was a prominent white southern Democrat at the time.

PRIVATE AND CONFIDENTIAL.

The White House

Washington

My dear Mr White,

Before I received your letter today I had been in to the President talking to him about your letter enclosing that of the Attorney General. I told him it seemed rather terrible that one could get nothing done and I did not blame you in feeling that there was no interest in this very serious question. I asked him if there was any possibility of getting even one step taken, and said the difficulty is that it is unconstitutional for the Federal government to step in in the lynching situation. The Government has only been allowed to do anything about kidnapping because of its interstate aspect, and even that has not yet been appealed and they are not sure that it will be declared constitutional.

The President feels that lynching is a question of education in the states, rallying good citizens and creating public opinion so that the localities themselves will wipe it out. However, if it were done by a Northerner, it will have an antagonistic effect. I will talk to him again about the Van Nuys resolution and will also talk to Senator Byrnes and get his point of view. I am deeply troubled about the whole situation as it seems to be a terrible thing to stand by and let it continue and feel that one cannot speak out about his feeling. I think your next step is to talk to prominent members of the Senate.

Very sincerely yours,

Eleanor Roosevelt

SOURCE
8

Eleanor Roosevelt speaking out against lynching at the Second Congress of Negro Youth in Washington DC on 13 January 1939. She is with Mary McLeod Bethune, director of Negro Youth Affairs at the National Youth Administration.

EXTEND YOUR KNOWLEDGE

Eleanor Roosevelt (1884–1962)

Eleanor was born into one of America's most privileged families, the Roosevelts. In 1905, she married another member of the Roosevelt family, Franklin, a distant cousin.

In the 1920s she began her own political career, speaking on issues such as women's rights, labour unions and black equality. When FDR became president, she championed these issues throughout the New Deal and war years. She constantly pressured FDR to appoint women and minority members to federal positions of influence and supported the appointment of Mary McLeod Bethune to the National Youth Administration. During the Second World War, she was a major defender of the black American Tuskegee airmen against white criticism in Congress. A fighter training school had been established, at Tuskegee, for black airmen, but many white politicians from the southern states thought black Americans should not have combat roles.

Eleanor survived her husband, who died in April 1945, by 17 years. Under his successor, President Truman, she represented the USA in the United Nations.

Impact of the New Deal on the voting patterns of black Americans

Before 1933, black Americans had primarily voted for the Republican Party. They had done so for a variety of reasons. The Republican Party was the party of Abraham Lincoln, who had issued the Emancipation Proclamation during the Civil War and had been responsible for the abolition of slavery in 1865. In addition, after Lincoln's assassination, Radical Republicans in the US Congress had been responsible for the creation of the Freedmen's Bureau, which offered financial help and assistance to freed black Americans. During the Republican presidencies of Andrew Johnson and Ulysses Grant, the Fourteenth and Fifteenth Amendments of the US Constitution had been passed. These granted black Americans equal protection of the law (under the Fourteenth Amendment) and the right to vote (under the Fifteenth Amendment). These amendments were passed during the period of Reconstruction when the Republicans encouraged black Americans, who at that time lived overwhelmingly in the former Confederacy, to participate in politics for the first time.

It was only in 1928 that the Democrat candidate for the presidency, Al Smith, made a concerted attempt to win the black American vote. Smith was a northerner from New York and the first Catholic to be nominated by a major party. He enlisted the support of James Weldon Johnson, the executive secretary of the NAACP, and Walter White, the assistant executive secretary of the NAACP, to win black support. Walter White even created a 'Smith for President Colored League'. However, Smith lost badly to Republican Herbert Hoover. In Chicago, one of the largest northern cities, the Democrat Party received 11 percent of the black vote in 1920, 10 percent in 1924 and 27 percent in 1928.

In 1932, in spite of the economic depression, black Americans voters still supported the Republican Party. However, the radical social and economic programmes of the New Deal began attracting black Americans in the north. The change in voting pattern began to appear in the 1934 congressional elections. In Chicago, black Democrat Arthur W. Mitchell defeated black Republican Oscar De Priest to become the first black Democrat elected to Congress.

The major breakthrough for the Democrats came in the presidential and congressional elections of 1936 when, for the first time, that party received the majority of black American votes. Many black Americans voted for F.D. Roosevelt as a person rather than for the Democrats, as his New Deal programmes offered jobs and hope to many poor and unemployed black Americans. From that election on, black Americans consistently voted Democrat in large numbers. In Chicago, the Democrat vote among black Americans was 49 percent, a very large increase on 1928 and 1932. Even though the Democrat Party still contained southern white Americans, who supported legal racial segregation, F.D. Roosevelt could put together a coalition of supporters, which made the Democrats the dominant political party in the USA until the 1970s. Its supporters included Irish, German and Italian Americans, Catholics, Jews, black Americans, trade unionists and southern white Americans. While the Roosevelt coalition of support began to come apart in the 1970s, black American support for the Democrat Party continued into the 21st century.

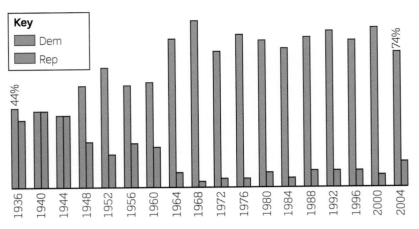

Figure 5.2 Party identification of black American voters from 1936 to 2004.

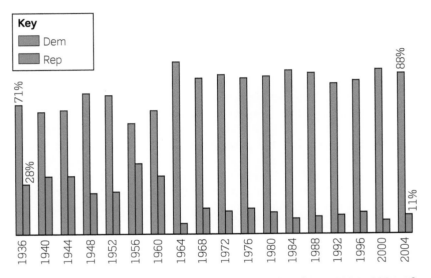

Figure 5.3 How black Americans voters voted in presidential elections from 1936 to 2004. After 1936, there was a major and permanent change in the voting pattern of black Americans.

ACTIVITY
KNOWLEDGE CHECK

Changing voting patterns

1 What reasons can you give for why black Americans tended to vote for the Republican Party up to the New Deal years?

2 What do Figures 5.2 and 5.3 tell us about the impact of the New Deal years on the voting patterns of black voters in presidential elections and in voter identification?

ACTIVITY
SUMMARY

The New Deal and race relations, 1933–41

1 Write a brief description of the position of black Americans in US society in 1933 with respect to grievances and lack of civil rights, and a brief description of the position of black Americans in 1941.

   a) What differences can you identify and what impact did these have on the lives of black Americans?

   b) What do you regard as the most important change which affected the position of black Americans in US society during the New Deal years?

2 Produce a spider diagram that shows the beneficial changes made during the New Deal years which affected black Americans.

3 Write notes on how the following affected the lives of black Americans:

   a) the federal anti-lynching campaign

   b) the creation of New Deal agencies, such as the CCC and the AAA

   c) the impact of the Wagner Act and the Social Security Act on black Americans.

 WIDER READING

Clements, P. *Prosperity, Depression and the New Deal*, Hodder Murray (2008)

Kelley, R. *To Make Our World Anew*, Oxford University Press (2005)

Murphy, D. *United States 1917–2008*, Collins (2008)

Patterson, D., Willoughby, S. and Willoughby, D. *Civil Rights in the USA*, Heinemann (2001)

Riches, W.T.M. *The Civil Rights Movement: Struggle and Resistance*, Palgrave (2010)

Sklaroff, L. *Black Culture and the New Deal*, University of North Carolina Press (2014)

Tuck, G.N. *We Ain't What We Ought to Be*, Harvard University Press (2011)

3.6 'I have a dream', 1954–68

KEY QUESTIONS

- To what extent did black American civil rights improve between 1954 and 1963?
- How significant were the Civil Rights Acts of 1964 and 1968 and the Voting Rights Act of 1965 in bringing change to black American civil rights?
- How far did internal divisions within the black American community affect the quest for greater civil rights?

INTRODUCTION

The years 1954–68 were seen as the height of the civil rights movement. Beginning with a landmark decision in the US Supreme Court in 1954, *Brown* v *the Board of Education, Topeka, Kansas*, and ending with the assassination of Martin Luther King Jr, this period saw the end of legal segregation in the USA. Across the USA, but beginning in the South, ordinary black Americans began taking direct action to gain full civil rights.

The period was also characterised by the importance of key individuals. In 1953, President Eisenhower nominated former California governor, Earl Warren, as chief justice to the US Supreme Court. Under his leadership, the US Supreme Court provided vital legal support for the ending of legal segregation. This period also produced the person most associated with the leadership of the civil rights movement, Martin Luther King. A Baptist Church minister, King became the symbol of peaceful, non-violent change, which was a dominant theme in the black struggle for equal civil rights. His example helped to create the Southern Christian Leadership Conference (SCLC) and the Student Non-Violent Co-ordinating Committee (SNCC), and enthused the growth of the Congress on Racial Equality (CORE). Throughout the period 1955–68, King dominated the struggle.

Martin Luther King's non-violent campaign for equal civil rights for black Americans was aided by the actions of presidents John F. Kennedy and Lyndon Johnson. Their actions were able to put into law many of the aims and hopes of the King-led civil rights movement.

However, although Martin Luther King may have been seen as the unofficial leader of the civil rights movement, the quest for full civil rights was a fragmented and multi-faceted movement containing many different groups. Some rejected Martin Luther King's non-violent approach and adopted more radical aims and tactics. The Black Panther Movement and Malcolm X and his supporters were centred in black communities in the north, rather than in the South where King received strong support.

By the time of King's assassination in April 1968, a revolution had occurred in the quest for full civil rights for black Americans. However, the black community was divided into various factions, many demanding radical social and economic change in addition to civil equality under the law.

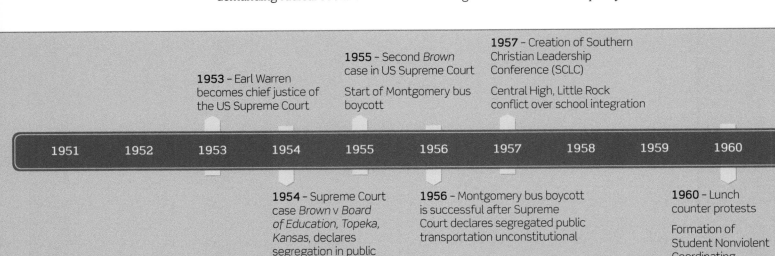

1953 – Earl Warren becomes chief justice of the US Supreme Court

1955 – Second *Brown* case in US Supreme Court

Start of Montgomery bus boycott

1957 – Creation of Southern Christian Leadership Conference (SCLC)

Central High, Little Rock conflict over school integration

1951   1952   1953   1954   1955   1956   1957   1958   1959   1960

1954 – Supreme Court case *Brown* v *Board of Education, Topeka, Kansas*, declares segregation in public schools unconstitutional

1956 – Montgomery bus boycott is successful after Supreme Court declares segregated public transportation unconstitutional

1960 – Lunch counter protests

Formation of Student Nonviolent Coordinating Committee (SNCC)

TO WHAT EXTENT DID BLACK AMERICAN CIVIL RIGHTS IMPROVE BETWEEN 1954 AND 1963?

The role of Earl Warren and the US Supreme Court

The beginning of the revolution in black American civil rights came with a landmark decision by the US Supreme Court. On 17 May 1954, in *Brown* v *Board of Education of Topeka, Kansas*, in a unanimous 9–0 decision, the Court overturned the previous Supreme Court decision of *Plessy* v *Ferguson* in 1896. That decision had created the concept of 'separate but equal' educational facilities for black and white children, and reinforced the policies of state governments that had introduced legal racial segregation.

The *Brown* v *Board of Education* case was brought to the US Supreme Court in 1953 by the NAACP. Its chief lawyer, black American Thurgood Marshall, argued that 'separate but equal' educational facilities in public schools was a breach of the Fourteenth Amendment of the US Constitution which granted all US citizens equal protection of the law. This was the culmination of efforts by the NAACP to overturn *Plessy* v *Ferguson*. For instance, in 1950, in the case of *Sweatt* v *Painter*, the US Supreme Court under Chief Justice Carl Vinson, had demanded a $3 million upgrade of the facilities at the all-black Prairie View University in Texas because its facilities were deemed inferior to those of all-white colleges in the state.

In the *Brown* v *Board of Education* case, the unanimity of the decision, where all nine Supreme Court justices agreed to overturn *Plessy* v *Ferguson*, was a great achievement for Earl Warren. He was able to persuade other justices, such as a supporter of segregation, Stanley Reed, that a unanimous decision was essential in order to ensure the significance of the change, in particular to those southern states that were likely to resist the decision. Justice Reed had argued that it was up to the US Congress to change the law on racial integration, not the Supreme Court.

This was the first major attack on legal segregation within the South. It met with considerable criticism from southern white politicians. As a result, the US Supreme Court issued a declaration in 1955, called the *Brown II* case, where it demanded the speedy integration of all **public schools** within the USA.

The Supreme Court did not limit itself to dealing with legal segregation in public schools. In 1956, in the case of *Browder* v *Gayle*, it declared legal segregation of black and white passengers on public transportation within cities unconstitutional. This decision gave a massive boost to Martin Luther King's campaign to end segregation in Montgomery, Alabama. In 1960, in the Supreme Court case *Boynton* v *Virginia*, the Court ruled that segregated bus depots were illegal. In 1962, in another case, *Bailey* v *Patterson*, the Supreme Court declared legal segregation on interstate public transportation also unconstitutional. Freedom Riders of the Congress of Racial Equality (CORE), beginning in 1961, tested the implementation of these decisions by highlighting racial discrimination on interstate buses and interstate bus waiting rooms. White violence and opposition to Freedom Rides forced the federal government to intervene to protect the protestors.

KEY TERM

Public school
In the USA, this is equivalent to a state-maintained school in the UK. Fee-paying schools in the USA are called private schools.

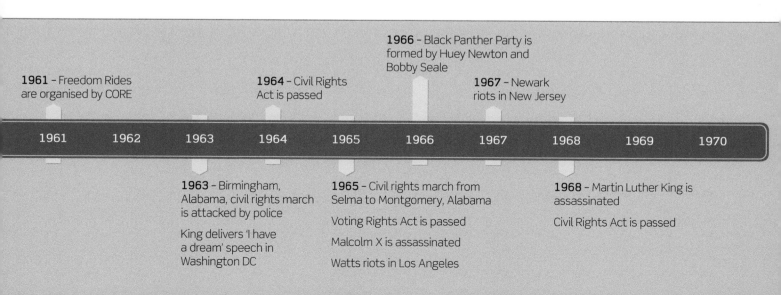

1961 – Freedom Rides are organised by CORE

1964 – Civil Rights Act is passed

1966 – Black Panther Party is formed by Huey Newton and Bobby Seale

1967 – Newark riots in New Jersey

| 1961 | 1962 | 1963 | 1964 | 1965 | 1966 | 1967 | 1968 | 1969 | 1970 |

1963 – Birmingham, Alabama, civil rights march is attacked by police

King delivers 'I have a dream' speech in Washington DC

1965 – Civil rights march from Selma to Montgomery, Alabama

Voting Rights Act is passed

Malcolm X is assassinated

Watts riots in Los Angeles

1968 – Martin Luther King is assassinated

Civil Rights Act is passed

The US Supreme Court had considerable constitutional power in interpreting the US Constitution. However, to implement its decisions it needed the support of federal and state governments. Without enforcement by either of these authorities, US Supreme Court decisions remained merely court decisions. The US Supreme Court did not have power of enforcement. The decision to end legal racial segregation in the South met with considerable resistance. White citizens councils were created to offer grass-roots resistance to racial integration. In Congress, 100 southern senators and members of Congress signed the Southern Manifesto, which declared outright opposition to these changes. Southern state governors, such as Ross Barnett in Mississippi, openly challenged the right of the federal government, in the form of the Supreme Court, to 'interfere' in southern politics. By the end of 1956, not one public school in the South had been racially integrated, in spite of the landmark Supreme Court decisions of the *Brown* case of 1954 and the *Brown II* case of 1955.

It would take direct action by the US president to force racial integration against local white opposition. In 1957, at Central High School, Little Rock, Arkansas, an attempt was made to allow nine black American students to attend an all-white school. The state governor, Orvil Faubus, and local white groups opposed the idea. A riot nearly occurred on the day the nine black students attempted to enrol at the school. Shown on national television, the episode caused national outrage. President Eisenhower had to dispatch 1,000 members of the 101st Airborne Division to protect the students and allow them to attend classes. The troops stayed at Central High School all year to protect the black students.

In 1962, a black American, James Meredith, attempted to enrol at the all-white University of Mississippi. The Mississippi governor, Ross Barnett, opposed the enrolment. President John F. Kennedy had to dispatch hundreds of **US marshals** and hundreds of federal troops to allow Meredith to enrol and attend the university.

The US Supreme Court provided the constitutional authority to bring an end to legal racial segregation, but its decisions had to be supported by the US president and the federal government.

KEY TERM

US marshal
In the USA, law enforcement is primarily a city and state responsibility. However, in the enforcement of federal (national) law, US marshals are law enforcement officers who have the power to implement that law.

A Level Exam-Style Question Section A

Study Source 1 before you answer this question.

Assess the value of the source for revealing the reasons why the US Supreme Court decided to desegregate public schooling as soon as possible in 1955.

Explain your answer, using the source, the information given about it and your own knowledge of the historical context. (20 marks)

Tip

In your answer it is important to refer to the provenance of the source as a way of assessing its value. Who wrote it? When was it written? Who was its intended audience? To support your answer, use relevant information from the content of the source and your own knowledge to help place the source in its historical context.

SOURCE

1 From Chief Justice Earl Warren's opinion in the Brown II case of 31 May 1955, following on from the *Brown* v *Board of Education, Topeka, Kansas* case of 17 May 1954. He puts forward the principles on which he declared 'separate but equal' educational provision in public schools was unconstitutional and the need for urgent action to implement the *Brown* decision of 1954. The plaintiffs were those bringing the case against racial discrimination. The defendants were those boards of education that had allowed racial discrimination.

The fundamental principle [is] that racial discrimination in public education is unconstitutional.

All provisions of federal, state or local law requiring or permitting such discrimination must yield to this principle.

In fashioning and effectuating the decrees, the courts will be guided by equitable principles. Traditionally, equity has been characterised by a practical flexibility in shaping remedies and by a facility for adjusting and reconciling public and private needs. These cases call for the exercise of these traditional attributes of equity power. At stake is the personal interest of the plaintiffs in admission to public schools as soon as is practicable on a non-discriminatory basis. To effectuate this interest may call for elimination of a variety of obstacles in making the transition to school systems operated in accordance with the constitutional principles set forth in our decision of 17 May 1954. Courts of equity may properly take into account the public interest in the elimination of such obstacles in a systematic and effective manner. But it should go without saying that the vitality of these constitutional principles cannot be allowed to yield simply because of disagreements with them.

While giving right to these public and private considerations the courts will require that the defendants make a prompt and reasonable start toward full compliance with our 17 May 1954 ruling. Once such a start has been made, the courts may find that additional time is necessary to carry out the ruling in an effective manner. The burden rests upon the defendants to establish that such time is necessary in the public interest and is consistent with good faith compliance at the earliest practicable date. To that end, the courts may consider problems relating to administration, arising from the physical condition of the school plant, the school transportation system, personnel, revision of school districts and attendance areas into compact units to achieve a system of determining admission to public schools on a non-racial basis and revision of local laws and regulations which may be necessary in solving the foregoing problems.

Such orders and decrees consistent with this opinion are necessary and proper to admit to public schools on a racially non-discriminatory basis with all deliberate speed.

The role of Earl Warren and the Supreme Court

1 What areas of US life did the US Supreme Court declare should see an end to legal segregation?

2 With a partner, identify areas where the US Supreme Court helped to gain civil rights for black Americans.

3 Which US Supreme Court action do you regard as the most important? Give a reason for your answer.

The impact of the Montgomery bus boycott victory

The issue that brought Martin Luther King to national prominence was the Montgomery bus boycott of 1955–56. The person who sparked off the bus boycott was Mrs Rosa Parks, an NAACP activist. She was deliberately chosen by the NAACP to test racial segregation on public buses. On 1 December 1955, she intentionally got herself arrested for refusing to move from her seat on a public bus in the state capital of Alabama to allow a white person to sit there. The bus company had a rule whereby the front seats were reserved for white Americans. When white people got on the bus, black Americans were expected to move to the back. This was not the first bus boycott against racial segregation. Baton Rouge, the state capital of Louisiana, had seen a boycott, but it had failed. The NAACP hoped that a bus boycott in Montgomery, if successful, would lead to the end of racially segregated bus transportation across the South.

The NAACP needed a local black American to publicise the protest. They chose a Baptist minister, newly arrived in the city, a native of Atlanta, Georgia. He was Martin Luther King. King had been appointed to the post of minister at the Dexter Avenue Baptist Church in central Montgomery. King proved to be a very effective public speaker. He also supported non-violent protest. He was greatly influenced by the Indian nationalist leader, Mahatma Ghandi, who had led the successful Indian independence movement against Britain in the first half of the 20th century. With King as the leader, a local organisation was formed to ensure the boycott was effective, the Montgomery Improvement Association (MIA). The MIA organised car lifts for black American workers and ensured that the boycott was supported by virtually all black residents of Montgomery. Without black passengers, the bus company in Montgomery faced severe financial difficulties. The MIA, to begin with, did not want an end to racial segregation on the buses. It simply wanted a more humane way of implementing bus policy that was not humiliating to black people when they were forced to give up their seats to white passengers.

However, under King's leadership, the bus boycott received national media coverage. King's eloquent oratory and his moderate, non-violent message gained enormous sympathy from black and white Americans across the country. A key turning point came on 5 June 1956, when a Montgomery federal court ruled that any law requiring racially segregated seating on buses violated the Fourteenth Amendment of the US Constitution. The City of Montgomery appealed to the US Supreme Court. The US Supreme Court decision of *Browder* v *Gayle* upheld the federal court decision made on 13 November 1956. This decision gave the MIA great constitutional and political backing. On 21 December 1956, the bus boycott came to an end after 381 days. When the Montgomery bus company ended legal segregation on the buses, one of the first black Americans to ride at the front of a Montgomery bus was Martin Luther King.

This did not end white resistance to bus integration. In January 1957, four black churches in Montgomery and the homes of prominent black Americans were bombed. A bomb at Martin Luther King's house was defused. On 30 January 1957, the Montgomery City Police arrested seven white men for the bombing. All were members of the Ku Klux Klan. This brought the initial violence against black Americans in Montgomery to an end.

The success of the Montgomery bus boycott was significant for a number of reasons. It was the result of a grass-roots mass protest by black Americans who adopted a non-violent way of voicing their grievances. It led to the rapid rise to prominence of Martin Luther King as a civil rights leader, a position he held until his assassination in April 1968. It also led to the creation, in 1957, of the Southern Christian Leadership Conference (SCLC).

A Level Exam-Style Question Section A

Study Source 2 before you answer this question.

Assess the value of the source for revealing the reasons for the Montgomery bus boycott.

Explain your answer, using the source, information given about its origins and your own knowledge about the historical context. (20 marks)

Tip

It is important to consider the intended audience for the source, and the extent to which the information contained within the source provides sufficient information on the reasons for the bus boycott.

SOURCE 2

Suggestion to black Americans from the Montgomery Improvement Association (MIA) on how to behave on the buses following the end of the bus boycott. The MIA was the black American organisation that led the boycott under the leadership of Martin Luther King.

December 19, 1956

This is a historic week because segregation on buses has now been declared unconstitutional. Within a few days the Supreme Court Mandate will reach Montgomery and you will be reboarding *integrated* buses. This places upon us all a tremendous responsibility of maintaining, in face of what could be some unpleasantness, a calm and loving dignity befitting good citizens and members of our Race. If there is violence in word or deed it must not be our people who commit it.

For your help and convenience the following suggestions are made. Will you read, study and memorize them so that our non-violent determination may not be endangered. First, some general suggestions:

1. Not all white people are opposed to integrated buses. Accept goodwill on the part of many.

2. The *whole* bus is now for the use of *all* people. Take a vacant seat.

3. Pray for guidance and commit yourself to *complete* non-violence in word and action as you enter the bus.

4. Demonstrate the calm dignity of our Montgomery people in your actions.

5. In all things observe ordinary rules of courtesy and good behavior.

6. Remember that this is not a victory for Negroes alone, but for all Montgomery and the South. Do not boast! Do not brag!

7. Be quiet but friendly; proud, but not arrogant; joyous, but not boisterous.

8. Be loving enough to absorb evil and understanding enough to turn an enemy into a friend.

Now for some specific suggestions:

1. The bus driver is in charge of the bus and has been instructed to obey the law. Assume that he will cooperate in helping you occupy any vacant seat.

2. Do not deliberately sit by a white person, unless there is no other seat.

3. In sitting down by a person, white or colored, say 'May I' or 'Pardon me' as you sit. This is a common courtesy.

4. If cursed, do not curse back. If pushed, do not push back. If struck, do not strike back, but evidence love and goodwill at all times.

6. For the first few days try to get on the bus with a friend in whose non-violence you have confidence. You can uphold one another by glance or prayer.

7. If another person is being molested, do not arise to go to his defense, but pray for the oppressor and use moral and spiritual forces to carry on the struggle for justice.

Southern Christian Leadership Conference (SCLC) and the work and impact of Martin Luther King

Martin Luther King's leadership of the Montgomery bus boycott had a lasting legacy. In 1957, the Southern Christian Leadership Conference was created in Montgomery. The organisation's main aim was to continue the fight for black American civil rights through non-violent means. King was made president, a post he held until his assassination in April 1968. Originally, the organisation was called the Southern Negro Leaders Conference on Transportation and Non-violent Integration, which underlined its origins, its composition and purpose. 'Christian' was added to the organisation's name later in 1957 mainly because it was led by Christian ministers,

It claimed to have three main aims:

- to encourage white Americans to participate in the organisation to bring change. As a result, the term 'negro' was dropped from its original title

- to encourage all black Americans to seek justice and reject all injustice

- to encourage the use of non-violent protest.

From its creation in Montgomery, the SCLC organisation spread across the southern states. It acted as an umbrella organisation, absorbing smaller civil rights groups into a much broader organisation. The SCLC organised protests across the South, highlighting segregation and civil rights issues. It was generally successful in gaining publicity and bringing change, yet positive results were limited initially. Between 1958 and 1960, the SCLC engaged in the Crusade for Citizenship, which was an attempt to double black American voter registration. The campaign was not very effective due to poor organisation and very limited financial support.

In 1961–62, at Albany, Georgia, the SCLC faced its biggest defeat. A protest against racial discrimination was effectively handled without violence by the city police chief, Laurie Pritchard, who had all the protestors jailed peacefully. Even when Martin Luther King was arrested, Pritchard quickly arranged for a court fine to be paid by an anonymous donor to secure an early release for the SCLC leader. This drew very limited national media coverage and scant change in the city with regard to racial discrimination. By August 1962, the SCLC called off its protest, having achieved little.

SOURCE 3

From a letter by the Albany Movement to the Albany, Georgia, City Commission, 23 January 1962. It sets out the aims of the Albany Movement which desired an end to racial discrimination in that city, by W.G. Anderson and M.S. Page on behalf of the Albany Movement.

The Albany Movement came into being as a result of repeated denials of redress for inadequacies and wrongs, and finally, for the refusal to even consider petitions which have been presented to your group as far back as 1957.

The first request was for sewage and paving relief in the Lincoln Heights area – nothing done. Next, the stoning of a Negro minister's house, following an inflammatory editorial in the local press, caused a request to be sent by registered mail to the Mayor that a joint group try to stop the worsening conditions – no official acknowledgement of this request has ever been received by us. Again, a request that segregated polling places, which we felt were used to counteract the effect of our vote, was made from the top to the bottom – the refusal of any attempt of any kind of redress necessitated a successful suit to be waged in the Federal Court by us. Finally, it was the refusal of Albany officials, through its police department, to comply with the Interstate Commerce Commission regulation which became effective last 1 November, that made the creation of this body a necessity. Test rides were conducted throughout the entire state of Georgia. Atlanta, Savannah, Augusta, Macon, Columbia, Valdosta and Waycross all complied. Only Albany resisted.

We the members of the Albany Movement, with the realisation that ultimately the people of Albany, Negro and white, will have to solve our difficulties; realising full well that racial hostility can be the downfall of our city; realising that what happens in Albany, as well as what does NOT happen in Albany; affects the whole free world, call upon you tonight to hear our position.

It is our belief that discrimination based on race, color or religion is fundamentally wrong and contrary to the letter and intent of the Constitution of the United States. It is our aim in the Albany Movement to seek means of ending discriminatory practices in public facilities, both in employment and in use.

Birmingham, Alabama, April and May 1963

The polar opposite to the SCLC defeat in Albany, Georgia, was the SCLC-inspired civil rights protest in April and May 1963 in Birmingham, Alabama, a major steel-producing city. Martin Luther King found the confrontation he was looking for to gain national media attention. The SCLC looked for the end to racial segregation in the city and organised a peaceful protest involving, among others, many young people. The SCLC wanted to see the end of segregation of shop facilities, dismissal of all charges in previous civil rights protests, equal job opportunities for black and white within the city government, the reopening on a desegregated basis of the city's recreational facilities and the establishment of a **biracial committee** to pursue further desegregation.

KEY TERM

Biracial committee
Consisting of both black and white Americans.

The Birmingham city police chief, Eugene 'Bull' Connor, was determined to stop the demonstration. Using police dogs and water cannon, Connor's police brutally attacked the protestors and arrested many of them. These incidents were filmed and shown on US television and broadcast across the country. King himself was arrested and wrote 'A Letter from Birmingham Jail' to highlight his non-violent civil rights credentials. A peaceful end to the confrontation was negotiated between the SCLC and local businessmen, which saw only limited concessions towards desegregation. However, the national impact of the media coverage made Martin Luther King a national civil rights figure.

SOURCE 4

The Birmingham, Alabama Truce Agreement, 10 May 1963. This was a written agreement between the SCLC and Birmingham's business leaders. The agreement was encouraged by the presence of US Assistant Attorney General Burke Marshall, a close adviser to President John F. Kennedy. The Truce Agreement brought to an end the violence following a peaceful civil rights demonstration organised by the SCLC.

The Birmingham Truce Agreement:-

1. Within 3 days after the close of demonstrations, fitting rooms will be desegregated.

2. Within 30 days after the city government is established by court order, signs on wash rooms, rest rooms and drinking fountains will be removed.

3. Within 60 days after the city government is established by court order, a program of lunchroom counter desegregation will be commenced.

4. When the city government is established by court order, a program of upgrading Negro employment will be continued and there will be meetings with responsible local leadership to consider further steps.

5. Within 60 days from the court order determining Birmingham's city government, the employment program will include at least one sales person or cashier.

6. Within 15 days from the cessation of demonstrations a Committee on racial Problems and Employment composed of members of the Senior Citizens' Committee will be established, with a membership made public and the publicly announced purpose of establishing liaison with members of the Negro community to carry out a program of up-grading and improving employment opportunities with the Negro citizens of the Birmingham community.

Impact of Martin Luther King up to 1963

To confirm Martin Luther King as unofficial leader of the civil rights movement, a march on Washington DC was organised by the SCLC to take place in August 1963. The idea of a mass march and protest in support of black American civil rights had a long history. In 1941, black civil rights activist A. Philip Randolph had planned such a protest, but the very thought of such a march persuaded President Franklin Roosevelt to set up the Equal Opportunities Commission of the Federal Government

135

to outlaw racial discrimination in factories with federal contracts. On 28 August 1963, in front of 250,000 people, Martin Luther King gave the keynote address on the steps of the Lincoln Memorial, in central Washington DC. His speech became one of the most famous in 20th-century US history. He called for racial integration and the end of segregation. He claimed, 'I have a dream' that one day soon racial discrimination would come to an end.

The combination of events in 1963 prompted President John F. Kennedy to go on nationwide television to announce that he would introduce a civil rights bill to Congress to outlaw racial discrimination. In 1964, Martin Luther King went to Oslo, Norway, to receive the Nobel Peace Prize for his work in gaining greater equality for black Americans through non-violent campaigning. This not only confirmed King's leading role in the civil rights movement within the USA, but also made him an international figure. In 1983, President Reagan signed into law 'Martin Luther King Day' as a national holiday on 15 January, King's birthday, and in 2011 the Martin Luther King National Historic Site was opened in central Washington DC, close to the Lincoln Memorial.

SOURCE

5 Civil rights demonstrators being attacked by police dogs while peacefully protesting against racial segregation in Birmingham, Alabama, on 3 May 1963.

ACTIVITY
KNOWLEDGE CHECK

The role of Martin Luther King: 1955 to 1963

1 Write down four possible reasons why Martin Luther King rose to prominence in the black civil rights movement from 1955 to 1963.

2 Produce a spider diagram that shows the various ways Martin Luther King and the SCLC were able to highlight racial discrimination against black Americans in the years 1957 to 1963.

SOURCE

President Kennedy's speech, which was broadcast across the USA on national television on 11 June 1963, followed protests in Birmingham, Alabama. Kennedy's speech led to his introduction of a proposed bill to the US Congress to deal with civil rights.

We are confronted primarily with a moral issue. It is as old as the Scriptures and is as clear as the American Constitution. The heart of the question is whether all Americans are to be afforded equal rights and equal opportunities; whether we are going to treat our fellow Americans as we want to be treated.

If an American, because his skin is dark, cannot eat lunch in a restaurant open to the public; if he cannot send his children to the best public schools available; if he cannot vote for the public officials who represent him; if in short, he cannot enjoy the full and free life which all of us want, then who among us would be content to have the color of his skin changed and stand in his place?

Now the time has come for this nation to fulfill its promise. The events in Birmingham and elsewhere have so increased the cries for equality that no city or state or legislative body can prudently choose to ignore them.

Student Non-Violent Co-ordinating Committee (SNCC)

Martin Luther King may have been seen as the unofficial leader of the civil rights movement, but the SCLC was only one of a number of civil rights organisations campaigning to end segregation and gain equality for black Americans. Much civil rights activity came from the grass roots, rather than from top-down leadership.

One such group was the Student Non-Violent Co-ordinating Committee (SNCC), known as 'snick'. It had its origins in February 1960. On 1 February of that year, a group of four black American students entered the Woolworth's department store in Greensboro, North Carolina. They sat down at a white Americans only lunch counter waiting to be served. They were Franklin McCain, David Richmond, Joseph McNeil and Izell Blair. They all attended the North Carolina Agricultural and Technical College. When staff refused to serve them, they stayed until the store closed. The actions of these students led to copycat lunch counter demonstrations across the South in February–April 1960. In a meeting held in Raleigh, North Carolina between 16 and 18 April, the SNCC emerged as the youth wing of the civil rights movement.

Like the protests organised by the SCLC, SNCC protests received widespread media publicity and led directly to the desegregation of lunch counters across the South. In 1964, the SNCC went on to engage in a major voter registration campaign centred on Lowndes County in Mississippi. Their activities in that state led to the creation of the Mississippi Free Democratic Party, which offered a rival to the white-led official Democrat Party in that state.

SOURCE

From the Student Non-violent Co-ordinating Committee (SNCC) Statement of Purpose, written by Reverend James Lawson, 14 May 1960.

We affirm the philosophical or religious ideal of non-violence as the foundation of our purpose, the pre-supposition of our faith, and the manner of our action. Non-violence as it grows from Judaic-Christian traditions seeks a social order of justice permeated by love. Integration of human endeavour represents the crucial first step towards such a society.

Through non-violence, courage displaces fear; love transforms hate. Acceptance dissipates prejudice; hope ends despair. Peace dominates war; faith reconciles doubt. Mutual regard cancels enmity. Justice for all overthrows injustice. The redemptive community supersedes systems of gross social immorality.

Love is the central motif of non-violence. Love is the force by which God binds man himself and man to man. Such love goes to the extreme; it remains loving and forgiving even in the midst of hostility. It matches the capacity of evil to inflict suffering with an even more enduring capacity to absorb evil, all the while persisting in love.

By appealing to conscience and standing on the moral nature of human existence, non-violence nurtures the atmosphere in which reconciliation and justice become actual possibilities.

The Congress of Racial Equality (CORE)

Unlike the SCLC and SNCC, the Congress of Racial Equality (CORE) was founded in the north at the University of Chicago in 1942. Like the SCLC and SNCC, CORE believed in non-violent protest.

The issue which brought CORE to national prominence in 1961 was the Freedom Rides. On 4 May 1961, four white and four black students took interstate buses from Virginia to Mississippi. Their aim was to test the existing law on desegregation. In 1946, in a Supreme Court case called *Morgan* v *Virginia*, and again in another case in 1960 called *Boynton* v *Virginia*, the US Supreme Court had declared racial segregation on interstate buses unconstitutional.

James Farmer, one of the founders of CORE, made clear the purpose of the Freedom Rides when he declared that their specific intention was to create a crisis that would force the federal government to enforce the Supreme Court decision. Farmer and CORE hoped the Freedom Rides would provoke the white southerners who were opposed to racial integration to react violently. CORE's aims for the Freedom Rides did not take long to materialise. At Anniston, Alabama, a Greyhound interstate bus carrying the Freedom Riders was violently attacked by a white mob and the bus was burnt. In other Freedom Rides, CORE members were attacked and beaten by mobs in Birmingham, Alabama, and Jackson, Mississippi. These events were televised and reported on by the national press, causing uproar outside the South.

James Farmer's aims were realised. The Federal Interstate Commerce Commission and the US Justice Department under President John F. Kennedy's brother, Robert F. Kennedy, issued orders to enforce racial integration on interstate buses. Effective from 1 November 1961, all interstate buses and interstate bus facilities, such as waiting rooms, had to be racially integrated.

The tactics and impact of the SCLC, SNCC and CORE, 1957–63

As Martin Luther King and other civil rights leaders realised, a violent campaign by those who wished for greater racial equality would lead to a major white backlash. State governments possessed the means through the police and the National Guard to defeat any violent action by civil rights groups. However, non-violent protest did not necessarily lead to a lack of violence. Civil rights groups, in many cases, deliberately provoked the authorities into violent reaction, such as at Birmingham, Alabama in 1963. Such reaction, when filmed on national television and reported by the national press, was used to pressure the federal government into action to protect civil rights protestors and implement change. The civil rights activists believed they had right on their side.

The different civil rights groups were aware that Supreme Court decisions and the terms of the US Constitution gave all Americans basic and equal civil rights. It was clear that racial segregation as practised in the southern states was unconstitutional. The SCLC, SNCC and CORE helped to publicise and expose racial inequality and force a reluctant federal government to act. That reluctanct action was shown by President Eisenhower at Central High, Little Rock, in 1957 and, again, by President John F. Kennedy over the Freedom Rides of 1961, James Meredith in 1962 and Birmingham in 1963. Perhaps the greatest triumph of the civil rights movement by the end of 1963 was to place the issue of legal segregation at the top of the political agenda in the USA. Rather than leading the cause of black American civil rights, the federal government was forced to act, often reluctantly, in response to actions and protests by civil rights groups.

ACTIVITY
KNOWLEDGE CHECK

The civil rights movement, 1957–63

1 Identify the ways in which the SCLC, SNCC and CORE helped to highlight injustices and racial discrimination against black Americans in the years 1957–63.

2 Which of the civil rights groups mentioned above (SCLC, SNCC and CORE) did most to improve the civil rights of black Americans? Give a reason for your answer.

HOW SIGNIFICANT WERE THE CIVIL RIGHTS ACTS OF 1964 AND 1968 AND THE VOTING RIGHTS ACT OF 1965 IN BRINGING CHANGE TO BLACK AMERICAN CIVIL RIGHTS?

By the beginning of 1964, the quest for greater equality for black Americans had made significant progress. The US Supreme Court, under Chief Justice Earl Warren, had made a number of significant judgments, which had attacked legal segregation. 'Separate but equal' facilities in public schools and transportation had been declared unconstitutional. Most importantly, a civil rights movement led by black Americans, most notably Martin Luther King, had highlighted the major areas of discrimination against black Americans in the southern states.

One of the most important aspects of the civil rights protests was to pressure the federal government into action to protect the rights of black Americans. At Central High School, Little Rock, in 1957, in the Freedom Rides of 1961, and at the University of Mississippi in 1962, the federal government was forced to act in support of greater equality for black Americans. However, the greatest contribution to the achievement of equal civil rights for black Americans came during the presidency of Lyndon B. Johnson (1963–69). During his presidency, three important civil rights acts were passed by the US Congress: the Civil Rights Act, 1964; the Voting Rights Act, 1965; and the Civil Rights Act, 1968.

The Civil Rights Act, 1964

President John F. Kennedy and civil rights, 1961–63

Following the brutal repression of the civil rights protest in Birmingham, Alabama, in the spring of 1963, President John F. Kennedy felt forced to act to bring an end to legal segregation in the southern states. On 11 June 1963, he made a nationwide television broadcast in which he stated that he would ask Congress to pass legislation to bring greater racial equality and end legal segregation, and provide greater protection for black Americans to vote. Unfortunately, before that legislation could be passed, Kennedy was assassinated on 22 November 1963, to be replaced as president by Vice President Lyndon B. Johnson.

Kennedy had been a reluctant supporter of black American civil rights during his presidency (1961–63). He had won the presidency by a very small margin over Republican Richard Nixon in 1960, which had given him a limited election mandate. He also faced a hostile southern Democrat group in Congress that was opposed to major civil rights changes. However, in March 1961, by Executive Order, Kennedy created the President's Committee on Equal Employment Opportunity (PCEEO). Its aim was to prevent racial discrimination for all those doing business with the federal government. It was placed under the chairmanship of Vice President Lyndon Johnson. Kennedy also introduced a programme of affirmative action, whereby the federal government followed an active policy of recruiting ethnic minorities to federal jobs.

President Johnson and civil rights

Johnson was from a southern state, Texas. He had been a keen supporter of F.D. Roosevelt's New Deal policies in the 1930s, which saw positive use of federal programmes to aid the unemployed and economic development. Johnson had become president by accident through the tragic death by assassination of Kennedy, ironically in a Texas city, Dallas. In the wave of sympathy for the dead president, Johnson announced that, in memory of Kennedy, he would work to pass the comprehensive Civil Rights Act, which Kennedy had proposed in June 1963.

In addition to the national desire to fulfil the dead president's outstanding proposals, Johnson was gifted in getting congressional leaders to support presidential policies. Johnson had been Democrat leader of the Senate in the 1950s and had developed a national reputation for getting things done in Congress. Using his wealth of experience, his great ability at persuasion and the exploitation of Kennedy's assassination, Johnson was able to guide through Congress a civil rights bill, which became law.

The House of Representatives Rules Committee, chaired by a southern Democrat, had deliberately delayed the passage of Kennedy's civil rights bill during the second half of 1963. The bill then went to the House Judiciary Committee, where Johnson's influence helped to push the bill through the House. Johnson's persuasive skills were able to overcome a 57-day filibuster by southern Democrats through gaining support from non-southern Democrats and Republicans. The bill became the Civil Rights Act on 2 July 1964, when Johnson signed the bill into law.

The Civil Rights Act of 1964 and its impact

The Act brought to an end legal segregation in the USA. In the second section of the Act, known as Title II, the Act outlawed racial segregation for all public facilities and accommodation. Title III also outlawed racial segregation in all federal government facilities. To aid the desegregation of public schools, federal financial assistance was to be given to schools to encourage racial integration. Following on from Kennedy's Executive Order of 1961, the Act forbade racial discrimination in any federal-funded programme. This aspect of the Act had a major impact on state governments who attempted to preserve segregation in some form. If they did so, they could and would lose federal funding.

Title VII of the Act went beyond ending racial segregation. It forbade all discrimination in employment on the grounds of race, colour, religion, national origin and sex. This was seen as a major triumph for those campaigning for gender equality in the USA. Finally, the Act set up the Equal Employment Opportunities Commission (EEOC) to ensure that the Civil Rights Act was implemented.

The Civil Rights Act attacked both *de jure* and *de facto* racial segregation across the USA. It was the first major Civil Rights Act since Reconstruction, although a very weak Civil Rights Act, with virtually no enforcement powers, had passed into law in 1957. In terms of basic civil rights, black Americans now had similar rights to all other Americans. The aims of the Civil War Amendments of 1865–70 (Thirteenth, Fourteenth and Fifteenth Amendments) were now given effective federal government backing. The age of Jim Crow had finally come to an end in terms of basic civil rights.

However, this did not mean that black Americans did not have major social, economic and political problems. The Civil Rights Act of 1964 did not address these. Black Americans still faced considerable discrimination in their attempts to register to vote in southern states. Also, across the country, many black Americans lived in very poor housing, with very limited job prospects. Within a year of the passage of the 1964 Civil Rights Act, a major race riot broke out in the Watts district of south central Los Angeles. Between 11 and 15 August 1965, 34 people were killed and over 1,000 rioters were arrested. The Watts riot was one of 239 outbreaks of racial violence in over 200 US cities that broke out in the five summers of 1964–68. Gaining equal civil rights was one thing; gaining social and economic advancement was another.

The Voting Rights Act, 1965

Freedom Summer, 1964

The Civil Rights Act of 1964 brought an end to legal segregation. However, black Americans still faced huge problems in gaining the right to vote in the southern states. Literacy tests, poll taxes and constitutional tests, among others, prevented large numbers of black Americans from registering to vote. Considerable attempts had been made before 1964 to encourage black registration by civil rights groups. In the summer of 1964, the SNCC organised committees across the South to encourage voter registration. Both black and white SNCC organisers faced extensive local white opposition. In 1964, in Mississippi, three activists, both black and white, were murdered. This episode formed the basis of the 1988 Hollywood film, *Mississippi Burning*. In Mississippi, in 1964, 69.9 percent of the adult white population was registered to vote, compared to 6.7 percent of black Mississippians.

SNCC activists found it very difficult to register black Mississippians by normal methods. As a result, they helped set up the Mississippi Freedom Democratic Party (MFDP) as an alternative to the white-dominated state party. At the Democrat Party National Convention, in August 1964, both the official white-dominated state party and the MFDP appeared. The attempted compromise by Lyndon Johnson's advisers of allowing two representatives of the MFDP to participate led to the official state delegation leaving. This created the atmosphere for more radical action on the issue of black American voting rights.

The march from Selma to Montgomery, 1965

To put pressure on the Johnson administration to introduce legislation giving black Americans equal voting rights, Martin Luther King and the SCLC organised a civil rights march from Selma to Montgomery, Alabama, in March 1965. Selma was chosen as it was a centre of white opposition to black civil rights. Montgomery was the destination, as it had been the first capital of the Confederacy in the Civil War and the city where King had triumphed in the bus boycott of 1955–56. The march became the subject of the 2014 Hollywood film, *Selma*, which was nominated for several Oscars.

The aim of the march was to gain national publicity for black American rights and it fulfilled its purpose. On 7 March 1965, at Pettus Bridge, black and white civil rights marchers, including several male and female members of the clergy, were attacked by Alabama State Troopers (police) and white opponents. The events became known as Bloody Sunday. Johnson was so shocked, he federalised the Alabama National Guard to protect the civil rights marchers. From 17 to 25 March, 25,000 civil rights marchers completed the walk to Montgomery. During the march, two white civil rights supporters, Viola Liuzzo and Protestant minister James Reeb, were murdered by white supremacists. The march and the murders provided sufficient pressure and national publicity to allow Johnson to get Congress to pass a Voting Rights Act. This had a much easier passage than the Civil Rights Act the year before. In November 1964, Johnson had won the presidential election by a landslide and the Democrats had greatly increased their numbers in both houses of Congress.

The Voting Rights Act of 1965 and its impact

In August 1965, Johnson signed the Voting Rights Act into law. It outlawed literacy tests and provided for federal examiners to replace state government officials with the power to register voters. The Act also followed a wording similar to that employed in the Fifteenth Amendment of the US Constitution of 1870, which guaranteed adult American males the right to vote by claiming that there should be no discrimination in registering a person to vote on the basis of race or colour. The issue of poll taxes had already been addressed in 1964 with the Twenty-fourth Amendment to the US Constitution, which outlawed their use.

The Voting Rights Act proved to be the most effective use of federal power in the electoral system since the end of Reconstruction in 1877. By the end of 1965, 250,000 new black voters had been added to the electorates of the southern states. By the end of 1966, only four of the 13 southern states had less than 50 percent of the potential black electorate as registered voters. The Act was readopted by the US Congress in 1970, 1975 and 1982, and stands out as a major landmark in enabling black Americans to play a full part in the US political system.

SOURCE

8 The Voting Rights Act: percentage of adult white and black Americans who had registered to vote in the southern states in 1964 (on the eve of the Act) and in 1969.

	1964		1969	
	White	**Black**	**White**	**Black**
Alabama	69.2	19.3	94.6	61.3
Arkansas	65.6	40.4	81.6	77.9
Florida	74.8	51.2	94.2	67.0
Georgia	62.6	27.4	88.5	60.4
Louisiana	80.5	31.6	87.1	60.8
Mississippi	69.9	6.7	89.8	60.8
North Carolina	96.8	46.8	78.4	53.7
South Carolina	75.7	37.3	71.5	54.6
Tennessee	72.9	69.5	92.0	92.1
Virginia	61.1	38.3	78.7	59.8

The Civil Rights Act, 1968

On 4 April 1968, the civil rights movement was dealt a major blow. At the Lorraine Motel, Memphis, Tennessee, Martin Luther King was assassinated, sending shockwaves around the USA. On 9 April, his funeral took place in Atlanta, Georgia. The following day, Congress passed another Civil Rights Act, which dealt with aspects of civil rights and racial discrimination not covered by either the Civil Rights Act of 1964 or the Voting Rights Act of 1965.

The Civil Rights Act of 1968 (also known as the Fair Housing Act) outlawed discrimination on the basis of colour, race, religion or national origin in the rent or sale of housing, except in owner-occupied or owner-managed units. This issue of *de facto* racial discrimination affected black Americans across the USA and was a significant cause of rioting in US cities from 1965. The Act also outlawed racial discrimination in jury selection.

In more general terms, the Act made it a federal crime to interfere with voting, work, schooling and participation in federally assisted programmes on the basis of race or colour. It also protected civil rights workers from attack, declaring that anyone who travelled across state lines to foment a riot would face fines and/or imprisonment.

The Act had limited impact on desegregated housing across the USA. This was due in part to the population movements of black and white people in urban areas. From 1950 to 1980, the total black population in cities in the USA rose from 6.1 million to 15.3 million. At the same time, the white populations of cities moved from city centres to suburbs known as 'white flight'. Associated with 'white flight' was the relocation of retail outlets into out-of-town shopping malls, and of businesses to out-of-town industrial and business parks. As a result, the inner cities became black ghettoes, with poor quality of life and very limited job opportunities. So *de facto* segregation caused by these demographic changes made it difficult to bring about a real change in the segregation of housing. In 1988, a Fair Housing Amendments Act attempted to address this problem again by prohibiting discrimination in housing based on disability or family status. It was also to be supervised by the Office of Fair Housing and Equal Opportunity, a subsection of the US Department of Housing and Urban Development (HUD).

The impact of President Johnson

During his presidency, Johnson had seen the passage of the most comprehensive civil rights legislation in US history since Reconstruction. In achieving these momentous changes, Johnson had a number of advantages. He benefited from the wave of sympathy following President Kennedy's assassination. In 1964, he also benefited from the election of the 89th Congress, which was dominated by liberal Democrats from outside the southern states, so he was not hamstrung by southern opposition to his proposals. He was also the president who appointed the first ever black American Cabinet member in Robert Weaver, and the first black American US Supreme Court judge in Thurgood Marshall.

However, what began so promisingly in 1964 to 1965 did not last long. The continuing problems associated with the US involvement in the Vietnam War (1965–73) began to alienate many black American leaders. In 1967, Martin Luther King came out publicly against US involvement. Also, the civil rights legislation led to a backlash from southern Democrats. In the 1968 presidential election, the former Democrat governor of Alabama, George Wallace, challenged for the leadership of the party and, when he failed, stood as presidential candidate for the American Independent Party after he failed to get the Democratic Party nomination. He polled 9.9 million votes and won majorities in five southern states, gaining an electoral college vote of 46. The split in the Democrat Party in 1968 helped Republican Richard Nixon to win the presidency in that year.

> **ACTIVITY**
> **KNOWLEDGE CHECK**
>
> **The Civil Rights Acts and Voting Rights Act**
> 1 What were the main changes made in race relations by the Civil Rights Act of 1964?
>
> 2 Why was the Voting Rights Act of 1965 so important to getting greater equality for black Americans?
>
> 3 How significant were the changes made during the presidency of Lyndon Johnson in the achievement of greater racial equality in the USA?

HOW FAR DID INTERNAL DIVISIONS WITHIN THE BLACK AMERICAN COMMUNITY AFFECT THE QUEST FOR GREATER CIVIL RIGHTS?

Although Martin Luther King was seen as the unofficial leader of the campaign for greater black American civil rights, the movement for that goal was never properly unified and contained a wide variety of different groups with differing aims. The moderate stance of Martin Luther King was not always followed by these other groups, which, as the 1960s wore on, became more radical.

Increasing divisions: the expulsion of white Americans from the SNCC and CORE

SNCC

Following the formation of the SNCC in 1960, many white Americans participated in its protest for greater civil equality for black Americans. In November 1960, a workshop was organised by the SNCC called 'The Role of the Student in the Changing South', and was attended by 80 black and white students from universities all across the South. In 1961, white students at the Presbyterian and Baptist seminaries were arrested for taking part in sit-in protests in Louisville, Kentucky. White and black students participated.

However, during the Freedom Summer of 1964, when the SNCC engaged in black voter registration across the South, many black Americans in the organisation resented the involvement of white students, many of whom were from the north.

A major change in the SNCC occurred in the summer of 1965. The leadership of the organisation was heavily influenced by two northern black Americans, James Forman and Stokely Carmichael. These two activists ensured that the SNCC became a more radical organisation, aligned to the growing support for black nationalism and growing disillusionment with the Democratic Party. A key shift in Carmichael's attitude occurred after the foundation of the Lowndes County Christian Movement for Human Rights in the spring of 1965. Lowndes County in Mississippi was an area of considerable black poverty and where the local Democrat Party was run by white Americans. Originally, the Lowndes County Christ ian Movement for Human Rights contained members from the SCLC as well as the SNCC, but Carmichael's experience in Lowndes County in the spring and summer of 1965 convinced him that the SNCC should be a radical, all-black organisation.

Carmichael's disillusionment with the federal government was reinforced when the white supremacist perpetrators of the murder of black activist Samuel Younge in 1966 in Mississippi were not brought to justice. In 1966, Carmichael took over as chairperson from the more moderate Al Lewis. Carmichael supported the exclusion of white Americans from the SNCC and espoused support for Black Power, where black Americans alone would fight for greater equality.

EXTEND YOUR KNOWLEDGE

Black Power

Black Power was a slogan associated with radical black activist groups in the 1960s and early 1970s. The first black activist leader to be linked to the slogan was Stokely Carmichael when he used it to encourage his supporters by exclaiming, 'What do we want?' The reply was 'Black Power'. Overall, Black Power represented a desire for black Americans to celebrate their culture and their demands for political, social and economic equality with other Americans.

The term meant different things to different black activist groups. The SNCC, CORE and the Black Panther Party were some of the groups associated with the slogan. To many, it meant the separation of black communities from white communities and a reliance on black self-help to run businesses and employ black workers. Some demanded that the US government pay reparations (money) to black Americans for the historic damage done to them by the institution of slavery before the Civil War (1861–65).

Others saw Black Power to be a call to support pride in black American culture. This included the wearing of an Afro-American haircut and black American fashion, music and dance. The black American festival of Kwanza was developed as a black alternative to Christmas where black Americans celebrated their African heritage.

Traditional black civil rights groups, such as the SCLC and NAACP, were critical of Black Power, as it suggested the separation rather than integration of black Americans into US society.

CORE

The idea of a civil rights movement that integrated the efforts of both black and white Americans was also increasingly challenged by black activists in CORE. By 1965, CORE black activists were also becoming disenchanted with the lack of support from the federal government and became more disillusioned with non-violent protest. With the end of legal segregation, CORE began to concentrate on issues such as black unemployment, slums, police brutality and substandard schooling. These issues were highlighted in the Watts riot of 1965 in Los Angeles, California, far away from the southern states.

By 1964, 80 percent of CORE's National Action Committee were black Americans, and the white American majority, which had dominated the organisation from 1942, was declining rapidly. This change had taken place because many black American members began questioning CORE's attachment to non-violent political action in the face of attacks and intimidation by white supremacist groups.

The murder of three CORE activists, Michael Schwerner, Andrew Goodman and James Chaney, in Mississippi during the black voter registration campaign started this major shift. In addition, the very limited success of the Mississippi Freedom Democratic Party increased disillusionment with mainstream white-dominated politics. In 1966, a power struggle occurred within CORE where the national director and supporter of non-violence, James Farmer, was forced to stand down from his position in the organisation. The more militant, radical Floyd McKissick took over as CORE leader. In the summer of 1966, CORE still worked with Martin Luther King and the SCLC in the Meredith March against Fear, but later, in 1968, McKissick supported the idea of Black Power, the expulsion of white members and the abandonment of non-violent political protest.

EXTEND YOUR KNOWLEDGE

Floyd McKissick (1922–91)

Born in Ashville, North Carolina, on 9 March 1922, McKissick graduated from North Carolina Law School. During the Second World War, he served in the US armed forces in Europe, returning after the war to North Carolina to practise law.

When Floyd McKissick replaced James Farmer as head of CORE on 3 January 1966, the organisation completed a major change in policy. It changed from an interracial civil rights organisation, pledged to uphold non-violence, into a militant, uncompromising supporter of the ideology of Black Power. McKissick and Roy Innis, who in 1966 was head of the Harlem, New York City, chapter of CORE, were close allies, and when McKissick left CORE in 1968, Innis took over.

After leaving CORE in 1969, McKissick launched a plan to build a new community, called Soul City, in Warren County, North Carolina. It was to be a community with sufficient industry to support itself, with a population of 55,000. He received $14 million from the federal Department of Housing and Urban Development and a loan of $500,000 from a bank. Soul City ran into problems, and in June 1980 the project was taken over by the federal government.

The role of Malcolm X

For much of the period 1954–68, Martin Luther King was seen as the unofficial leader of the civil rights movement. He was highly educated, gaining a PhD from Boston College, and was a religious leader, like his father. He came from the South, preached non-violent protest and spoke with eloquence. Malcolm X was almost the exact opposite as a civil rights leader.

Malcolm X was born in Omaha, Nebraska in 1925, to a West Indian mother and a black Baptist minister. When Malcolm was six years old, his father was murdered by white supremacists. Malcolm was later convicted as a drug dealer and spent time in prison. Born Malcolm Little, he changed his last name to 'X' to signify that Little had been a slave name and he did not know his real African name.

When in prison, in 1952, Malcolm X converted to Islam and became a follower of Elijah Muhammed, the founder and leader of the Nation of Islam, a black American Islamic group. They were known as the Black Muslims. Elijah Muhammed supported racial separatism between black and white, black self-determination, and the creation of an independent black republic within the borders of the USA or a return to Africa. Black Muslims published their own black history books, which stressed the glories of black African history and culture. They rejected the term 'negro' as racially derogatory and preferred 'Afro-American'. Converts to the Nation of Islam usually discarded their original names and chose their own Muslim names. Perhaps the most famous convert to the Nation of Islam, apart from Malcolm X, was Muhammed Ali, the world heavyweight boxing champion from 1964 to 1967. He was stripped of his title when he refused to be drafted into the US army to fight in the Vietnam War. He later regained the title in the 1970s. He had been born Cassius Marcellus Clay, the name of a former slave owner who had owned his ancestors at the time of the Civil War.

SOURCE

'Malcolm' by Sonia Sanchez, a poet and playwright who was working for CORE when Malcom X was assassinated in February 1965. It was written shortly after his death.

Do not speak to me of martyrdom
Of men who die to be remembered
On some parish day.
I don't believe in dying
Though I too shall die
And violets like castanets
Will echo me.

Yet this man
This dreamer,
Thick-lipped with words
Will never speak again
And in each winter
When the cold air cracks
With frost, I'll breathe
His breath and mourn
My gun-filled nights.

He was the sun that tagged
The western sky and
Melted tiger-scholars
While they searched for stripes.
Man, We have been curled too long. Nothing
Is sacred now. Not your
White face nor any
Land that separates
Until some voices
squat with spasms.

Do not speak to me of living.
Life is obscene with crowds
Of white on black.
Death is my pulse.
What might have been
Is not for him or me
But what could have been
Floods the womb until I drown.

A Level Exam-Style Question Section B

How far did increasing tensions within the campaign for black civil rights damage the move towards greater racial equality in the USA? (20 marks)

Tip

You will need to address the factionalisation of the civil rights movement and the change in aims and methods of CORE and the SNCC, and the rise of the Black Panther Party. To balance this view, it could be argued that the new aims and focus of groups such as the SNCC and CORE and the views of Malcolm X highlighted the need to address the social and economic problems faced by many black Americans across the USA.

In 1952, after he left prison, Malcolm X was given a ministry within the Nation of Islam at Temple Number 7 at Lennox Avenue and 116th Street in Harlem, the black ghetto in New York City. His ability to speak in public made him a popular guest on television and radio shows, so by 1964 Malcolm X had become the second most popular speaker on university campuses. The most popular was Senator Barry Goldwater of Arizona, a right-wing Republican who was that party's candidate in the 1964 presidential election.

In March 1964, Malcolm X broke with the Nation of Islam and worked independently, forming Muslim Mosque Incorporated for the last 18 months of his life. He continued to support the idea of black separatism and an ultimate return to Africa, but he wanted to address the concerns of black youths living in the ghettoes of northern cities. He rejected the non-violent approach of Martin Luther King and the SCLC. He felt that, when black people were faced with police brutality and attacks by white people, they had to fight back. To achieve his aims, Malcolm X attempted to form an alliance with the rising radical leadership of the SNCC and CORE, but both of these organisations rejected his overtures.

Even with the Civil Rights Act of 1964 and Voting Rights Act of 1965, black Americans still suffered second-class status. In 1966, unemployment among black Americans was 7.8 percent, twice the figure for white Americans. Forty percent of black families lived in poverty on less than $3,000 a year. Ten years after the Brown case had declared segregated schools unconstitutional, the US Commissioner of Education reported that the majority of US children still attended racially segregated schools. This was the world that was attracted by Malcolm X's message, and black anger was reflected in riots in Watts in 1965, Newark in 1967, and Detroit and Cleveland in 1968.

In February 1965, Malcolm X was assassinated by Nation of Islam gunmen. His legacy was an important aspect of the rising splits and tensions within the black civil rights movement, which became increasingly popular in the black ghettoes of the north and west. Malcolm X emphasised the spiritual regeneration of black Americans. This would be achieved through black racial separatism. His support for black nationalism was popular with the new SNCC leader, Stokely Carmichael, and the new CORE leader, Floyd McKissick. Malcolm X believed that the best way to make white Americans respect black people was if the latter were able to organise themselves effectively.

The growth of the Black Panther Party

By the summer of 1966, Stokely Carmichael of the SCNC was using the phrase 'Black Power' to describe the new radical activism of some civil rights groups. In 1966, at Greenwood, Mississippi, Stokely Carmichael said that the only way to stop white men keeping black men as second-class citizens was to take over. He said the term 'freedom' was no longer appropriate as their aim. Instead, it should be 'Black Power'.

Perhaps the most radical black American group to adopt the idea of Black Power was the Black Panther Party. This was formed in Oakland, California, by two black college students, Huey Newton and Bobby Seale, in 1966. It adopted a ten-point programme that set out its radical agenda.

SOURCE

The Black Panther Party Ten-Point Programme of 1966.

1. We want freedom. We want power to determine our destiny of our black community.

2. We want full employment for our people.

3. We want an end to robbery by the white men of our black community.

4. We want decent homes.

5. We want education for our people that exposes the true nature of this decadent American society. We want education that teaches us our true history and our role in present day society.

6. We want all black men to be exempt from military service.

7. We want an immediate end to police brutality and murder of black people.

8. We want freedom for all black men held in federal state and county and city prisons and jails.

9. We want all black men when brought to trial to be tried in a court by a jury of their peer group or people from their black communities, as defined by the US Constitution.

10. We want land, bread, housing, education, clothing, justice and peace.

The Black Panther Party was seen by US society as the most radical black activist group. Members wore black berets, black gloves and carried firearms. The internal organisation of the Black Panther Party was hierarchical and centralised. The party's key decision-making body was the non-elected National Central Committee. This comprised a black revolutionary **shadow government** to the USA. Huey Newton was minister of defence, Bobby Seale was central committee chairman, and Eldridge Cleaver was minister of information. Other important people on the committee were: Kathleen Cleaver, Eldridge's wife, who was communications secretary; David Hilliard, chief of staff; Don Cox, field marshal; Roy Hewitt, minister of education; and Emory Douglas, minister of culture. In February 1968, it formed an alliance with the SNCC and, as a result, Stokely Carmichael was appointed to the National Central Committee as prime minister, and James Forman of the SNCC as minister of foreign affairs. However, both Carmichael and Forman resigned by the end of 1968 because they no longer agreed with the new direction of the Party.

Membership of the Black Panther Party never exceeded 5,000 people. It was largely confined to 30 specific groups in urban areas of California, such as Oakland, and in northern cities, such as Chicago, Boston and New York.

However, initially the Black Panther Party aimed at reform rather than revolution. In 1967, it began a free breakfast programme for black children in Oakland and offered medical advice to the black residents in the Oakland ghetto. It also monitored the levels of police brutality and the harassment of black communities by law enforcement officers.

However, from 1968 it became a more radical group, adopting Marxist socialism as its ideology, which advocated the overthrow of American society. The Black Panthers sought to develop links with Third World liberation movements in Africa, Asia and South America. Within the USA, it developed links with the SNCC and with Mexican American activists the Brown Berets and the Chinese American Red Guards, which were similar radical groups.

As a result, it became a particular target for the US law enforcement community, including the FBI. In 1969, 27 Black Panthers were shot by police and 750 were arrested. By 1970, FBI infiltration had broken the back of the Black Panther Party leadership through arrests and imprisonment.

SOURCE 11

A Black Panther Party rally held as a memorial for Bobby Hutton, a young Panther killed by police in Oakland, California, in April 1968.

ACTIVITY
KNOWLEDGE CHECK

Increasing divisions in the civil rights movement

1 What does Source 9 tell us about why Malcolm X was seen by other black Americans as an important influence on the issue of black civil rights?

2 What evidence is there in Source 10 about the way in which the black civil rights movement had changed by 1966?

3 Describe the ways in which the SNCC, CORE and the Black Panther Party had developed different aims and methods from 1966 in the civil rights movement.

4 Give reasons why the SNCC, CORE and the Black Panther Party had adopted new aims and methods from 1966.

Martin Luther King: the last years, 1966–68

The failure in Chicago, 1966

At the time of the radicalisation of both the SNCC and CORE and the rise of the Black Panther Party, Martin Luther King made a fateful decision. Up to 1966, King had campaigned and protested against racial discrimination in the southern states. In 1966, he decided to take his campaign north to Chicago, where black Americans faced discrimination in housing and employment. Unfortunately, the SCLC was poorly organised in Chicago. In opposition stood one of the top city bosses in the USA, the Hon. Richard Daley, a key member of the Democrat Party and mayor of Chicago. When King tried to highlight poor housing accommodation for black Americans, Daley sent in building inspectors, who handed out housing violations to the landlords concerned.

The biggest confrontation in King's Chicago campaign came at the white suburb of Gage Park. An SCLC protest march to highlight *de facto* racial segregation was met with hostile white residents who hurled missiles at the black protestors. Mayor Daley accused the SCLC of encouraging rioting. King failed to persuade the Chicago city council, Mayor Daley or most of the Chicago population to move on the issue of housing segregation. In 1967, Daley was returned as mayor in a landslide victory.

King's stance on the Vietnam War

King's failure in Chicago occurred when protests against the US involvement in the Vietnam War were increasing. The USA had sent ground troops to Vietnam in March 1965. By early 1967, there seemed no sign of victory, as the USA increased its military commitment to almost half a million men and carried out extensive bombing of North Vietnam by the US air force.

Protests against the war began on university campuses, but spread around the country. The SNCC and CORE protested against sending black Americans to fight in the USA's war. World heavyweight boxing champion, Muhammed Ali, refused to be drafted into the US army, claiming that no Vietnamese communist had ever called him 'nigger'. He was subsequently stripped of his boxing crown.

The first time King spoke out against the war was in 1965, but he was aware at that time that the SCLC was opposed to any identification with the peace movement against the war. The change came on 4 April 1967, when he delivered a speech at the Riverside Church, New York City. In that speech, he expressed sympathy for the Vietnamese communists who were fighting US forces and South Vietnamese forces in South Vietnam. He also expressed support for other left-wing revolutionary movements around the world. In 1967, wars against pro-Western and colonial governments were taking place in South America, Africa and Asia. King went so far as to compare US military tactics in Vietnam to the Nazis in the Second World War. He said that US forces were destroying two important institutions in Vietnamese society: the family and the village. He claimed that US forces had destroyed land and crops and had killed women and children.

Later in April, King was the main speaker at the Spring Mobilisation to End the War in Vietnam, organised by James Bevel of the SCLC. One hundred and twenty-five thousand protestors marched from Central Park, in the middle of New York City, to United Nations Plaza, in front of the United Nations building. Also involved in the march were Floyd McKissick of CORE and Stokely Carmichael of the SNCC. It was a deliberate attempt by King to align himself with the younger, more radical element of the black civil rights movement.

However, King's stance on the Vietnam War came at a cost. Two important black civil rights leaders condemned his position: Whitney Young of the Urban League and Roy Wilkins of the NAACP. Moreover, King alienated President Lyndon Johnson and his administration. King had worked closely with the Johnson administration on civil rights, particularly over the Voting Rights Act of 1965. Now, King lost his influence with Johnson and became more isolated politically from national decision-making. In addition, the director of the FBI, J. Edgar Hoover, kept Johnson informed of King's anti-war activities and King's private life. Throughout King's public life, Hoover had been an implacable opponent and used his influence with Johnson to increase surveillance of King and the SCLC.

The Poor People's Campaign and the assassination of Martin Luther King

By the end of 1967, King had come up with a new idea for a campaign. He wanted to reassert his idea of non-violent protest and to unite a coalition of groups to aid the poor, not just the black poor. His idea was the Poor People's Campaign. In an article published just after his assassination, King explained the aims of the campaign. He highlighted the triumphs of non-violent protest in ending legal racial segregation. He now felt the time was right to use the same tactics to address the serious economic problems faced by America's deprived. King planned a march to highlight the fact that the USA required a major redistribution in economic wealth downward to aid the poor. The march's aim was to try to persuade the US Congress to enact King's proposed bill of rights for the disadvantaged. This would involve massive federal funding for poor relief programmes, far beyond the monies already granted by Congress for Johnson's **Great Society programme**.

In February 1968, the sanitation workers in Memphis, Tennessee, went on strike to win union recognition and improve their wages and working conditions. King saw the strike as a suitable cause to launch his Poor People's Campaign. Demonstrations in favour of the strikers ended in chaos, and King's visit to Memphis in aid of the strikers ended abruptly. However, on 3 April 1968, King returned to Memphis. In a speech at the Mason Temple, he foresaw his own death when he claimed that although he would enjoy a long life, that was not the most important thing in life. He said that he was not worried about anything and he did not fear any man. The following day, he was assassinated at the Lorraine Motel, Memphis by a white assassin, James Earl Ray.

SOURCE
12

From 'My Last Letter to Martin' by the Reverend Ralph Abernathy, a speech delivered on 7 April 1968 at the West Hunter Street Baptist Church, Atlanta, which was Martin Luther King's home city. Ralph Abernathy was one of King's closest associates and became acting leader of the SCLC on King's death. Martin Luther King had been assassinated on 4 April 1968 in Memphis, Tennessee.

My dear friend, Martin, now that you have gone, there are some special thoughts that come to me during this Lenten season. There are so many parallels. You were our leader and we were your disciples. Those who killed you did not know that you loved them and that you worked for them as well. For, so often, you said to us: 'Love your enemies. Bless them that curse you and pray for them that despitefully use you.' They did not know, Martin, that you were a good man, that you hated nobody. But you loved everybody. They did not know that you loved them with a love that would not let go. They thought they could kill our movement by killing you, Martin.

But Martin, I want you to know that black people loved you. Some people say that they were just burning and looting in the cities of the nation at the time. But you and I know that just folk, poor people, have had a hard time during these difficult days in which we have lived on earth. And, in spite of the burning, I think they are saying, 'He died for us'. It may seem that they are denying our nonviolence for they are acting out their frustrations. And even a man of good, as you were, was killed in such an evil world we live in today. And they are merely seeking to express their frustrations. They do not see a way out.

The immediate effect of Martin Luther King's assassination

The assassination of Martin Luther King by a white assassin caused national outrage and an outpouring of grief. King's funeral, in Atlanta, Georgia, was attended by most of the major political figures in America as it was an election year. Widespread rioting by black Americans occurred across the USA. The National Guard was called out to protect federal government buildings in the capital, Washington DC.

The SCLC lacked leadership following King's death. Under the nominal leadership of the Reverend Ralph Abernathy, one of King's closest associates, the SCLC was riven with factionalism.

KEY TERM

Great Society programme
Lyndon Johnson's attempt to eradicate poverty in the USA. Also termed the War on Poverty, it was launched at the University of Michigan in 1965 and lasted until 1969. It involved a variety of federal programmes aiming to eradicate poverty in inner cities and poor rural areas.

A Level Exam-Style Question Section B

How successful, by 1968, was the campaign to achieve equal civil rights for black Americans? (20 marks)

Tip

This question requires a balanced analysis. You will be expected to explain where the civil rights movement had been successful, such as in the area of legal segregation, but also to balance this view with areas where black Americans were still facing discrimination, such as housing, job opportunities and quality education.

Abernathy decided to stage a Poor People's Campaign event in the capital. Resurrection City was created on the National Mall, between the Lincoln Memorial and Capitol Hill, home of the US Congress. It was a canvas and wooden encampment and quickly deteriorated into a sea of mud due to poor weather. The National Parks Service, which owned the National Mall, served the SCLC with a bill for $71,000 to pay for the mess. Inadequately funded and without clear leadership, Resurrection City was dismantled on 24 June 1968. At its height, 2,500 protestors camped there.

SOURCE 13

Black American looters participating in a riot in Chicago immediately after the announcement of Martin Luther King's assassination in April 1968.

Martin Luther King's impact on the move for greater equality

With King's death, the semblance of unity in the civil rights movement evaporated. Radicalised groups, such as the SNCC, CORE and the Black Panthers, abandoned non-violent campaigning. The SCLC declined into irrelevance. King had focused the USA on the abolition of legal segregation in the southern states. In this, he was very successful. However, in trying to deal with the social and economic problems facing black Americans across the USA, King failed. *De facto* segregation still existed and black Americans suffered from higher unemployment, poorer housing and worse educational opportunities than white Americans.

ACTIVITY
KNOWLEDGE CHECK

Martin Luther King: The last years, 1966–68

1 In what ways did Martin Luther King change his views on the issue of civil rights in the years 1966–68?

2 With a partner, write down what you regard as Martin Luther King's most significant achievements and what were his most notable failures. Place them in order of importance.

THINKING HISTORICALLY   Interpretations (6a)

Ever-changing history

Our interpretations of the past change as we change. This may be because our social attitudes have changed over time, or perhaps a historian has constructed a new theory, or perhaps technology has allowed archaeologists to discover something new.

Work in pairs.

1 Make a timeline that starts with Reconstruction (1865–77) and ends 50 years in the future. Construct reactions that illustrate the point that time changes history. In the future box, you can speculate how people might react to the event in 50 years' time. Here is an example:

1865	1870	1896	1968	2066
Event: Abolition of slavery	Frederick Douglass, black American civil rights activist: 'free at last' Former Confederate soldier: 'a disaster'	Southern white politician: '*Plessy* v *Ferguson* allows legal segregation' Southern black American: 'a disaster'	Black American: 'at long last black Americans get full civil rights' Southern white politician: 'the end of the old southern way of life' A member of Black Panther Party: 'still a long way to go for full black equality'	?

Answer the following questions.

2 Identify three factors that have affected how Reconstruction is interpreted over time, or might affect it in the future.

3 If a historian were to write a book proposing a radically new interpretation of Martin Luther King and the civil rights movement, how might other historians react? What would affect their reaction?

4 How will the future change the past?

ACTIVITY
SUMMARY

'I have a dream', 1954–68

1 How important was the role of presidents in helping to achieve greater equality for black Americans in the years 1957 to 1968?

2 Which civil rights group did most to help achieve greater equality for black Americans in the years 1957 to 1968?

- SCLC
- SNCC
- CORE
- Black Panther Party

Give reasons for your choice.

WIDER READING

Bunce, R. and Gallagher, L. *Pursuing Life and Liberty: Equality in the USA 1945–1968*, Pearson (2009)

Fairclough, A. *To Redeem the Soul of America; the SCLC and Martin Luther King*, University of Georgia (2001)

Murphy, D. *United States 1917–2008*, Collins Educational (2008)

Paterson, D., Willoughby, S. and Willoughby, D. *Civil Rights in the USA*, Heinemann (2001)

Sanders, V. *Civil Rights in the USA, 1945–1968*, Hodder (2005)

3.7

Obama's campaign for the presidency, 2004–09

KEY QUESTIONS

- How important was Obama's political career from 2004 to 2006 in his rise to the presidency?
- Why was Obama successful in gaining the Democrat Party nomination for the presidency in 2008?
- How far was Obama's success in winning the presidential election of 2008 due to the weakness of his opponents?

INTRODUCTION

On 20 January 2009, Barack Obama was sworn in as the 44th president of the United States. He took the oath of office using the same Bible used by Abraham Lincoln in 1861. Lincoln had freed the black slaves of the USA through the passage of the Thirteenth Amendment of the US Constitution in 1865. Barack Obama was the first black American to become US president. When he was sworn in as president in front of the Capitol Building in Washington DC, which houses the US Congress, he was standing in front of a building built by black slaves before the US Civil War.

Such an idea, that a black American could become president, seemed inconceivable before the advent of the 21st century. Obama's rise to the highest political office in the USA was meteoric. He was the first US president born in Hawaii, which did not become a state until 1959. He was also from a background completely different from other black American politicians. He had no links with ancestors who were black slaves. His father was a black Kenyan from east Africa and his mother was white. Barack Obama rose to prominence through the politics of the city of Chicago and the state of Illinois. In his campaign to become president, he received the overwhelming majority of black American votes. However, to win a majority in the election, he also received considerable support from both Hispanic and white Americans. Was Obama's rise to the presidency the culmination of the moves towards greater equality for black Americans which had begun during the Civil War in the middle of the 19th century?

1961 – 4 August: Barack Obama is born in Honolulu, Hawaii, to Barack Obama Sr and Stanley Ann Dunham

1967 – Obama's mother marries Lolo Soetoro and moves family to Indonesia

1983 – Receives BA in Political Science from Columbia University; works in New York City

1992 – 18 October: Marries attorney Michelle Robinson

1988 – Enrols at Harvard Law School

1960	1965	1970	1985	1990

1964 – His parents divorce

1985 – Moves to Chicago and works as a community organiser

1990 – Is elected editor of *Harvard Law Review* (first black American elected to the position)

SOURCE 1

The inauguration of Barack Obama, 20 January 2009. He is shaking hands with John Ashcroft, the US Supreme Court chief justice who administered the oath of office. Also in the photograph are Obama's wife and daughters.

HOW IMPORTANT WAS OBAMA'S POLITICAL CAREER FROM 2004 TO 2006 IN HIS RISE TO THE PRESIDENCY?

Obama's career to 2006

Obama's early life

Barack Obama's early life reinforces the view that he had a unique upbringing among all US presidents. He was born on 4 August 1961, in Honolulu, Hawaii, just two years after Hawaii was

1995 – Mother dies of cancer, aged 52

Obama's first book, *Dreams from My Father*, is published

1998 – Re-elected to the Illinois state senate (second term)

2002 – Re-elected to the Illinois state senate (third term)

2004 – Elected to the US Senate (IL-Dem)

2008 – June: Wins Democratic Party presidential primary election process

August: Is officially nominated by the Democratic Party at August Convention (first black American to win a major party nomination)

1995	2000	2005	2010	2015

1993 – Begins lecturing at University of Chicago Law School and works at a law firm

2000 – Loses Illinois Democratic primary election for US House of Representatives seat

1996 – Elected to the Illinois state senate (first term)

2006 – Obama's second book, *The Audacity of Hope*, is published

2009 – 20 January: Inaugurated as president of the USA

2008 – 4 November: Elected 44th president of the USA (first black American elected to the position)

admitted to the USA as a state. Obama's father was a member of the Luo tribe from Kenya, east Africa. His mother was Ann Dunham, a white woman originally from Kansas. They married on 2 February 1961 and Barack was born six months later. His parents divorced in March 1964 when Barack was two years old. Shortly afterwards, his father returned to Kenya. In 1965, his mother remarried.

In the 1980s, Barack Obama became a member of the Trinity United Church of Christ, a Christian Church. However, in the 2008 presidential campaign, Obama's background was questioned by his Republican Party opponents. They questioned whether or not he had been born in the USA, a constitutional requirement to stand for president. Obama was the first presidential candidate who made his birth certificate public to confirm his place of birth. He was also accused of being Muslim. His middle name, Hussein, was used as evidence to support this fallacy.

SOURCE 2

A family photograph showing Barack Obama as a young man with his mother and his stepfather, Lolo Soetoro, and his step-sister as a baby. It was released to the media by the Obama campaign on 4 February 2008, during the Super Tuesday primary election campaign, to show his multi-ethnic upbringing.

Illinois state senator, 1997–2004

Obama's first success at winning elective office came in 1996, when he won a seat in the Illinois state senate for the 13th District. This included the South Side of Chicago and the area of Hyde Park, both predominantly black American areas of poverty and social deprivation, where Obama had worked as a social worker. Although he won as a Democrat, Obama developed a reputation for working with both Democrats and Republicans to pass legislation. He was able to get legislation passed to expand health care and early years education programmes for the poor. He became chairperson of the Illinois senate Health and Human Services Committee. In that role, he helped improve the rights of suspects held by the police by requiring video-taping of police interrogations.

In 2000, he suffered his first electoral setback. In that year, he tried to become the Democrat candidate for the 1st Congressional District of Illinois for the US House of Representatives. The district covered the South Side of Chicago and was 65 percent black American. The seat was held for the Democrats by black American Bobby Rush, who had been a founder of the Black Panther Party in Chicago in 1968. He had won the seat in 1992 and had been re-elected in 1994, 1996 and 1998.

Obama displayed a mixture of ambition and naivety in thinking he could replace Rush. Bobby Rush won the Democrat primary election by a decisive 60 percent to 31 percent against Obama. Rush then went on to retain the seat with 88 percent of the vote. However, Obama's experience of campaigning for a national election laid the groundwork for his campaign of 2004 to become a US senator.

The race for the US Senate in 2004

The turning point in Barack Obama's national political career was 2004. In what proved to be a monumental year for him, he won a seat in the US Senate and gave the keynote speech at the Democratic National Convention which chose the Democrat presidential and vice-presidential candidates.

The 2004 national elections took place against a backdrop of war. In 2003, the USA, with its allies, had invaded and occupied Iraq. The Republican president, George W. Bush, was seeking re-election.

For Obama, the opportunity for election to the US Senate looked very promising. In 2003, the incumbent senator for Illinois, Republican Peter Fitzgerald, who had won the Senate seat in 1998, announced he was giving up the seat to return to private business.

The Democrat Party primary election, March 2004

However, Obama still faced a major task. The Democrat Party in Illinois had five major candidates for the post. Before the national election in November 2004, Obama had to win the Democrat Party primary. The primary election was to be held on 16 March 2004. The most prominent Democrat opponent was the state comptroller, Daniel Hynes. He already held this state-wide office and was more widely known than Obama. Hynes was also a member of a well-known Chicago political family. His father, Tom Hynes, had been a state Senator and president of the Illinois state senate. Another serious opponent was Blair Hull of Chicago, a wealthy businessman with a personal fortune of between $131 million and $444 million. In 2002, he had financed a number of Democrat campaigns within Illinois. He was seen as the early leader in the primary campaign.

In addition, Obama faced two other serious candidates – Maria Pappas, who was Cook County treasurer (Chicago was in Cook County) and Gery Chico. Chico had been chief of staff to Chicago mayor, Richard M. Daley. Compared to all these candidates, Obama was a relative unknown. He had a good reputation in the Illinois state senate, but was not known much outside his own 13th District. Within Chicago, both Pappas and Chico were more prominent figures.

Opinion polls run by the major media in the Chicago area during the campaign reflected the rise of Obama in popularity among Democrat supporters. Polls conducted in February 2004 had Obama on 15 percent, behind Blair Hull who had 24 percent. By March, Obama was leading the polls with a more than 10 percent greater share of the vote than his nearest rivals, Dan Hayes and Blair Hull. Maria Pappas and Gery Chico lagged well behind.

The media coverage in the final week of the campaign emphasised the Obama surge in support. This was aided by an effective advertising campaign paid for by Obama, which recounted his life's story. He also got some very high-profile endorsements. Sheila Simon, the daughter of former popular Democrat, Senator Paul Simon, and the Chicago Bulls basketball star, Michael Jordan, backed Obama. Jordan donated a $10,000 cheque to the Obama campaign. A significant feature in Obama's rise and the collapse of the Hull campaign was the announcement, in February, that Hull's divorce of his ex-wife had become controversial. Hull's ex-wife had placed two restraining orders on her ex-husband and there had been a physical quarrel between them. The clear beneficiary of the collapse of Hull's campaign was Obama.

Ultimately, when the Democrat Party electorate got to know Obama, his natural oratory and personality came to the fore. On 16 March 2004, he won the Democrat Party primary election with 53 percent of the vote.

SOURCE 3

From an article in the *New Yorker* magazine on 31 May 2004 by William Finnegan, called 'How the son of a Kenyan economist became an Illinois Everyman'. It deals with Obama and his role in the race to gain the US Senate seat for Illinois in November 2004.

People in Illinois seem largely unaware of Obama's long, annealing trip into their midst, although they often remark on his unusual calm. Now forty-two and a state senator, Obama emerged, in March, from a raucous primary as the Democratic nominee for the United States Senate. In a seven-person field, he received a remarkable fifty-three per cent of the vote—he even won the 'collar' counties around Chicago, communities that supposedly would never support a black candidate.

Obama's Republican opponent in November will be Jack Ryan. The seat they are competing for is now held by a Republican who is retiring. An Obama victory thus would move the Senate Democrats, at present outnumbered fifty-one to forty-eight, one seat closer to a majority. It also would make Obama only the third African-American to serve in the Senate since Reconstruction.

Obama, lanky and dapper in a dark suit, his shoulders almost strangely relaxed, seemed to know most of the men there. He broke the ice with a joke at the expense of Ed Smith, a huge, tough-looking delegate. Obama had met Smith's mother on a recent downstate swing and had discovered that 'she's the one who really calls the shots there.' Smith laughed, and the other delegates said they wanted her phone number.

The questions were terse, specific, well informed. They dealt with federal highway funding, [and] non-union companies coming in from out of state on big contracts. Obama listened closely, and his answers were fluent and dauntingly knowledgeable, but he kept his language colloquial. 'It's not enough just to vote right,' he said. 'You gotta advocate. A lot of these bills coming up now are lose-lose for Democrats.'

Back at the statehouse, Obama, who is chairman of the Health and Human Services Committee, rushed from meeting to floor vote to committee room. Everybody seemed to want a word with him. Kirk Dillard, a leading Republican senator from the Chicago suburbs, looked chagrined when I asked him about Obama. 'I knew from the day he walked into this chamber that he was destined for great things,' he said. 'In Republican circles, we've always feared that Barack would become a rock star of American politics.' Still, Dillard was gracious. 'Obama is an extraordinary man,' he said. 'His intellect, his charisma. He's to the left of me on gun control, abortion. But he can really work with Republicans.' Dillard and Obama have co-sponsored many bills.

The Senate election, November 2004

Even though Obama won the Democrat primary election, he still had to face a very serious challenger in the Republican Party which had held the Illinois Senate seat vacated by Peter Fitzgerald. The winner of the Republican primary election was Jack Ryan. He had won a hard-fought Republican primary campaign. However, he was University of Harvard educated, and married to a television star, Jeri Ryan, both often vote-winning qualities in US elections. Ryan won the primary election with 36 percent of the vote. Both Obama and Ryan were seen as well-educated, photogenic and charismatic. In addition, the Democrat and Republican parties were evenly represented in Illinois. The Democrats held ten congressional districts against nine held by the Republicans. Ryan's personal wealth, as a successful businessman, and the financial power of the Republican Party made winning the Senate seat very challenging for Obama.

However, Obama did possess a number of advantages. In the Democrat primary election, Obama won a total of 655,923 votes and 52.77 percent of the vote. On the Republican side, Ryan won 234,717 votes (35 percent of the total). Based on these figures, Obama had a distinct advantage in the Senate election if he could get out the Democrat vote. The Democrats dominated the vote in Chicago, by far the largest city in Illinois. In the suburban areas surrounding Chicago, in Cook County, the Republican vote was in decline where the Democrats had won a number of Illinois state elections. This was the bedrock support for Obama. He also won well in Champaign County, the home of the University of Illinois, and Sangamon County, home of the Illinois state government. Ultimately though, the election was decided by a major problem in the Republican Party campaign.

As in his Democrat primary campaign, Obama benefited from a massive stroke of luck. Republican Jack Ryan was involved in an acrimonious divorce case. Accusations by his wife Jeri resulted in considerable media coverage. The result was the withdrawal of Jack Ryan as the Republican candidate. In his place, the Republican National Committee chose a conservative black American commentator, Alan Keyes, who had previously tried to be senator for the state of Maryland on the eastern seaboard. The Illinois Senate contest was the only one in the USA where the two challengers for the Democratic and Republican parties were both black Americans. The media response across Illinois was almost uniformly negative towards Keyes. His campaign failed to win over many undecided voters. He was strongly against abortion and gay rights, and in favour of increasing the role of religion in US society. Obama, in contrast, ran a very energetic campaign concentrating on key social issues. He used his experience of community-based projects in Chicago to organise a grass-roots campaign which dealt with local issues.

In addition, Obama's profile was enhanced nationally when he became keynote speaker at the Democratic Party National Convention held in late July in Boston, Massachusetts. It gave him considerable positive media publicity and made him into a national political figure. His engaging personality, his moderate views, his attractive wife and family all endeared him to the electorate. Following the Democratic National Convention, Obama became a sought-after speaker across the USA. Also, his decision to ignore his Republican opponent, Alan Keyes, enhanced his reputation, because he engaged in positive campaigning on the issues rather than negative campaigning against his opponent. When the election took place on 2 November 2004, Obama won with 69.9 percent of the vote against Keyes 27.05 percent. Obama had won the vast majority of votes in Chicago. Over the whole state, Obama won in 92 of 102 counties in Illinois. Nearly three-quarters of female voters and two-thirds of male voters voted Democrat. An analysis of votes by party identification (being asked about party loyalty and whether they identify with either the Democrats, Republicans or Independents) showed that almost all people who identified with the Democrats voted for Obama, while only just over half of voters who identified with the Republican party voted for Keyes – just over a third of these Republican supporters voted for Obama.

Obama's success in the Illinois Senate race gave him both state-wide and national recognition. The Democrats had not performed well in the elections of 2004. Republican George W. Bush was re-elected president and Democrat Senate majority leader, Tom Daschle, lost his seat. As a young, photogenic black American senator, Obama's victory was one of the high spots for the Democrat Party. He became a regular guest on television shows and at political events. In 2005, he re-released his autobiography, *Dreams From My Father*, which became a best-seller nationally. The book's success made him a millionaire. His national career had been established. The following year, Obama published a second book, *The Audacity of Hope*. This book discussed his vision of the future for the USA. Like his autobiography, this second book became a best-seller in both US bookshops and on Amazon.

SOURCE 4

US Senate election results in Illinois in November 2004, when Barack Obama became the only black American in the US Senate from January 2005.

Status	Candidate	Political Party	Vote	Vote %
✓	D Obama	Democrat	3,597,456	70%
	R Keyes	Republican	1,390,690	27%
	I Franzen	Independent	81,164	2%
	L Kohn	Libertarian	69,253	1%

ACTIVITY
KNOWLEDGE CHECK

Obama's success in winning elections

1 With a partner, find five reasons why you think Obama was successful in winning elections in 2004.

2 With a partner, place the reasons in order of importance. Give reasons for your choice.

US senator for Illinois

Obama was sworn in as junior senator for Illinois in January 2005. He was only the third black American senator since Reconstruction. For the next two years, his work in the US Congress helped cement his reputation as a rising star within the Democrat Party. When he arrived in the Senate, he was 99th in terms of seniority out of 100 senators. He was 43 years old in an institution where the average age was 60 years. He was also a member of the minority party, as the Republicans held a majority. In committee hearings, he had to wait until all other senators had asked questions before he could speak.

However, Obama did use his time as US senator to increase his national profile. He was able to persuade the Democrat leadership in the Senate to get him a seat on the Foreign Relations Committee. Although a liberal Democrat, he developed a reputation for cross-party collaboration. With Senator Tom Coburn, a Republican from Oklahoma, he created a website that tracked federal spending, aiming at rebuilding citizen trust in national government after the debacle of the federal response to Hurricane Katrina in New Orleans. In August 2005, Hurricane Katrina had wrought havoc in the Gulf of Mexico region of the USA, in particular the city of New Orleans, which had been flooded. Obama partnered Republican Senator Richard Lugar of Indiana in sponsoring a bill to destroy nuclear weapons in Eastern Europe and Russia. He also voted against troop withdrawals from Iraq, which disappointed the Democrat leadership in the US Senate, most notably Senators John Kerry of Massachusetts and Russ Feingold of Wisconsin.

As a rising star of the Democrat Party, Obama used his time acquiring money for his attempt to win the presidential nomination of his party in 2008. He created a **Political Action Committee (PAC)** called the Hopefund. It raised $1.8 million in its first year. During the **midterm elections** of 2006, Obama became a sought-after campaign speaker and helped to raise $1 million for the campaign of

KEY TERMS

Political Action Committee (PAC)

A popular term for a political committee organised for the purpose of raising and spending money to elect and defeat candidates. Most PACs represent business, labour or ideological interests. PACs can give $5,000 to a candidate committee per election (primary or general). They can also give up to $15,000 annually to any national party committee, and $5,000 annually to any other PAC. PACs may receive up to $5,000 from any one individual, PAC or party committee per calendar year. A PAC must register with the Federal Election Commission within ten days of its formation, providing a name and address for the PAC, its treasurer and any connected organisations. Affiliated PACs are treated as one donor for the purpose of contribution limits.

Midterm election

A general election that does not coincide with a presidential election year, but occurs two years into the term of a president, i.e. in the middle of a president's term in office. While presidential elections are held every four years, general elections for other positions are held every two years. In a midterm election, some members of the US Senate, all members of the House of Representatives, and many state and local positions are voted on.

the veteran Democrat senator from West Virginia, Robert Byrd. In the midterm elections, the Democrats scored a stunning victory. They retook control of both the House of Representatives and the Senate. Obama, as a key speaker during the campaign, rose in stature in both the Democrat Party and the country. This confirmed his status as a future leader within the Democrat Party. In the House, the Democrats increased their seats from 202 to 233; in the Senate, they increased their seats from 44 to 51.

Obama's performance as US senator and in the midterm elections laid the foundations for his ultimate ambition, to run for president. On 10 February 2007, he declared he would be a candidate for the Democratic nomination for president in the 2008 presidential election.

SOURCE 5

From Barack Obama's keynote speech at the Democratic National Convention on 27 July 2004. The Convention confirmed John Kerry as Democratic presidential candidate. The keynote speech is the most important speech apart from that made by the candidate.

Tonight, we gather to affirm the greatness of our nation not because of the height of our skyscrapers, or the power of our military, or the size of our economy; our pride is based on a very simple premise, summed up in a declaration made over two hundred years ago: 'We hold these truths to be self-evident, that all men are created equal that they are endowed by their Creator with certain inalienable rights, that among these are life, liberty and the pursuit of happiness.'

That is the true genius of America, a faith, a faith in simple dreams, an insistence on small miracles; that we can tuck in our children at night and know that they are fed and clothed and safe from harm; that we can say what we think, write what we think, without hearing a sudden knock on the door; that we can have an idea and start our own business without paying a bribe; that we can participate in the political process without fear of retribution; and that our votes will be counted – or at least, most of the time.

This year, in this election, we are called to reaffirm our values and our commitments, to hold them against a hard reality and see how we are measuring up, to the legacy of our forbearers and the promise of future generations have the drive, have the will, but doesn't have the money to go to college.

In this election, we offer that choice. Our party has chosen a man to lead us who embodies the best this country has to offer. And that man is John Kerry.

Well, I say to them tonight, there's not a liberal America and a conservative America; there's the United States of America.

There's not a black America and white America and Latino America and Asian America; there's the United States of America.

I believe that we can give our middle class relief and provide working families with a road to opportunity.

I believe we can provide jobs for the jobless, homes to the homeless, and reclaim young people in cities across America from violence and despair.

I believe that we have a righteous wind at our backs, and that as we stand on the crossroads of history, we can make the right choices and meet the challenges that face us.

A Level Exam-Style Question Section A

Study Source 5 before you answer this question.

Assess the value of the source for revealing the reasons why Barack Obama was seen as a future political leader in the Democratic Party.

Explain your answer, using the source, the information given about its origin and your own knowledge about the historical context. (20 marks)

Tip

In your answer, it is important to refer to the provenance of the source as a way of assessing its value. Who wrote it? When was it written? Who was its intended audience? To support your answer, use relevant information from the content of the source and your own knowledge to help place the source in its historical context.

A Level Exam-Style Question Section B

How far was Obama's election to the Illinois state senate a turning point in his career to become a possible future Democratic Party candidate for the presidency? (20 marks)

Tip

You will need to address the importance of his election to the Illinois state senate and explain why this was important in Obama's career. In doing so, you will need to examine his career before his election and the impact it had on his career after 2008.

ACTIVITY
KNOWLEDGE CHECK

Obama's early political career

Identify which personal qualities Barack Obama possessed that made him a rising star in the Democratic Party.

WHY WAS OBAMA SUCCESSFUL IN GAINING THE DEMOCRAT PARTY NOMINATION FOR THE PRESIDENCY IN 2008?

EXTEND YOUR KNOWLEDGE

The race to the White House

The USA is a federal country where political power is divided between a central (federal) government and 50 state governments. To emphasise the federal nature of the US political system, the main political parties are organised at state level. There are 50 Democrat and 50 Republican Party organisations. They come together every four years to elect a president.

The process of becoming president is long and arduous and involves a considerable amount of funding. The official party process for choosing a presidential candidate begins at the beginning of January in the presidential election year. Traditionally, the first way of showing support for both parties is the Iowa state caucus. A caucus is a meeting of party members to show which candidate they prefer. This is followed by a series of primary elections, of which the New Hampshire state primary is traditionally the first.

The aim of candidates is to get as many delegates as they can to attend the party's national convention in the summer. The candidate with a majority of delegates becomes the party's presidential candidate.

Traditionally, the presidential candidate chooses the vice-presidential candidate. The announcement usually takes place at the party national convention.

The official election for president usually occurs between the start of September and the first Tuesday in November.

Personal and speaking skills

In 2000, Barack Obama's political career faced a major setback. He failed to win the Democratic Party primary election for a seat in the House of Representatives. Yet within eight years he had become the first black American president of the United States. Such a meteoric rise for any politician was astonishing.

Keynote speech at the Democratic National Convention, 27 July 2004

A key event in Obama's rise was his keynote speech at the Democratic National Convention in late July 2004. The National Convention is the coming together of the Democrat Party to choose their presidential and vice-presidential candidates. It is the most important national event in the party and takes place every four years.

Obama was only the third black American to deliver such a speech to a major party national convention. The entire national media were present. John Kerry of Massachusetts was announced as the Democrat Party presidential candidate against the incumbent George W. Bush. Kerry wanted to win the black American, Latino American and Asian American votes in the election. Obama was seen as a person who would win over these voters. The keynote speech received a very positive response. He was introduced as someone who, one day, would be president of the USA.

Obama's personal qualities and speech-making helped to transform him into a nationally known politician. His appeal in his keynote address was to all Americans from all types of economic background, not just black Americans or the poor and disadvantaged. In particular, his speech appealed to white Americans through references to President Lincoln, to Thomas Jefferson and to the Declaration of Independence. In many ways, Obama distanced himself from, and broke the link with, other black Americans who had tried to enter the national stage. The most notable of Obama's predecessors in this sphere was the Reverend Jesse Jackson. He had been a close aide of Martin Luther King. He had campaigned to be the Democrat presidential candidate in 1984 and 1988. In the latter year, he won some primary elections. Yet Jackson was closely associated with the civil rights movement and was initially from the South. Obama came from a completely different background. Obama was from a northern city and was not tainted with the divisive nature of the civil rights movement.

Obama's performance stood in marked contrast to that of another speaker at the Democratic National Convention, black American activist Al Sharpton. Sharpton spoke of the failings of President Lincoln and the civil rights movement, and the need to provide reparation payments to black Americans for past wrongs. Sharpton was seen as a traditional black American politician, speaking primarily to a black American audience. Obama represented a new style of black American politician from a younger generation, not linked to black radicalism and speaking to all Americans. This was the key to Obama's success. He spoke for all Americans of all classes. This approach was one of the main secrets of his success over the following four years.

His keynote speech was followed by his success in the 2004 Illinois senatorial election. In a year when the Democrats failed to win the presidential election and lost four seats in the Senate, Obama won a formerly Republican Senate seat with 70 percent of the vote. His ability to campaign well in 2004, combined with his excellent speaking skills, made him a very sought after politician in the Democrat Party. Such skill was clearly evident during his campaign to win the Democrat Party nomination against other candidates who were far more well known.

Democrat Party opponents

The 2008 presidential election gave the Democrats a clear opportunity to return their candidate to the White House. The Twenty-Second Amendment of the US Constitution, passed in 1951, limited any president to two terms in office. George W. Bush had been elected in 2000 and had to stand down as president in January 2009. President Bush was also deeply unpopular and would see his popularity slip to 33 percent, while only 31 percent of polled Americans believed that their country was heading in the right direction.

As a result, several senior Democrat politicians sought their party's nomination. In the initial list of possible contenders, Obama was seen as the outsider. He was the only black American in the US Senate and had been a US senator for only three years. However, a poll conducted by *Newsweek* magazine in 2006 showed that if their party nominated a black American, 93 percent of respondents said they would vote for them. A February 2007 *Associated Press* poll had put Hillary Clinton ahead of Obama, with a 41 percent lead over his 17 percent, with John Edwards close behind at 16 percent. However, by the end of the month, Clinton's lead was reduced from 36 percent to 24 percent and Edwards' to 12 percent.

SOURCE

An article on Obama from Fox News, a conservative media organisation. It announced Barack Obama's decision to stand for the Democratic Party nomination as their presidential candidate, 11 February 2007.

Barack Obama announced his bid for president Saturday, a black man evoking Abraham Lincoln's ability to unite a nation and a Democrat portraying himself as a fresh face capable of leading a new generation. 'Let us transform this nation,' he told thousands shivering in the cold at the campaign's kickoff. Obama, 45, is the youngest candidate in the Democrats' 2008 primary field dominated by front-runner Sen. Hillary Rodham Clinton and filled with more experienced lawmakers. In an address from the state capital where he began his elective career 10 years ago, the first-term U.S. senator sought to distinguish himself as a staunch opponent of the Iraq war and a White House hopeful whose lack of political experience is an asset. Obama is looking to cap his remarkable, rapid rise to prominence with the biggest political prize of all — the presidency. His elective career began just 10 years ago in the Illinois Legislature. He lost a bid for a U.S. House seat, then won the Senate seat in 2004, a relatively smooth election made easier by GOP stumbles. In his speech, Obama did not mention his roots as the son of a man from Kenya and a woman from Kansas, his childhood in Hawaii and Indonesia or the history he would make if elected. That compelling biography has turned him into a political celebrity.

Instead, he focused on his life in Illinois over the past two decades, beginning with a job as a community organizer with a $13,000-a-year salary that strengthened his Christian faith. He said the struggles he saw people face inspired him to get a law degree and run for the Legislature, where he served eight years.

'He's young and he's fresh,' said 22-year-old Rachel Holtz, a graduate student from DeKalb, Ill., who plans to work in education.

Brenda and Michael Talkington, who live near Muncie, Ind., said they have never been involved in a political campaign, but both were laid off from jobs with a lighting company and plan to volunteer for Obama.

'He makes you feel like it is possible to change things,' Brenda Talkington said.

He spoke of reshaping the economy for the digital age, investing in education, protecting employee benefits, insuring those who do not have health care, ending poverty, weaning America from foreign oil and fighting terrorism while rebuilding global alliances. But he said the first priority must be to end the war in Iraq.

> **A Level Exam-Style Question Section A**
>
> *Study Source 6 before you answer this question.*
>
> Assess the value of the source for revealing the reasons why Barack Obama was regarded as a serious contender for the Democrat presidential candidate in 2008.
>
> Explain your answer, using the source, the information given about its origin and your own knowledge about the historical context. (20 marks)
>
> **Tip**
>
> *In your answer, it is important to refer to the provenance of the source as a way of assessing its value. Who wrote it? When was it written? Who was its intended audience? To support your answer, use relevant information from the content of the source and your own knowledge to help place the source in its historical context.*

Hillary Rodham Clinton

A favourite to win the nomination was Hillary Rodham Clinton, wife of former Democrat president, Bill Clinton (1993–2001). She had a very high profile as First Lady during her husband's presidency and played a leading role in Bill Clinton's attempt to reform medical provision in 1993. In January 2001, she became the first ever female senator for the state of New York and was re-elected as senator in 2006. Her national reputation was higher than that of any other Democrat and she also benefited from the considerable campaigning skills of her husband. A poll conducted by *Newsweek* in 2006 found that 55 percent of Americans said that they were ready to elect a female president.

John Edwards

John Edwards had even more experience than Hillary Rodham Clinton in running for president. He had sought the Democrat Party nomination in 2004 and was defeated by John Kerry of Massachusetts. However, he accepted the role as vice-presidential running mate to Kerry in the 2004 election. He was a lawyer and senator for North Carolina from 1999 to 2005. He was a very effective speaker, and as a white southerner would appeal to the voters in the southern states. In October 2006, Edwards trailed Hillary Rodham Clinton by 11 points in a poll among Democrats about who they would prefer as their presidential candidate.

Joe Biden

Biden had been a senator for the small state of Delaware since 1973 and had run for the Democrat Party nomination in 1988. He withdrew at that time when accused of plagiarising speeches from British Labour Party leader Neil Kinnock.

Other candidates

Christopher Dodd, senator for Connecticut from 1981, decided to run, along with former senator Mike Gravel, senator for Alaska from 1969 to 1981, Dennis Kucinich, congressman for the 10th district of Ohio, and Governor Bill Richardson of New Mexico, who was governor from 2003.

The impact of the Iowa state caucus election contest

Unlike the British general election, the US presidential election campaign is long and arduous. It begins with gaining the nomination of a political party. This began with the Iowa state caucus in January 2008. Even though only one percent of delegates to the Democratic National Convention are chosen by the Iowa caucus, it gives an early indication of how popular candidates may be. It is seen as an important sounding board of party opinion before the first primary election in New Hampshire.

Following their poor showing in the Iowa state caucus election, Governor Bill Richardson, Senator Christopher Dodd and Dennis Kucinich withdrew. At the end of January 2008, John Edwards also withdrew due to his poor performance.

SOURCE

7

From an article, 'Have You Come a Long Way, Baby? Hillary Clinton, Sarah Palin, and Sexism in 2008 Campaign Coverage' by Diana B. Carlin and Kelly L. Winfrey in *Communication Studies*, Vol. 60, No. 4, September–October 2009. © 2009 Routledge. It comments on the portrayal of Hillary Rodham Clinton and why she did not win the Democratic Party nomination in 2008.

Iron Maiden

Portrayals of Hillary Clinton as weak or needing a man to carry her campaign were relatively rare. The common media frame for Clinton was that she was not feminine enough. An analysis of 'the media's negative attitudes about Clinton as a career-oriented woman' by media critic Ashleigh Crowther (2007) identified the following common terms to describe Clinton: 'overly ambitious', 'calculating', 'cold', 'scary', and 'intimidating'. When Clinton nearly cried in New Hampshire when asked how she did it every day, the incident grabbed headlines and was reported as breaking news largely because it went against the tough image Clinton projected. The overt sexism resulted in frequent vulgar overtones. 'At Christmas, Hillary Clinton nutcrackers were quite the snapped-up item'. The 'device [was] ... a pantsuit-clad Clinton doll [who] opens her legs to reveal stainless steel thighs that, well, bust nuts'. The theme was repeated by MSNBC's Tucker Carlson who commented that 'When she comes on television, I involuntarily cross my legs', and by Chris Matthews who called her male supporters 'castratos in the eunuch chorus'. Once again, it is difficult to find a male counterpart to the portrayal or comments.

Projecting competence through demonstration of masculine traits such as toughness not only can result in crude humor but it is also the primary cause of the double bind. The double bind is most obvious when women need to go negative as Peggy Simpson of the Women's Media Center noted: 'Normally, a politician trying to check an opponent's surge will go negative to alert voters to his flaws, to bring up his foibles, to say he's not ready for prime time. It's not clear that works for a female politician without doing more harm to her than to her opponent. But what is clear is that, so far, it's not working for this woman.'

ACTIVITY
KNOWLEDGE CHECK

Obama's campaign for the Democratic nomination

1 Describe four ways in which Obama's campaign for the Democratic nomination for president was successful.

2 What do you regard as the most important reason why Obama won the Democratic Party nomination?

- Personal qualities
- Election strategies
- Weaknesses of his main opponent

Give reasons to support your answer.

Obama's election strategies

The Iowa caucus election on 3 January 2008 was a defining moment in Obama's campaign for the Democratic nomination and showed that his election strategy was the key to his success. Obama offered a striking contrast to Hillary Rodham Clinton. She was in her late fifties and Obama was in his forties. She was tainted by her link to her husband Bill among independent and Republican voters. Obama offered a new future; Clinton a reversal to the past of the 1990s.

Obama built on his grass-roots campaigning approach that won him his seat in both the Illinois and US senates. The Obama 'brand' was sold effectively using the internet. The number of Americans using the internet had risen from 2 percent in 1996 to 26 percent in 2007, while the use of newspapers for opinion forming fell from 49 percent to 30 percent over the same period.

This use of the social media became a feature of Obama's campaign. His campaign team effectively used Facebook, Twitter, YouTube and www.barackobama.com to connect with young voters. Research had shown that 42 percent of 18- to 29-year-olds used the internet as the basis of their coverage of campaign news.

This approach suggested that the Obama campaign was inclusive of all age groups. It was through these social media that Obama was able to get ahead of Clinton in the polls, even though Clinton began the campaign with the advantages of more money and greater voter recognition.

Long before the Iowa delegates made their views known in January 2008, Obama's social media campaign was having results. By the spring of 2007, over 450,000 people had signed up to the Obama campaign online.

This strategy also proved very effective in fundraising. Using the internet, Obama raised $6.9 million compared to only $4.2 million for the Clinton campaign. Campaign contributions to Obama came from large numbers of small donations rather than large contributors. The average contribution was less than $200.

Clinton's campaign team tried to exploit Obama's relative political inexperience and referred to Clinton as the candidate of experience. This allowed the Obama team to portray him as the candidate for change, speaking for a new generation. His best-selling book, *The Audacity of Hope* published in 2006, aided this ploy. In the Iowa caucus, Clinton won four percent of Democrat supporters but hardly any from non-Democrats. Thirty-six percent of Obama's supporters declared themselves non-Democrats. This made it clear that Obama had the greatest appeal to those voters who were not registered Democrats, which made his chances of defeating a Republican much greater.

Iowa confirmed a trend in Obama's campaign for the Democratic Party nomination. The use of IT and social networking proved very effective in both fundraising and citizen participation in elections. It greatly reduced Clinton's pre-election advantages.

After the victory in the Iowa caucus, Obama lost to Clinton in the first primary election in New Hampshire on 8 January 2008. Clinton won 39.1 percent of the vote to Obama's 36.5 percent. However, in a *New York Times* poll at the time, 55 percent of voters claimed Obama was most likely to bring the change most US voters felt they needed in 2008. Also, 53 percent of voters claimed that Obama had a better chance than Clinton in defeating the Republicans in the presidential election. Clinton had done well with the core Democratic vote, but Obama did well among independents, which augured well for the rest of his campaign. Also, Clinton was almost universally disliked by Republican **registered voters**.

A big breakthrough occurred in the South Carolina primary election on 26 January 2008, when Obama won an overwhelming endorsement from black American voters. He also won 55.4 percent of the vote compared to Clinton's 26.5 percent. More significantly, after that primary election victory, he received the endorsement of Edward and Caroline Kennedy, the brother and daughter of former president, John F. Kennedy.

On **Super Tuesday**, 5 February, when 23 states and American Samoa held their primaries and caucus elections, Obama won 13 to Clinton's 10.

As the primary election contests progressed, Obama attracted support as the underdog and the person most likely to bring change. His campaign slogan, 'Yes We Can', increasingly became a central feature

KEY TERMS

Registered voter
Unlike the UK, in the USA, a voter must register personally to vote. In that process, they must identify themselves as Democrat, Republican or Independent. In the vast majority of primary elections, only registered Democrats or Republicans can vote in their own primary elections. These are known as closed primaries. Open primaries are elections when any type of registered voter can vote.

Super Tuesday
The day in the cycle of primary elections when 24 states hold primary and caucus elections. Usually the day when the frontrunner in the Democratic and Republican nomination contest becomes apparent.

of the campaign. Young, full of energy, a new face and a black American all proved to be attractive qualities across ethnic and social groups of voters. By June 2008, the long battle for the primaries was over. Obama's campaign strategy, headed by David Plouffe, had won by concentrating on grass-roots and social media campaigning. He had outmanoeuvred and outspent the Clinton campaign.

A critical factor in the campaign was the readiness of Democrat voters to accept a male black American as their candidate rather than a woman. Also, while David Plouffe ran an effective campaign, the Clinton campaign was dogged by in-fighting between her chief strategists Mark Penn and Harold Ickes.

Even so, the Democrat campaign for presidential nomination was very close. In caucus elections, Obama won 383,317 votes (66.7 percent) against Clinton's 179,604 votes (31.2 percent). But in the primary elections, Obama polled 17.6 million votes (47.1 percent) to Clinton's 18 million (48.3 percent).

An important factor was Obama's success in attracting 'superdelegate' votes from Democrat politicians and leading party members. These were extra delegates not chosen in caucuses or in primary elections and who are not committed to any one candidate. Before the Democratic National Convention, Obama had 1,741 delegates (41.8 percent) compared to Clinton's 1,643 (39.4 percent). In superdelegate votes, Obama received 543 against Clinton's 209, which secured Obama the necessary majority to be the Democratic Party candidate.

Policies

In terms of policy, Obama's positive emphasis on America's strength and the need to change from the Republican presidency of George W. Bush were constant themes. To Obama, Bush had taken the USA in the wrong direction. Bush had involved the USA in costly wars in Iraq and Afghanistan, and the US economy by 2008 had entered a period of crisis. He emphasised the poor performance of the economy and the high costs of health care. As president, Obama claimed he would provide decisive leadership from a new generation, he would end economic recession and make sure the hard-working American received a decent standard of living.

To achieve these ends, he offered an emergency economic plan, and to restore trust in government and fiscal responsibility. He also aimed to promote the energy independence of the USA and create five million green jobs. Like John F. Kennedy before him, he offered the idea of service to the USA, with voluntary citizen service and greater opportunity for all. In foreign affairs, he advocated the end of involvement in Iraq and spoke about turning the tide against global terrorism. Taken together, these policy statements resonated with a wide cross-section of Democrat voters.

On 27 August 2008, at the Democratic National Convention in Denver, Colorado, Barack Obama was confirmed as the Democrat Party presidential candidate. This was the first time in history a black American had achieved such a position. Before 2004, he was virtually unknown in national politics. Now he was just over two months away from the ultimate prize of the presidency itself. What stood in the way was a gruelling national election campaign and his Republican Party opponent.

SOURCE 8

From a speech made by Barack Obama in Flint, Michigan, on 16 June 2008. Flint was an area affected by very high unemployment. Obama sets out his planned policies for economic recovery.

So these are challenging times. That's why I spent last week talking about immediate steps we need to take to provide working Americans with relief. A broad-based, middle class tax cut, to help offset the rising cost of gas and food. A foreclosure prevention fund, to help stabilize the housing market. A health care plan that lowers costs and gives those without health insurance the same kind of coverage members of Congress have. A commitment to retirement security that stabilizes Social Security and provides workers a means of increased savings. And a plan to crack down on unfair and sometimes deceptive lending in the credit card and housing markets, to help families climb out of crippling debt and stay out of debt in the first place.

These steps are all paid for and designed to restore balance and fairness to the American economy after years of the Bush administration policies that tilted the playing field in favor of the wealthy and the well-connected. But the truth is, none of these short-term steps alone will ensure America's future. Yes, we have to make sure that the economic pie is sliced more fairly, but we need to provide immediate help to families who are struggling in places like Flint, but we also need a serious plan to create new jobs and industry.

SOURCE
9
Street mural of Barack Obama in Chicago and his campaign slogan for the 2008 presidential election, 'Yes We Can'.

ACTIVITY
KNOWLEDGE CHECK

Obama's policies and campaign
Study Sources 8 and 9.

How important are these two sources in providing reasons why Obama won the Democratic Party nomination in 2008?

HOW FAR WAS OBAMA'S SUCCESS IN WINNING THE PRESIDENTIAL ELECTION OF 2008 DUE TO THE WEAKNESS OF HIS OPPONENTS?

The context

On 1 September 2008, the Republican Party held its National Convention to confirm John McCain of Arizona as its candidate for the presidency. Like Obama, McCain faced a number of opponents to win the Republican Party nomination. Most serious was Mitt Romney, former Governor of Massachusetts. He also faced opposition from a large number of candidates who dropped out early in the campaign. One was Alan Keyes, the black American opponent to Barack Obama in the Illinois Senate election of 2004.

From the beginning of September to the first Tuesday in November, the actual presidential election contest occurred primarily between Obama and McCain. However, as in all presidential elections, other parties fielded candidates who had no chance of winning. These included: Ralph Nader, an Independent; Bob Barr, Libertarian; Cynthia McKinney, Green; and Alan Keyes, who decided to run as an Independent having failed to win support in the Republican Party.

The economic situation

A key concern in the 2008 presidential election was the condition of the US economy. In the election, 60 percent of the voters who cast their ballots claimed the economy was their main concern. After a period of moderate economic growth in the early part of the 21st century, the US economy had entered a recession by 2008. At the height of the presidential election, it seemed that the US economy was in freefall. The chairman of the Federal Reserve Board (equivalent to the governor of the Bank of England), Alan Greenspan, claimed it was the worst economic crisis facing the USA since the end of the Second World War.

In one week in September 2008, Lehman Brothers Bank, one of the most prestigious in the USA, filed for bankruptcy. The insurance corporation AIG, who at the time sponsored Manchester United, was loaned $85 billion by the federal government as emergency funds to prevent its financial collapse. In the economy as a whole, the gross domestic product of the USA shrank as low as −3.8 percent and unemployment rose to 10 percent.

In the wake of these serious economic problems, President George Bush asked Congress for new powers that would allow a bailout plan for the US banking sector, which would cost US taxpayers billions of dollars. Senator John McCain suspended his campaign in September to return to Washington DC to vote on Bush's rescue package for the US economy. Similar problems were faced by other western economies, such as the United Kingdom. The world economic system seemed on the verge of collapse.

All these developments benefited a candidate who had consistently advocated that 2008 was a time of change for the US federal government. In 2008, Obama published a book which set out his plans for a future America under his presidency, entitled *Change We Can Believe In*. In that book, Warren Buffett, a multi-billionaire, stated that he thought Obama had the right vision for where the USA needed to go. Elizabeth Warren, co-author of *The Two-Income Trap: Why Middle Class Mothers and Fathers are Going Broke*, believed Obama boldly addressed the issues critical to family economic security.

At the beginning of the campaign in early September, Obama and McCain had similar ratings in the polls at 46 percent each, but as the economic crisis developed, Obama's lead increased. As the campaign entered October, Obama was seen as the person who could bring change. As a Republican, McCain was tarnished with being associated with the Bush administration.

The choice of vice-presidential candidates

The choice of a vice-presidential running mate was the preserve of the presidential candidate. Normally, presidential candidates attempt to 'balance the ticket' by choosing someone from another part of the country to increase electoral appeal. John F. Kennedy of Massachusetts, in 1960, chose Texan Lyndon Johnson; Ronald Reagan of California chose G.H.W Bush of Texas as vice-presidential candidate.

In 2008, Barack Obama chose Joe Biden of Delaware as vice-presidential candidate. Biden was from one of the smallest states, but was chosen because of his experience and his expertise in foreign affairs, an area where Obama was weak. He had been a US senator since 1973.

John McCain chose former Alaska governor, Sarah Palin, as his running mate. She was only the second woman chosen for that position. (Geraldine Ferraro had been Walter Mondale's running mate for the Democrats in the 1984 presidential election. Mondale had suffered a heavy defeat.) Initially, this was seen as a bold decision by McCain. Following the announcement of Palin's candidacy, poll ratings for McCain rose to the point where McCain led Obama by 48 percent to 45 percent. McCain hoped Palin would appeal to women voters. Palin claimed to appeal to the small town 'hockey moms' of America who worked hard to bring up families. She also was an avid supporter of the National Rifle Association, which was opposed to any form of gun control.

However, 'the Palin effect' soon became apparent. Palin displayed a widespread ignorance of key policy areas. Her lack of knowledge of foreign affairs opened the Republican campaign up to ridicule. Her lack of experience of national politics, her homespun demeanour and an ability to make gaffes during the campaign damaged McCain's chances. The very popular television show *Saturday Night Live* ran a regular feature where a comedian posing as Palin portrayed her as a bumpkin. Far from being a bold move, the choice of Sarah Palin began to damage McCain's chances of success.

SOURCE

10 From an article called 'Sarah Palin's Very Bad Interview' written for the liberal news website AlterNet on 25 September 2008. The article is about Sarah Palin's interview with Katie Couric of CBS News, shown live on US television in two parts. The first part was aired on 24 September and dealt with Palin's view on the financial crisis. The second part was aired on 25 September and dealt with foreign policy. Sarah Palin was formerly governor of Alaska.

The more time Sarah Palin spends on the national stage, the worse she gets.

The first half of the Katie Couric interview with Sarah Palin did not start off well. It was a complete disaster, in fact it's like watching a train wreck, she seems to have no idea what she is talking about. But hey, people sometimes get off on the wrong foot. Well, no. If the first half of the interview was bad, well then the second half of the interview was much, much worse. In the second part of the interview with Palin, Couric asks Palin to explain what this talking point means: COURIC: You've cited Alaska's proximity to Russia as part of your foreign policy experience. What did you mean by that?

PALIN: That Alaska has a very narrow maritime border between a foreign country, Russia, and on our other side, the land – boundary that we have with – Canada. [...]

COURIC: Explain to me why that enhances your foreign policy credentials.

PALIN: Well, it certainly does because our – our next door neighbors are foreign countries. They're in the state that I am the executive of. And there in Russia --

COURIC: Have you ever been involved with any negotiations with the Russians?

PALIN: We do, it's very important when you consider even national security issues with Russia as Putin rears his head and comes into the air space of the United States of America, where – where do they go? It's Alaska. It's just right over the border. They are right next to – to our state.

Usually, candidates for national office get better as time goes on. Palin is clearly getting worse. I mean, really, think about Palin's argument here. She has foreign policy experience because Russian leaders fly over Alaskan air space on their way to the U.S.? Seriously, that's what Palin told a national television audience. First, it's probably not true. Moscow is in Western Russia, and if a Russian leader were flying to the U.S., he or she would probably fly over the Atlantic. But geography aside, *what does this have to do with foreign policy experience*? If a head of state flies over you, you necessarily gain a background in international affairs? I'm afraid Sarah Palin is not only embarrassing herself, she's quickly become a national joke.

It'd be funny, if it wasn't so painful to watch.

A Level Exam-Style Question Section A

Study Source 10 before you answer this question.

Assess the value of the source for revealing how far Obama's race for the White House was aided by the weakness of his opponents.

Explain your answer, using the source, the information given about its origin and your own knowledge about the historical context. (20 marks)

Tip

In your answer, it is important to refer to the provenance of the source as a way of assessing its value. Who wrote it? When was it written? Who was its intended audience? To support your answer, use relevant information from the content of the source and your own knowledge to help place the source in its historical context.

SOURCE 11

From a Gallup Poll, 15 September 2008, entitled 'Republicans Cry Foul Over Media Coverage of Palin' by Lydia Saad. It deals with media coverage of Republican presidential and vice-presidential candidates, John Mc Cain and Sarah Palin.

The pundit-fueled firestorm around media coverage of John McCain's running mate Sarah Palin is evident in Americans' highly mixed views on the subject. About the same proportion of Americans say media coverage of Palin has been unfairly negative (33%) as say it has been about right (36%). An additional 21% say coverage of her has been unfairly positive.

These views – taken from a Sept. 8-11 Gallup Poll conducted mostly before the airing of Palin's interview with ABC News' Charlie Gibson – are sharply partisan. A majority of Republicans (54%), compared with only 29% of independents and 18% of Democrats, think Palin is getting a raw deal from the press. Three times as many Democrats as Republicans (34% vs. 11%) think coverage of her has been too positive.

Americans' Evaluation of Media Coverage of Sarah Palin

	Unfairly positive %	About right %	Unfairly negative %	No opinion %
National adults	21	36	33	9
Republicans	11	31	54	4
Independents	18	38	29	15
Democrats	34	39	18	8

By contrast, a majority of Americans say media treatment of McCain has been about right (53%). However, among the remainder, the balance tilts more than 2-to-1 toward saying coverage of him has been unfairly negative: 30% vs. 13%. Republicans are closely divided on this, with the slight majority (51%) saying coverage of McCain has been too negative and close to half (43%) saying it has been about right.

These perceptions haven't changed much since they were previously measured, in late July. The view that coverage of McCain is about right has increased slightly (from 46% to 53%), as the percentage with no opinion on the issue has declined. But there has been no meaningful change in perceptions that he is getting either unfair positive treatment or unfair negative treatment.

Americans' Evaluation of Media Coverage of John McCain

	Unfairly positive %	About right %	Unfairly negative %	No opinion %
2008 Sep 8–11*	13	53	30	4
Republicans	5	43	51	1
Independents	12	58	22	9
Democrats	23	57	16	3
2008 Jul 25–27*	12	46	32	10

*Among national adults

ACTIVITY
KNOWLEDGE CHECK

Why Obama became president

Study Source 11.

What information contained in Source 12 helps to explain why Obama won the presidential race to the White House?

The presidential election result of 4 November 2008

Barack Obama was a clear winner. At 11.00pm on the evening of 4 November 2008, McCain conceded the election and Obama was the 44th president. He polled 69,499,428 votes (52.86 percent). He won 365 electoral college votes (67.8 percent). McCain polled 59,950,323 votes (45.60 percent), winning 173 electoral college votes.

The third-placed candidate was Ralph Nader (Independent), who polled 739,278 votes (0.56 percent) and did not win any electoral colleges votes. Obama was the first Democrat to win a majority of the popular vote since Jimmy Carter in 1976.

Obama benefited from his personal qualities and speaking skills. He struck the right note by suggesting the USA needed change following the unpopular presidency of G.W. Bush. Dislike of the aftermath of the Iraq War and the economic crisis proved big problems for the McCain campaign. Obama did not suffer from what was known as the **Bradley Effect**, where white voters told pollsters they would vote for an ethnic candidate in public and then on polling day voted for the other white candidate.

Obama won 44 percent of the white vote in general, but 54 percent of the below 30-year-old white vote, confirming his claim that he stood for a new generation of voters. Obama was 47 years old, while McCain was 72 years old, the oldest candidate for a major political party. Obama won 95 percent of the black American vote, up from 84 percent who had voted for the Democrat Party candidate John Kerry in 2004. He also received 65 percent of the Latino vote, which was 13 percent higher than in 2004.

On 5 November 2008, the BBC made its own assessment of why Obama won. One reason was Obama's ability to raise funds. His campaign attracted over three million donors, and $650 million more than the combined spending of both major candidates in the 2004 presidential election. This was translated into campaign offices, with Obama having four times as many as McCain. In the final weeks of the campaign, Obama was outspending McCain by a factor of 4 to 1 in the key **swing states**. Obama also engaged in a major voter registration campaign. In Florida alone, he added 300,000 to the registered Democrat list.

Obama's use of social media proved to be a decisive factor. His well-planned campaign was able to get Obama's message across in a way that other candidates failed to do. It helped to get across that Obama was the candidate for change, representing a young generation. He was a wholesome family man with two young daughters. In contrast, McCain was portrayed as yesterday's man, 72 years old, linked to outgoing President Bush. His wealth worked against him at a time of economic crisis, when he could not even remember how many houses he owned when asked by the media.

KEY TERMS

Bradley Effect
Named after black American, Tom Bradley, who was mayor of Los Angeles. It refers to the phenomenon whereby voters when asked who they might vote for tend to say they may support an ethnic minority candidate but actually vote for a white candidate. For instance, in 1989, Virginia black American candidate, Douglas Wilder, enjoyed a 15 percentage point lead two weeks before the election, yet he only won by 6,000 votes.

Swing state
Most states are traditionally Democrat or Republican. Also some states are small and have a small number of electoral college votes. Therefore, candidates concentrate on states where both major parties have a similar level of support and also have a large number of electoral college votes. In the 21st century, two of the most important swing states are Ohio and Florida.

SOURCE

12 From Obama's speech on election night, 4 November 2008, when he had become aware he had won the presidential election. It was made in Grant Park, central Chicago.

If there is anyone out there who still doubts all things are possible; who still wonders if the dream of our founders is alive in our time; who still questions the power of our democracy, tonight is your answer.

It's the answer told by lines that stretched around schools and churches in numbers this nation has never seen; by people who waited three hours and four hours, many for the first time in their lives, because they believed that this time must be different; that their voices could be that difference.

It's the answer spoken by young and old, rich and poor, Democrat and Republican, black, white, Hispanic, Asian, Native American, gay, straight, disabled and not disabled – Americans who sent a message to the world that we have never been just a collection of individuals or a collection of Red States and Blue States; we are, and always will be, the United States of America.

It's the answer that led those who've been told for so long by so many to be cynical, and fearful, and doubtful about what we can achieve to put their hands on the arc of history and bend it once more toward the hope of a better day.

It's been a long time coming, but tonight, because of what we did on this date, in this election, at this defining moment, change has come to America.

America has come so far. We have seen so much. But there is so much more to do. So tonight, let us ask ourselves – if our children should live to see the next century; what change will they see? What progress will we have made?

This is our chance to answer that call. This is our moment. This is our time – to put our people back to work and open doors of opportunity to our kids; to restore prosperity and promote the cause of peace; to reclaim the American Dream and reaffirm that fundamental truth – that out of many, we are one; that while we breathe, we hope; and where we are met with cynicism, and doubts, and those who tell us that we can't, we respond with that timeless creed that sums up the spirit of our people: Yes we can.

A Level Exam-Style Question Section A

Study Source 12 before you answer this question.

Assess the value of the source for revealing why Obama won the presidential election of 2008.

Explain your answer, using the source, the information given about its origin and your own knowledge about the historical context. (20 marks)

Tip

In your answer it is important to refer to the provenance of the source as a way of assessing its value. Who wrote it? When was it written? Who was its intended audience? To support your answer, use relevant information from the content of the source and your own knowledge to help place the source in its historical context.

The significance of Obama's victory and the response to it by black Americans

The election of Obama was seen at the time as historic. A black American as president had been something unheard of in 2000. In Grant Park, central Chicago, 125,000 people assembled to hear the result. At 11.00pm on 4 November 2008, Jesse Jackson, the seasoned civil rights campaigner, adviser to Martin Luther King and former Democrat presidential contender, was caught weeping openly on television.

When it was clear that Obama had won sufficient electoral college votes to be president, he made a short speech to the crowds assembled in Grant Park. His election was hailed as the beginning of post-racial America. The scourge of colour, the heritage of slavery and centuries of discrimination seemed to be over. Around the world, Obama's election was heralded as the start of a new era.

SOURCE 13 President Barack Obama speaking at the Security Council meeting at the UN in September 2009.

Many black Americans believed they were 'free at last' and that Obama's presidency would be the signal for significant change. In a study of the 2008 election, two University of California academics, Michael Tesler and David Sears, claimed shortly after the election that US politics was becoming increasingly organised on racial lines. In a repeated study, one year after Obama became president, they claimed that Obama was being judged as president not just as a black American, but also as someone distinctly different from previous holders of the office of president. As a person of mixed race, whose father was from east Africa, he stood out. In addition, the slurs that he was not really born in the USA and that he was a Muslim persisted even into his presidency. In his first year, although economic problems persisted, his approval ratings remained high. His popularity outside the USA was even higher. In October 2009, he was informed that he had won the Nobel Peace Prize for his actions in foreign affairs, an area he felt was one of his weaknesses in the presidential campaign.

However, problems of racism and racially motivated violence continued. In 2014, major race riots occurred in Ferguson, a suburb of St Louis, following the shooting of a young black man, Michael Brown, by a white policeman on 9 August 2014. On 17 June 2015, a white racist, Dylann Roof, murdered nine black American members of a church congregation in Charleston, South Carolina. The mere fact that a black American was in the White House had not brought racial harmony.

A Level Exam-Style Question Section B

How far was Obama's victory in the presidential election of 2008 due to the weakness of his opponents? (20 marks)

Tip

You will be expected to provide a balanced, analytical answer. Firstly, you will need to identify reasons associated with the weakness of his Republican opponents, both McCain and Palin. You will also need to balance this section of your answer with other factors, such as Obama's personal qualities, his election strategy, the economic crisis and Obama's policies.

ACTIVITY
KNOWLEDGE CHECK

Significance of Obama's victory

1 Identify three reasons why Obama's victory in gaining the US presidency was seen as important in US politics.

2 Why do you think Obama's victory in the presidential election of 2008 was a significant event in the history of black Americans and race relations?

THINKING HISTORICALLY Cause and consequence (7a & b)

Questions and answers

Questions that historians ask vary, depending on what they think is important. It is the questions that interest us that define the history that is written. These questions change with time and place. Different historians will also come up with different answers to the same questions, depending on their perspectives and methods of interpretation, as well as the evidence they use.

Read the information below about three historians who had different areas of interest, and look at the key events in the history of US race relations from 1850 to 2009.

Three historians with different areas of interest		
Thomas Carlyle	**Karl Marx**	**Edward P. Thompson**
A political historian who lived in the 19th century. He was interested in the idea that great men shape history.	An economic and political historian who lived in the 19th century. He was interested in the role of the lower classes and how they contributed to historical change.	A social, political and economic historian who lived in the 20th century. He was very interested in the social and economic forces in creating political and social movements.

Some key events in the history of race relations in the USA, 1850–2009		
The abolition of slavery, 1865	Jim Crow Laws, 1883– c1900	The role of Martin Luther King
The Fourteenth and Fifteenth Amendments to the US Constitution	The migration of black Americans north and west from 1865	The Montgomery bus boycott, 1955–56
The activities of the Ku Klux Klan	The New Deal, 1933–41	The election of Barack Obama as president

Work in groups of between three and six to complete the following task.

1 a) Which of these events would have been of most interest to each historian? Explain your answer.

b) Each take the role of one historian and devise a question that would interest them about each of the events.

c) Discuss each event in turn. Present the questions that have been devised for each historian and offer some ideas about how they would have answered them.

d) For each event, decide as a group which question is the most interesting and worthwhile of the three.

Answer the following questions in pairs.

2 Identify the different ways that each historian would approach writing an account of the role of Martin Luther King.

3 In what ways would Carlyle and Marx differ in their explanations of the significance of the New Deal of 1933–41? What would be the focus of their arguments?

Answer the following questions individually.

4 All three historians may produce very different accounts and explanations of the same piece of history. Of the three historians, whose account would you prefer to read first? Explain your answer.

5 Do the differences in these accounts mean that one is more valid than the others?

6 Explain why different historical explanations are written by different historians.

7 Explain why different explanations of the same event can be equally valid.

ACTIVITY
SUMMARY

Obama's campaign for the presidency, 2004–09

1 How important was Obama's political career up to 2006 in laying the foundation for his successful campaign to become US president?

2 Which of the following reasons were most responsible for his success in becoming the Democratic candidate?

   a) Personal qualities and speaking skills

   b) Weakness of his opponents

   c) Obama's election strategies

   d) Obama's policies

Give reasons for your choice.

3 Why was Obama able to become US president in November 2008? How important were the following factors?

   a) The economic crisis

   b) The weaknesses of McCain and Palin

   c) Obama's policies and desire for change

WIDER READING

Martin Riches, W.T. *The Civil Rights Movement: Struggle and Resistance*, Palgrave (2010)

Painter, A. *Barack Obama, the Movement for Change*, Arcadia (2008)

Porterfield, J. *The Election of Barack Obama: Race and Politics in America*, Rosen (2010)

Tesler, M. and Sears, D. *Obama's Race: The 2008 Election and the Dream of a Post-Racial America*, Chicago University Press (2010)

Tuck, E. (ed.) *We Ain't What We Ought to Be*, Harvard University Press (2011)

Preparing for your A Level Paper 3 exam

Advance planning

Draw up a timetable for your revision and try to keep to it. Spend longer on topics which you have found difficult, and revise them several times. Aim to be confident about all aspects of your Paper 3 work, because this will ensure that you have a choice of questions in Sections B and C.

Paper 3 Overview

Paper 3	Time: 2 hours 15 minutes	
Section A	Answer one compulsory question for the option studied, assessing source analysis and evaluation skills.	20 marks
Section B	Answer one question from a choice of two on an aspect in depth for the option studied.	20 marks
Section C	Answer one question from a choice of two on an aspect in breadth for the option studied	20 marks
	Total marks =	60 marks

Section A questions

There is no choice of question in Section A. You will be referred to a source of about 350 words long, printed in a Sources Booklet. The source will be a primary source or one that is contemporary to the period you have studied, and will relate to one of the key topics in the Aspect in Depth. You will be expected to analyse and evaluate the source in its historical context. The question will ask you to assess the value of the source for revealing something specific about the period, and will expect you to explain your answer, using the source, the information given about its origin and your own knowledge about the historical context.

Section B questions

You will have a choice of one from two questions in Section B. They will aim to assess your understanding of one or more of the key topics in the Aspect in Depth you have studied. Questions may relate to a single, momentous year, but will normally cover longer periods. You will be required to write an essay evaluating an aspect of the period. You may be asked about change and continuity, similarity and difference, consequences, significance or causation, or you may be given a quotation and asked to explain how far you agree with it. All questions will require you to reach a substantiated judgement.

Section C questions

You will have a choice of one from two questions in Section C. Questions will relate to the themes of the Aspects in Breadth you have studied, and will aim to assess your understanding of change over time. They will cover a period of not less than 100 years and will relate either to the factors that brought about change, the extent of change over the period or patterns of change as demonstrated by turning points.

Use of time

Do not write solidly for 45 minutes on each question. For Section B and C answers, you should spend a few minutes working out what the question is asking you to do, and drawing up a plan of your answer. This is especially important for Section C answers, which cover an extended period of time.

For Section A, it is essential that you have a clear understanding of the content of the source and its historical context. Pay particular attention to the provenance: was the author in a position to know what he or she was writing about? Read it carefully and underline important points. You might decide to spend up to ten minutes reading the source and drawing up your plan, and 35 minutes writing your answer.

Preparing for your A Level exams

Paper 3: A Level sample answer with comments

Section A

These questions require you to analyse and evaluate source material with respect to its historical context.

For these questions remember to:

- look at the evidence given in the source and consider how the source could be used in differing ways to provide historical understanding
- use your knowledge of the historical context to discuss any limitations the source may have
- use your historical understanding to evaluate the source, considering how much weight you would give to its argument
- come to a judgement on the overall value of the source in respect to the question.

Study Source 2 in Chapter 4 (page 92) before you answer this question.

Assess the value of the source for revealing the reaction within the USA to the US Supreme Court decision in the civil rights cases of 1883, to declare the Civil Rights Act of 1875 unconstitutional.

Explain your answer, using the source, the information given about its origin and your own knowledge about its historical context.
(20 marks)

Average student response

The extract has value to historians writing about the black American reaction to the civil rights cases of 1883. The extract is very critical of the US Supreme Court decision to declare the 1875 Civil Rights Act unconstitutional. This is clear in the title of the article where Bishop Turner uses strong language to show his anger at the Supreme Court decision. The source itself follows in the use of very strong language, accusing the US Supreme Court of allowing racial discrimination against black Americans. It says that the Court decision would anger both black and white Americans as the decision goes against racial equality. The author, black American bishop Turner, claims that most American people, both black and white, were ignorant of the real meaning and significance of the civil rights cases, decision on civil rights. He claims that most Americans are unaware of the 'cruel, disgraceful and inhuman condition of things affecting the colored race'. He claims that the laws of the USA have a brutal and degrading effect on the lives of black Americans. He even refers to the USA as a savage country. He believed that all the Jim Crow Laws in the USA, which brought about segregation of the black and white races, were due to the Supreme Court decision of 1883. It says the decision allows Jim Crow Laws to be implemented, which takes away the civil rights of black Americans. It also says, without naming them specifically, that the Supreme Court decision denies black Americans their civil rights as given to them under the Thirteenth, Fourteenth and Fifteenth Amendments of the US Constitution. From my own knowledge, I know that during the period of Reconstruction, in the years 1865–77, black Americans were given the same civil rights as all other Americans. Slavery was abolished in 1865. In 1868, black Americans, along with other Americans, received equal protection of the law. Finally, in 1870, they received the right to vote. To back up these newly acquired rights, the Civil Rights Act of 1875 ensured equality of treatment for both black and white Americans in the use of public facilities. All these points help explain why the source by Bishop Turner would be of value to historians writing about the impact of the Civil Rights cases of 1883 on race relations.

The opening paragraph is linked directly to the issue in the question. It refers to the issue of value to historians and also is able to refer directly to the source material and selects and summarises information from the source. However, information taken from the source is limited in the sense that it is used to make undeveloped inferences relevant to the question, but without providing links between the source material extracted and the precise reasons why this source material may be valuable.

Clearly the civil rights cases of 1883 and their impact are important for a number of reasons. The source is valuable because it is written in 1893, ten years after the cases, by a leading black American clergyman, a bishop from Atlanta, Georgia. The source is a personal attack on the civil rights cases, and their impact, and the fact that Bishop Turner had researched, compiled and published the article shows the importance of the cases to black Americans. Bishop Turner believes that all of the Jim Crow Laws, which introduced legal segregation from 1883 to when the article was published, in 1893, were the result of that decision.

The source material provides lots of information about different reasons for the black American reaction to the civil rights cases and why they were such an important event in the history of black civil rights and race relations in the USA. Bishop Turner uses strong language to support and sustain his case against the Supreme Court decisions. From my own knowledge, I know that by 1893, in the wake of the civil rights cases, Jim Crow Laws had begun to be introduced in many southern states. These laws introduced legal racial segregation and denied many black Americans the right to vote. Bishop Turner's article of 1893 was as much against these developments as the civil rights cases themselves.

> This section develops the information contained in the opening paragraph through referring to the provenance of the source. The paragraph is linked to the 'value' aspect of the question because it refers directly to the value of the date of writing and to the authorship of the source, which states that the author, a black American bishop, researched and published the article on his own. There is some repetition of the impact of the Supreme Court case on the subsequent introduction of Jim Crow Laws, which introduced legal segregation in the USA between black and white Americans.

> The concluding paragraph refers back to the issue of value by making general comments about the value of the extract. This is supported by accurate and detailed own knowledge, which reinforces the value of the source by linking the timing of the speech to the civil rights cases of 1883.

Verdict

This is an average answer because:

- it demonstrates some understanding of the source material but does not provide sufficient analysis
- it provides some contextual evidence to the source material, which helps expand and explain information from the extract

- it does mention the utility of the extract, but mainly through noting some aspects of the provenance of the extract, including some brief references to the authorship.

Use the feedback on this answer to rewrite it, making as many improvements as you can.

Paper 3: A Level sample answer with comments

Section A

These questions require you to analyse and evaluate source material with respect to its historical context.

For these questions remember to:

- look at the evidence given in the source and consider how the source could be used in differing ways to provide historical understanding
- use your knowledge of the historical context to discuss any limitations the source may have
- use your historical understanding to evaluate the source, considering how much weight you would give to its argument
- come to a judgement on the overall value of the source in respect to the question.

Study Source 2 in Chapter 4 (page 92) before you answer this question.

Assess the value of the source for revealing the reaction within the USA to the US Supreme Court decision in the civil rights cases of 1883, to declare the Civil Rights Act of 1875 unconstitutional.

Explain your answer, using the source, the information given about its origin and your own knowledge about its historical context. (20 marks)

Strong student response

The source by Bishop Turner is of considerable value in revealing the reaction of black Americans to the Supreme Court decision in the civil rights cases of 1863. It makes direct reference to the cases, in general terms, and makes direct reference to the impact of the Supreme Court decision on black civil rights. It claims that the Supreme Court action in the civil rights cases had compromised the three Civil War Amendments of the US Constitution, which had granted black Americans equal civil rights with other Americans. The Thirteenth Amendment, passed in 1865, abolished slavery, the Fourteenth Amendment, passed in 1868, granted all Americans equal protection of the law, and the Fifteenth Amendment, passed in 1870, granted black Americans the right to vote.

The source's value is reinforced by the fact that it has been written by a prominent black American, a bishop from Atlanta, Georgia, one of the largest cities in the South. The attribution of the source states that the information contained within it was compiled by the Bishop, who then decided to publish his findings in an article, published in 1893. The publication date was ten years after the US Supreme Court decision in the civil rights cases. This gave Bishop Turner the opportunity to place the impact of these cases in a broader historical perspective. In doing so, he links the Supreme Court decision of 1883 to the imposition of Jim Crow Laws in the southern states. These laws introduced legal racial segregation, thus denying black Americans equal civil rights. In 1887, the state of Florida introduced legal segregation in railway travel. In 1890, the state of Mississippi amended its state constitution to include clauses making it very difficult for black Americans to register to vote, thereby denying black Americans their civil rights under the Fifteenth Amendment of the US Constitution.

However, the source does possess a number of limitations. It was written ten years after the Supreme Court decision, which has value in placing the black American reaction in a broader

> A very strong opening, which is sharply focused on the specific question and indicates a top-level response. There is some thorough deployment of own knowledge, which places the information in the extract in broader historical context and makes clear links between the issue of black American equality, its importance in US society and the timing of the speech following a major incident which highlighted the need to address the issue.

> This section places the value of the extract in broader historical context through assessment of the provenance of the extract. It displays very sound, detailed own knowledge and makes direct reference to the source's value to the historian writing on the reaction of a prominent black American to the impact of the civil rights cases of 1883 from the perspective of a decade later, in 1893, and how the cases enabled southern state governments to introduce Jim Crow Laws.

perspective, but clearly does not provide information on the immediate black American reaction in 1883. The language of the source, both in its title and in its content, contains very strong language which reflects Bishop Turner's anger but limits the source's value in terms of being a balanced, logical response to the civil rights cases of 1883. The attribution regards the Supreme Court decision as 'the most cruel and inhuman verdict against a loyal people in the history of the world'. Within the body of the source, this view is again mentioned when Bishop Turner states: 'The world has never seen such barbarous laws entailed upon a free people as have grown out of the decision of the United States Supreme Court, issued October 15, 1883. For that decision now sustains all the unjust discriminations, proscriptions and robberies perpetrated by public carriers upon millions of the nation's most loyal defenders.' In addition, Bishop Turner makes some wild claims which he fails to substantiate, such as the statement that the Supreme Court decision has resulted in thousands of deaths.

The nature of the source, its content, authorship and the date it was written make it of considerable value to the historian in an enquiry into the reaction of black Americans to the civil rights cases of 1883. It focuses on an important event in relation to the broader historical context of the introduction of Jim Crow Laws, which created legal racial segregation in the southern states. However, it deals with the views of one person, ten years after the event. The source also contains considerable intemperate language and phrases, which offers clear evidence of anger against the cases, but is limited in its provision of detailed factual evidence to reveal the impact of the decision on black American civil rights.

> The answer refers directly to the provenance of the source and also uses own knowledge to place it in the wider context of the civil rights cases of 1883 on black civil rights, particularly in the southern states.

Verdict

This is a strong answer because:

- it has sharp focus on the specific question
- it makes use of evidence in the source and in the introduction to the source
- it deploys appropriate own knowledge accurately and effectively.

Paper 3: A Level sample answer with comments

Section B

These questions require you to show your understanding of a period in depth. They will ask you about a quite specific period of time and require you to make a substantiated judgement about a specific aspect you have studied.

For these questions remember to:

- organise your essay and communicate it in a manner that is clear and comprehensible
- use historical knowledge to analyse and evaluate the key aspect of the question
- make a balanced argument that weighs up differing opinions
- make a substantiated overall judgement on the question.

'Martin Luther King was the person most responsible for the improvement in black American civil rights between 1955 and 1965.'
How far do you agree with this statement? (20 marks)

Average student answer

In many ways, the civil rights movement from 1955 to 1965 owes an enormous amount to Martin Luther King. When he became the leader of the Montgomery Improvement Association in 1955, legal racial segregation was the norm across the southern states. In the years 1955–65, Martin Luther King was a leading force in bringing an end to legal segregation, which came to an end with the Voting Rights Act of 1965. Martin Luther King was leader of the Southern Christian Leadership Conference and through that organisation he helped mobilise support from black and white Americans to campaign against segregation. His non-violent methods won respect for the cause of black American civil rights and largely explain why the campaign against segregation was successful.

One important way Martin Luther King was clearly responsible for improving black American civil rights was his work during the Montgomery bus boycott of 1955–56. As Pastor of the Dexter Avenue Baptist Church in Montgomery, Alabama, King was able to act as the leader and spokesman for the boycotters. His ability to offer a non-violent way of protesting proved to be very effective. The vast majority of black Americans in Montgomery boycotted the public buses for almost a year, nearly bankrupting the bus company. King was also a very effective speaker and gave the boycott a strong public presence through the media. The boycott proved to be successful by 1956 and it helped propel Martin Luther King into the public limelight across the USA.

In the following year, King was made leader of the Southern Christian Leadership Conference (SCLC). This was an organisation led by religious ministers across the South and aimed to end legal segregation. It campaigned in a number of places. In Albany, Georgia, in 1962 it attempted to desegregate local facilities, but it failed mainly due to the activities of local police chief Laurie Prichard. However, in Birmingham, Alabama, in 1963 King and the SCLC organised a peaceful protest which turned into a major confrontation with the local police. The police used strong-arm tactics such as using water cannon and police dogs against the protestors. Hundreds of protestors were arrested, including Martin Luther King. King's non-violence and the heavy-handed tactics

The response deals directly with the role of Martin Luther King in the civil rights movement in bringing about improvements in the position of black Americans in US society. Some historical context is provided in the early part of the paragraph. However, most of the paragraph is descriptive, with only limited links to an assessment of the question.

This deals directly with the role of the civil rights movement in campaigning against the racial discrimination in public transportation. The response deploys detailed, accurate factual information, but in a narrative-descriptive way. There is a brief attempt at assessment in the last sentence.

This paragraph follows on from the first, chronologically, and offers accurate information concerning the achievements of King and the SCLC in using non-violent protest to highlight the injustices of legal segregation and how these tactics helped pressurise the US president to introduce a proposal to Congress to end legal segregation. The candidate deploys detailed, accurate factual information, but in a narrative-descriptive way. There is a brief attempt at assessment in the last sentence.

of the police made events in Birmingham national television news. In reaction to the public outrage at the scenes shown on national television, President John F. Kennedy made a national broadcast where he promised to introduce a civil rights bill into Congress to help to give black Americans full civil rights. To highlight King's national position, in August 1963 he gave the keynote speech in the SCLC march on Washington DC which demanded the end of legal segregation. His 'I have a dream' speech became the watch phrase of the civil rights movement and gave the movement a strong national platform to get over its case.

Although President Kennedy was assassinated in November 1963, his successor, President Johnson, persuaded Congress to pass the Civil Rights Act of 1964. This Act brought to an end much of the legal segregation and racial discrimination against black Americans in the southern states. It was the actions of Martin Luther King and the SCLC through the use of non-violent protest that helped bring these important changes about.

> The fourth paragraph offers a brief analysis of the impact of Martin Luther King in bringing an end to legal segregation.

Although legal segregation in public facilities had come to an end with the Civil Rights Act of 1964, the majority of black Americans in southern states were still denied the right to vote through discriminatory registration to vote practices in many states. To pressure the federal government into action, Martin Luther King and the SCLC organised a protest march from Selma to Montgomery, Alabama, in the spring of 1965. The protestors were viciously attacked by a white mob aided by local police. In reaction, President Johnson had to federalise the Alabama National Guard to protect the marchers. The march from Selma was a national media event and highlighted the issue of the denial of black voting rights. It forced Johnson to introduce a bill in Congress to protect black voting rights. Congress passed the Voting Rights Act of 1965, which brought to an end discriminatory registration to vote practices, which finally allowed black Americans in southern states to take part in the democratic process.

> Again, a descriptive paragraph, which contains accurate information and makes a limited link between the actions of Martin Luther King in the civil rights movement and attempts to improve the position of black Americans in US society.

Overall, Martin Luther King played a central role in gaining civil rights for black Americans, in particular in the southern states where black people faced legal racial segregation. His oratory and non-violent tactics had won respect and national support for the cause of black Americans and helped persuade the federal government into introducing legislation in 1964 and 1965 which brought to an end legal segregation and gave black Americans protection in acquiring their voting rights.

> The conclusion is brief and consists largely of the repetition of points made in the body of the answer.

Verdict

This is an average answer because:

- an important weakness in the structure of the answer is the tendency to provide narrative description rather than analysis
- the knowledge deployed is adequate and deals directly with the issue of Martin Luther King and his role in the civil rights movement
- the answer fails to identify other factors which aided the achievement of black American civil rights in the period, such as the role of the US Supreme Court, the role of other civil rights organisations such as the Student Non-Violent Co-ordinating Committee and lunch counter protests in 1961, and the Congress of Racial Equality (CORE) Freedom Rides of 1962. It also mentions only briefly the very important role of the US president and Congress in helping to pass the legislation necessary to get black American civil rights.

Use the feedback on this essay to rewrite it, making as many improvements as you can.

Paper 3: A Level sample answer with comments

Section B

These questions require you to show your understanding of a period in depth. They will ask you about a quite specific period of time and require you to make a substantiated judgement about a specific aspect you have studied.

For these questions remember to:

* organise your essay and communicate it in a manner that is clear and comprehensible
* use historical knowledge to analyse and evaluate the key aspect of the question
* make a balanced argument that weighs up differing opinions
* make a substantiated overall judgement on the question.

'Martin Luther King was the person most responsible for the improvement in black American civil rights between 1955 and 1965.'
How far do you agree with this statement? (20 marks)

Strong student answer

I agree that Martin Luther King played a very important role in the civil rights movement and the achievement of greater equality for black Americans in the years 1955–65. During that period, legal segregation came to an end and the voting rights of black Americans were guaranteed. During that period, Martin Luther King played a central role in the Montgomery bus boycott, the foundation and work of the Southern Christian Leadership Conference (SCLC) and the campaign to end segregation in public facilities across the southern states, most notably in Alabama. His 'I have a dream' speech in Washington DC in August 1963, to many, encapsulated the entire movement for greater racial equality. The fact that Martin Luther King won the Nobel Peace Prize in 1964 suggests he was seen by the international community as a pivotal figure in the civil rights movement. However, to see Martin Luther King as mostly responsible is to simplify what was a complex and multi-faceted civil rights movement and a broad-based desire to end segregation which included branches of the federal government.

Perhaps the most significant aspect of Martin Luther King's role in the improvement of black American civil rights in the period 1955–65 was his position as leader of the SCLC. Formed in 1957, following the successful conclusion of the Montgomery bus boycott, the SCLC led a campaign to end legal segregation in the southern states. Perhaps the highlight of SCLC activity was the peaceful protest in Birmingham, Alabama, in the spring of 1963, where civil rights protestors were attacked by the city police. King had deliberately chosen Birmingham for the protest because of the poor reputation of police chief Bull Connor in enforcing segregation. The violent reaction by the Birmingham police against protestors, which included school children, placed the issue of greater civil equality at the top of the domestic political agenda. This led directly to President John F. Kennedy's national announcement that he intended to propose a civil rights bill to end legal segregation.

What propelled Martin Luther King into the national and international limelight was his role in the SCLC-sponsored march on Washington DC in August 1963. This mass multi-racial rally saw King give the keynote speech which was broadcast around the world. In his 'I have a dream' speech, King called for a nation that was integrated racially, not separated by legal segregation. It was the culmination of the rise of Martin Luther King as unofficial leader of the civil rights movement. It also led directly to his award of the Nobel Peace Prize the following year in 1964. King's leadership of the SCLC helped keep up the pressure on the federal government to introduce change. Following J.F. Kennedy's assassination, his successor President Lyndon

This is a strong opening paragraph. It links clearly the role of Martin Luther King in the civil rights movement and the achievement of greater civil equality for black Americans. It provides a clear reference to King's role and the role of other factors in the process of gaining greater civil equality in the years 1955–65.

This is a well-developed paragraph. The response identifies a significant set of changes in which Martin Luther King played a key role in the civil rights movement. The paragraph contains accurate and detailed factual information which is used to support and sustain a consistent argument leading to a judgement.

This paragraph continues a coherent and consistent argument about Martin Luther King's role. The argument is balanced and is supported and sustained by the inclusion of accurate own knowledge.

Johnson helped pass the Civil Rights Act through Congress in 1964. This landmark Act brought to an end the legal racial segregation in the southern states. So Martin Luther King played a pivotal role in the achievement of greater equality for black Americans in the southern states.

In the following year, King and the SCLC helped pressure the federal government into passing the Voting Rights Act. This Act of 1965 brought to an end discriminatory practices by southern states which prevented many black Americans from acquiring the right to vote. King's leadership of the SCLC-sponsored march from Selma to Montgomery, Alabama, focused national media attention on the issue. When white mobs attacked the peaceful marchers, President Johnson had to intervene to protect the marchers and also assisted his plan to persuade Congress to pass the Voting Rights Act. Therefore Martin Luther King played a central role in gaining an improvement in the civil rights of black Americans in the years 1955–65.

> This paragraph continues a coherent and consistent argument about Martin Luther King's role. The argument is balanced and is supported and sustained by the inclusion of accurate own knowledge.

However, to see the achievement in greater equality of black Americans as a result of Martin Luther King's efforts would be over-simplistic. A key institution which aided the improvement of greater equality for black Americans was the US Supreme Court. The Court's Brown and Brown II decisions of 1954 and 1955 gave the constitutional authority for the desegregation of public schooling. The Browder v Gayle decision of 1956 forced the racial integration of public transportation in Montgomery. Finally, in Boynton v Painter, the Court laid the legal foundation for the desegregation of interstate public transportation which gave legal authority to the Freedom Rides of 1962.

> This paragraph continues a coherent and consistent argument through comparing King's role with that of the US Supreme Court. The argument is balanced and is supported and sustained by the inclusion of accurate own knowledge.

Even within the civil rights movement, other groups apart from King and the SCLC played a very important role in ending segregation. The lunch counter protests organised by the Student Non-Violent Co-ordinating Committee (SNCC) helped end discrimination in department store lunch counters. The Freedom Riders of CORE helped end the segregation on interstate public transportation. In many ways, the civil rights movement was a grass-roots movement over which King was seen as an unofficial leader. The movement made Martin Luther King, rather than King making the movement.

> The response makes it clear that the civil rights movement contained a number of grass-roots organisations which all played a role in gaining extra racial equality. Again, sound evidence is produced, which is used to support a clear argument linked to the issue in the question.

Finally, the role of US presidents should not be underestimated. President Eisenhower sent federal troops to Little Rock, Arkansas, to enforce racial integration at Central High School in 1957. John F. Kennedy helped integrate the University of Mississippi in 1962 and proposed a civil rights bill in 1963. President Johnson and his administration were pivotal in passing the laws which ended legal segregation in 1964 and guaranteed black voting rights in the Voting Rights Act of 1965. King provided the pressure, but the presidents and Congress either enforced or changed the law.

> This is a strong evaluative paragraph dealing with the role of president and sustains the analytical approach of the answer.

Therefore, Martin Luther King played a very important role in gaining greater equality for black Americans, but in his quest he was aided by a wide variety of individuals and groups.

> This is an evaluative conclusion. The response notes the role of King and places it against the contribution of other groups and individuals.

Verdict

This is a strong answer because:

- the key issues relevant to the question are all explored, and the answer offers a balanced, analytical approach to the question

- there is a wide range of accurate material deployed to support the points made
- the argument throughout the answer is well-organised, coherent, logical and persuasive.

Paper 3: A Level sample answer with comments

Section C

These questions require you to show your understanding of a subject over a considerable period of time. They will ask you to assess a long-term historical topic and its development over a period of at least 100 years, and they require you to make a substantiated judgement in relation to the question.

For these questions remember to:

- organise your essay and communicate it in a manner that is clear and comprehensible
- use historical knowledge to analyse and evaluate the key aspect of the question covering the entire period
- make a balanced argument that weighs up differing opinions
- make a substantiated overall judgement on the question.

How far can the First World War be regarded as the key turning point in the changing geography of civil rights issues in the USA in the period 1850–2009? (20 marks)

Average student answer

During the period 1850–2009, the location of black Americans within the USA changed dramatically. In 1850, the vast majority of black Americans lived in the South as slaves. They were owned by and worked for their white masters and usually lived on plantations. Most black slaves were agricultural labourers or domestic servants. In the northern states, where slavery was once allowed but had been banned by 1850, there were a small number of freed black slaves. By 2009, black Americans were no longer located primarily in the South. Black Americans could be found all over the USA. In the South in 1850, most black Americans lived as slaves in rural areas. By 2009, a majority of black Americans lived in urban areas. Large numbers of black Americans lived in northern and western cities, as well as the South. In 2009, cities such as Baltimore and Washington DC had black majorities, while other cities such as Chicago, New York and Philadelphia had large black communities. In these cities, black communities faced many social and economic problems, which occasionally led to riots. These changes took place over a long period of time.

An important development in the changing geography of civil rights came with the abolition of slavery in 1865. This monumental change allowed the freed slaves to move away from their plantations in the South. A slow migration of freed slaves took place to the north and west. However, as former slaves possessed very little money and property, the vast majority of freed slaves remained in the South. Following the end of Reconstruction in 1877, these black Americans increasingly became subject to Jim Crow Laws which reduced their social position to one of second-class citizenship.

A much more important aspect of the changing geography of civil rights issues came from 1905, when large numbers of black Americans migrated to the Harlem district of New York City. Within a decade, the area became predominantly black in ethnic composition. However,

> The response deals directly with the changing geography of civil rights issues over the whole period 1850–2009 and juxtaposes the position in 1850 with that in 2009. The paragraph also contains some descriptive material about the location of black Americans in 1850. The paragraph is descriptive, with only limited links to an assessment of the question.

> This paragraph deals with some changes in the geography of civil rights issues and does provide a reason for the change. However, the paragraph is in narrative-descriptive format and does not address the question directly.

> This section deals directly with the impact of the First World War on the changing geography of civil rights issues. Detailed factual information is deployed and a direct reference is made to the changing nature of civil rights issues outside the area affected by Jim Crow Laws. The response deploys detailed, accurate factual information but in a narrative-descriptive way. There is a brief attempt at assessment in the final sentences.

of far greater significance was the impact of the First World War. The demand for armaments, even before the USA became actively involved in the war in 1917, led to the demand for labour in war industries. Hundreds of thousands of black Americans moved north into these factories. It began a process known as the Great Migration, which began in 1915. In the following 25 years, the biggest migration of black Americans took place. By the outbreak of the Second World War, the majority of northern and western cities had black communities. Until this Great Migration, civil rights issues centred on the South, where Jim Crow Laws introduced legal racial segregation and denied black Americans the right to vote. Following the impact of the First World War, black Americans faced de facto segregation in matters such as housing in the north and west. Racial discrimination was no longer peculiar to the South. This discrimination occasionally led to major race riots such as in Chicago in 1919.

Following the major impact of the First World War causing the Great Migration, a further major move north occurred during the Second World War. The desire to flee legal segregation and the draw of war work in northern industries meant that ten percent of the black American population migrated during the war from 1941 to 1945.

> This paragraph offers a brief assessment of the impact of the Second World War as a continuation of the migration following the First World War. There is brief, undeveloped analysis.

After the end of the Second World War, the north and west had large settled black communities. However, these areas were associated with social problems such as poor housing and poor job opportunities. In addition, these black communities faced occasional police brutality. In the 1960s, these civil rights issues flared up into major riots in the Watts district of Los Angeles in 1965 and in Newark in 1967. These occurred just at the time when legal segregation was coming to an end in the South.

> Again, a descriptive paragraph which contains accurate information and makes a link to the changing geography and nature of civil rights issues.

Overall, over the period 1850–2009, there was a dramatic change in the geography of civil rights issues. Migration from the South, the traditional home of most black Americans, created extra and different civil rights issues. However, in the years after the 1970s, migration of black Americans changed to a movement back to the post-segregation south. But the migration associated with the First World War was clearly the most important development in the changing geography of civil rights issues and must be seen as a key turning point.

> This final paragraph offers a brief summary of the points raised in the answer which is primarily narrative-descriptive with some analytical links. It addresses the question eventually, but by inference.

Verdict

This is an average answer because:

- an important weakness in the structure of the answer is the tendency to provide narrative description rather than analysis
- the knowledge deployed is adequate and deals directly with the issue of the changing geography of civil rights issues over the whole period of 1850 to 2009
- the answer fails to address directly the issue of the First World War as a turning point. A brief reference to turning point is made in the final, concluding paragraph, but this is not explained in relation to other developments in the period 1850–2009
- much of the analysis is inferred and partial and is secondary to a narrative-descriptive coverage of the subject.

Use the feedback on this essay to rewrite it, making as many improvements as you can.

Paper 3: A Level sample answer with comments

Section C

These questions require you to show your understanding of a subject over a considerable period of time. They will ask you to assess a long-term historical topic and its development over a period of at least 100 years, and they require you to make a substantiated judgement in relation to the question.

For these questions remember to:

- organise your essay and communicate it in a manner that is clear and comprehensible
- use historical knowledge to analyse and evaluate the key aspect of the question covering the entire period
- make a balanced argument that weighs up differing opinions
- make a substantiated overall judgement on the question.

How far can the First World War be regarded as the key turning point in the changing geography of civil rights issues in the USA in the period 1850–2009? (20 marks)

Strong student answer

I agree that the First World War was an important turning point in the changing geography of civil rights issues. In the period 1850–2009, a considerable change occurred in the demographics of the black American community. In 1850, the vast majority of black Americans lived as slaves in the southern states. By 2009, black Americans lived across the USA. Vibrant black communities had been created in virtually every city and town across the country. In 2009, the first black American president was inaugurated. Barack Obama came from the northern city of Chicago, which reflects the changing geography of civil rights issues. However, was the First World War the key turning point in this process?

The First World War saw a considerable change in the geography of civil rights issues. Before the First World War, civil rights issues involving black Americans meant the imposition of Jim Crow Laws in the southern states. In the period of Reconstruction after the Civil War, black Americans had been granted civil equality through changes to the US Constitution and an Act of Congress. However, from the 1880s, Jim Crow Laws had introduced legal racial segregation and had deprived the majority of black Americans in the southern states of the right to vote. Migration of black Americans from the South to the north and west had occurred before the First World War, but it had been slow and involved a relatively small number of black Americans. The only major black community in the north was in Harlem, New York City, which had developed since 1905.

With the coming of the First World War, the move to the north, in particular, became a flood. Black Americans moved for two interconnected reasons. One was push factors associated with the desire to leave the South and its Jim Crow Laws, and the violence and intimidation against the black communities there. The other was pull factors associated with the rapid increase in demand for jobs in war-related industries. The beginning of the biggest migration of black Americans in US history had begun. This Great Migration began in 1915 and continued to the outbreak of the Second World War. New, vibrant black communities were created in cities such as Chicago, Philadelphia and Washington DC among others. However, the push factor of

> This is a strong opening paragraph. It links clearly the changing geography of civil rights issues with the assertion in the question that the First World War was the key turning point in the process of change between 1850 and 2009. It provides a clear reference to the changing geography and the role of the First World War. It ends with a rhetorical question which allows a response to be addressed within the body of the answer.

> This is a well-developed paragraph. The response identifies the importance of the First World War as a possible turning point and supports this assertion with accurate factual evidence to support and sustain the case made.

> This paragraph continues a coherent and consistent argument about the importance of the First World War in the changing geography of civil rights issues. The argument is balanced and is supported and sustained by the inclusion of accurate own knowledge.

avoiding racial discrimination proved illusory. Black Americans in the north and west also faced discrimination in housing and employment. This de facto segregation, although less pervasive than the legal segregation of the South, was still discriminatory. Therefore, the First World War saw a major shift in the location of the black American community and a change in the nature and extent of civil rights issues affecting black Americans. In the north and west, race riots occurred due to the increased tensions between black and white Americans, created by the migration. In Chicago, Illinois, in 1919 and in Tulsa, Oklahoma, in 1921, black people faced violence from white racist mobs.

However, although the First World War was a turning point in the changing geography of civil rights issues, was it the key turning point? A second major wave of migration occurred during the Second World War. Again fuelled by the demand for workers in war-related industries, approximately ten percent of the black American population migrated to northern cities such as Detroit, Michigan, home of the US automotive industry. This migration also created new social and economic issues between black and white Americans. In 1942, serious race riots broke out in Detroit which were only quelled by the introduction of the US army.

> This paragraph continues a coherent and consistent argument on the issue of turning point and addresses the term 'key turning point' which appears in the question, through a comparison with migration in the Second World War. The argument is balanced and is supported and sustained by the inclusion of accurate own knowledge.

The migration of black Americans to the north and west did not end with the conclusion of the Second World War. Nor did it end racial tensions in those areas. Even after the end of legal racial segregation in the South, which had occurred by 1965, serious civil rights issues surrounding racial discrimination sparked off riots in the Los Angeles district of Watts in 1965 and in Newark, New Jersey in 1967. It also saw the rise of radical civil rights groups such as the Black Panther Party, which was urban based, in the north and west rather than in the South where Martin Luther King had the base of his civil rights organisation.

> This paragraph continues a coherent and consistent argument by referring to the post-Second World War era. The argument is balanced and is supported and sustained by the inclusion of accurate own knowledge.

In the 1970s to 2009, with the end of legal segregation in the South, the decline of heavy industry in the north and the continued issue of de facto segregation in the north and west, black Americans began to migrate back to the South. Again this was fuelled by both push and pull factors. Push factors included the desire to leave inner-city black communities in the north and west, where black Americans faced crime, poor housing and limited job opportunities. Pull factors involved a desire to follow the better job opportunities associated with the Sun Belt area of the South.

It is clear that the First World War was a turning point in the changing geography of civil rights issues. It led to a major shift in the black American population and created new civil rights issues associated with de facto segregation and racial discrimination. I think it was the key turning point because it began the shift in population which continued during the Second World War and up to the 1970s. It was only from the 1970s that a migration back to the South began, following the end of legal segregation there.

> The response makes it clear that black American migration involved a number of phases and was associated with pull and push factors. Again, sound evidence is produced which is used to support a clear argument linked to the issue in the question.

> This is a strong evaluative conclusion which deals with the term 'key turning point'. It provides a substantiated judgement through the development of a balanced, analytical argument throughout the answer.

Verdict

This is a strong answer because:

- the key issues relevant to the question are all explored, and the answer offers a balanced, analytical approach to the question
- there is a wide range of accurate material deployed to support the points made
- the argument throughout the answer is well-organised, coherent, logical and persuasive
- it has a wide range of evidence which is used to support the points made
- it reaches a secure concluding judgement
- it is well organised and communication of material is clear and precise.

Index

Acknowledgements

The authors and publisher would like to thank the following individuals and organisations for permission to reproduce photographs and text in this book.

Photographs
(Key: b–bottom; c–centre; l–left; r–right; t–top)

Alamy Images: National Geographic Image Collection 6, Everett Collection Historical (t) 32; **The Art Archive:** Granger Collection 9, 60, 71, 84; **Corbis:** Bettman (b) 32, Tyrone Turner/ National Geographic Creative 57, Bettman 58, Corbis 59, Stefano Bianchetti 72, Tarker 73, Underwood & Underwood 120, Bettmann 126, Reuters/Jason Reed 153, HO/Reuters 154 Frederic Soltan 165**; Getty Images:** Chicago History Museum 27, Paul Popper/Popperfoto 94, Afro Newspaper/Gado 136, New York Daily News Archive 147; **The Kobal Collection:** SELZNICK/ MGM 47; **TopFoto:** The Granger Collection 16, 17, 22, 44, 104, Topfoto 19, World History Archive (b) **61,** Roger-Viollet 106, ImageWorks 150, 170.

Cover images: Getty Images: Joe Raedle

All other images © Pearson Education

Figures
Figures 5.2 and 5.3, on page 128 adapted from 'Party identification of black American voters from 1936 to 2004', and 'How black Americans voters voted in presidential elections from 1936 to 2004. After 1936, there was a major and permanent change in the voting pattern of black Americans', data source: Joint Center for Political and Economic Studies. Reproduced with permission.

Maps
Maps on pp.10, 31 from *American History Atlas/The Routledge Atlas of American History,* Weidenfeld and Nicholson and Routledge (Sir Martin Gilbert) pp.50, 107, copyright © 1968, 1985, 1993, 1995, 2003, 2006, 2009, reproduced by permission of The Orion Publishing Group, London and Taylor & Francis Books UK, www.martingilbert.com.

Tables
Table p.12 'The Number of Black Americans in the USA and the proportion of the total population they compromised from 1790 to 2009'. Sources: Statistical Abstract of the United States: 2003, 'We, The American Blacks', US Census Bureau, 1993, 2009; Table p.20 from *Race Relations in the USA since 1900*, second edition, Hodder Education (Vivienne Sanders) 2003, p.38; Table p.31 from 'Black Migration Reversal in the United States', *Geographical Review*, Vol. 77 (2), pp.171–182 (Kevin E. McHugh) 1987 copyright © American Geographical Society; Tables p.168 from 'Republicans Cry Foul Over Media Coverage of Palin' by Lydia Saad, 15 September 2008, http://www.gallup.com, copyright © Gallup, Inc.

Text
Extract p.21 from 'Migration and Jobs: The New Black Workers in Pittsburgh, 1916–1930', *The Western Pennsylvania Historical Magazine*, Vol. 61 (1) (Peter Gottlieb) 1978, Heinz History Center, reproduced with permission; Extract p.23 from *Black San Francisco: The Struggle for Racial Equality in the West, 1900–54*, University Press of Kansas (Albert S. Broussard) 1993, p.166, copyright © 1993, www. kansaspress.ku.edu, reproduced by permission; Extract p.26 from *Freedomways* (Langston Hughes) 1963, reproduced by permission of David Higham Associates; Extract p.47 from *Gone with the Wind* (Margaret Mitchell) by permission of GWTW Partners, LLC; Extracts p.50 from *To Kill a Mockingbird* (Harper Lee), copyright © 1960 Harper Lee, renewed © 1988 by Harper Lee, reproduced by permission of The Random House Group Limited, and HarperCollins Publishers; Extract p.52 from 'The Unspoken Spoken: Toni Morrison's "Beloved" in the context of the African American Experience of Slavery, and slave narrative', by Marie Burns, December 2008, http://www.literature-study-online. com/essays/morrison-slavery.html, reproduced by permission of Marie C.E. Burns; Extract p.54 from *The Help*, Penguin Books (Kathryn Stockett) 2011, pp.150–151, copyright © 2009 Kathryn Stockett, reproduced by permission of Penguin Books Limited and G.P. Putnam's Sons, an imprint of

Penguin Publishing Group, a division of Penguin Random House LLC; Extracts pp.55 and 100 from *Reconstruction, America's Unfinished Revolution: 1863 to 1877*, HarperCollins (Eric Foner) 2002, pp.8, 591, reproduced by permission of HarperCollins Publishers; Extract p.55 from *Sweet Land of Liberty? The African American Struggle for Civil Rights in the Twentieth Century*, Routledge (Robert Cook) 1998, pp.218–220, reproduced by permission of Routledge; Extract p.56 from *The Unfinished Journey*, Oxford University Press Inc. (William H. Chafe) 1995, p.153, copyright © Oxford University Press, reproduced by permission; Extract p.61 from *The Rise and Fall of Jim Crow: Jim Crow Stories: D.W. Griffith's Birth of a Nation (1915)*, copyright © Thirteen Productions LLC, reproduced by permission; Extract p.62 from the film review 'In the Heat of the Night', by Tim Dirks, 2015, http://www.filmsite.org/inth.html, copyright © 2015 American Movie Classics Company LLC. All rights reserved; Extract p.64 from '*Malcolm X*: Spike Lee's biopic is still absolutely necessary', *The Guardian*, 19/02/2015 (Ashley Clark with comments from Dr Althea Legal-Miller), reproduced with permission of Dr Althea Legal-Miller, Ashley Clark and Guardian News & Media Ltd; Extract p.64 from the film review 'Malcolm X' by Clayborne Carson, American professor of History at Stanford University and Director of the Martin Luther King Research and Education Institute, standford.edu; Newspaper headline p.66 '*The Wire*: arguably the greatest television programme ever made', *The Telegraph*, 02/04/2009, copyright © Telegraph Media Group Limited 2013; Extract p.96 from 'The Separation of the Races in Public Conveyances', *American Political Science Review*, Vol. 3 (02), pp.180–204 (Gilbert Thomas Stephenson) 1909, Cambridge University Press, copyright © American Political Science Association 1909; Extract p.100 from 'More than the Woodward Thesis: Assessing the Strange Career of Jim Crow', *The Journal of American History*, Vol. 75 (3), pp.842–856 (H.N. Rabinowitz) 1988, copyright © Oxford University Press Journals; Extract p.112 from *Freedom from Fear, The American People in Depression and War, 1929 to 1945*, Oxford University Press (David M. Kennedy) 2002, p.357 copyright © Oxford University Press, reproduced by permission; Extract p.115 from *The Shaping of Southern Politics: Suffrage Restriction and the Establishment of the One-Party South 1880–1910*. Yale University Press (J. Morgan Kousser), 1977, reproduced with permission of Yale University Press; Extracts pp.118 and 121 from 'Segregation', *The Crisis*, (W.E.B. Du Bois) and 'A Negro in the CCC', *The Crisis*, Vol. 42, pp.244, 253–254 (Luther C. Wandall), http://www.thecrisismagazine.com. The publisher wishes to thank the Crisis Publishing Co., Inc., the publisher of the magazine of the National Association for the Advancement of Colored People, for the use of this material first published in the August 1935 and January 1934 issues of *Crisis*; Extract p.123 from *Race Relations in the USA since 1900*, Second Edition, Hodder Education (Vivienne Sanders) 2003, p.44, reproduced by permission of Hodder Education; Extract p.123 from *The New Deal: A Modern History*, The Free Press (Michael Hiltzik) copyright © 2011 Michael Hiltzik, reproduced by permission of Simon & Schuster, Inc., All rights reserved; Extract p.123 from *Anxious Decades, America in Prosperity and Depression, 1920–41*, W.W. Norton (Michael E. Parrish) 1992 p.397, copyright © 1992 by Michael E. Parish, reproduced by permission of W.W. Norton & Company, Inc.; Extract p.124 from *Who Built America? Working People and the Nation's Economy, Politics, Culture and Society*, Vol. 2, pp.405–406 (Joshua Freeman et al) 1992, Pantheon, reproduced by permission of Pantheon Books, an imprint of Knopf Doubleday Publishing Group, a division of Penguin Random House LLC. All rights reserved and American Social History Project; Extract p.134 from 'Integrated Bus Suggestions, December 19, 1955', Source: Inez Jessie Baskin Papers, http://www.alabamamoments.state.al.us/sec55ps.html, reproduced with permission from Alabama Department of Archives and History, Montgomery, Alabama; Extract p.135 from 'Letter from the Albany Movement to the Albany City Commission'. African-American History Online. Facts On File, Inc. http://www.fofweb.com (accessed 27/01/2016), copyright © Facts on File, 2014. Reproduced by permission of the publisher; Extract p.135 from The Burke Marshall Papers, Assistant Attorney General Files, 1958–1965 (bulk 1961–1964), No. 1.09; BMPP-018-004, John F. Kennedy Library, Boston, http://www.jfklibrary.org; Poetry on page 145 from 'Malcolm' published in *Homecoming*, Broadside Press (Sonia Sanchez) 1965, reproduced by permission of Broadside Lotus Press; Extract p.149 from *And the Walls Came Tumbling Down*, Harper, NY (Ralph D. Abernathy) 1990, p.425, copyright © 1989 Ralph David Abernathy, reproduced by permission of HarperCollins Publishers; Extract p.156 from 'The Candidate: How the son of a Kenyan economist became an Illinois Everyman', *New Yorker Magazine*, 31/05/2004 (William Finnegan), copyright © William Finnegan, reproduced with kind permission; Extracts p.161 from 'Obama Launches Bid to "Transform" U.S', *Washington Post*, (Nedra Pickler), and 'Obama is in the race' *The Ledger* (Deanr Bellandi & John O'Connor), 11/02/2007, The Associated Press, copyright © 2016, reproduced with permission of The Associated Press. All Rights Reserved; Extract p.162 from 'Have You Come a Long Way, Baby? Hillary Clinton, Sarah Palin, and Sexism in 2008 Campaign Coverage', *Communication Studies* Vol. 60 (4), pp.326–343 (Diana B. Carlin & Kelly L. Winfrey) 2009, copyright © 2009 Routledge; Extract p.167 from 'Sarah Palin's Very Bad Interview', 25 September 2008, http://www.alternet.org/story/100397/sarah_palin's_very_bad_interview, copyright © AlterNet, reproduced with permission; Extract p.168 from 'Republicans Cry Foul Over Media Coverage of Palin' by Lydia Saad, 15 September 2008, http://www.gallup.com, copyright © Gallup, Inc.